SOLDIER BOY

→ → → → → ← ← ← ← ←

SOLDIER BOY

→ → → → → ← ← ← ← ←

The CIVIL WAR LETTERS of
CHARLES O. MUSSER,
29TH IOWA

Edited by

Barry Popchock

→ ←

UNIVERSITY OF IOWA PRESS

IOWA CITY

University of Iowa Press, Iowa City 52242

Copyright © 1995 by the University of Iowa Press

All rights reserved

Printed in the United States of America

Design by Omega Clay

Printed on acid-free paper

Library of Congress Cataloging-in-Publication Data

Musser, Charles O. (Charles Oliver), 1842–1938.

Soldier boy: the Civil War letters of Charles O.
Musser, 29th Iowa / edited by Barry Popchock.

p.   cm.

Includes bibliographical references and index.

ISBN 0-87745-523-6

1. Musser, Charles O. (Charles Oliver), 1842–1938—
Correspondence.   2. United States—History—Civil
War, 1861–1865—Personal narratives.   3. United
States. Army. Iowa Infantry Regiment, 29th (1862–
1865). Company A.   4. Iowa—History—Civil War,
1861–1865—Personal narratives.   5. Soldiers—
Iowa—Council Bluffs—Correspondence.   6. Council
Bluffs (Iowa)—Biography.   I. Popchock, Barry,
1950–   . II. Title.

E507.5 29th.M87   1995

973.7′77—dc20   95-17660

                                        CIP

01 00 99 98 97 96 95 C 5 4 3 2 1

For Mom, who is reading this

CONTENTS

•

ACKNOWLEDGMENTS

A small but select circle of people have contributed to this book.

First, Civil War scholars owe a debt of gratitude to Hester Alice Musser, Charles O. Musser's daughter, who lovingly read and preserved his letters. Hester's son, Floyd Pierce of Lexington, Nebraska, has shown an equal appreciation of their historical importance, and it is through his kind permission that this book has emerged.

Kudos as well to the following: Becki Peterson, archivist at the State Historical Society of Iowa, and her staff for providing substantial material on the 29th Iowa and its campaigns; Judy Mingus, my "hired gun" from Methuen, Massachusetts, who unearthed invaluable data at the National Archives on William Musser; and the Social Sciences Department of the Carnegie Library's main branch in Pittsburgh, which helped with interlibrary loan.

I would like to express appreciation to Dad for sparking my interest in Civil War history.

Finally, an old adage is in need of revision: behind every successful man, you will find *two* women. In this case, they are Gaile Beatty and Carole Popchock, whose chance meeting at a copy machine was the genesis of *Soldier Boy*. Without Gaile's generous cooperation, her great-grandfather's correspondence would not have become part of the published record. I am grateful, too, for her splendid maps and her willingness to suffer the tedium of proofreading. My wife, Carole, also served as a proofreader and performed numerous clerical tasks. More important, she brought the Musser letters to my attention after discovering their existence. The rest is history of a different sort.

SOLDIER BOY

INTRODUCTION

As hostilities dragged into the summer of 1862, Abraham Lincoln allowed that he would need more men to put down the Southern rebellion. On July 2, the president called for 300,000 additional volunteers to serve three years in the Union army. Governor Samuel J. Kirkwood of Iowa echoed Lincoln's call to arms: "The time has come when men must make . . . sacrifices of ease, comfort and business for the cause of the country."[1] The state's response was not overwhelming at first. Farmers were busy with the harvest, lengthening casualty lists had dampened patriotic fervor, and Southern sympathizers discouraged enlistment. But volunteering accelerated in August when the men were threatened with national conscription. Iowa finally furnished twenty-two infantry regiments.[2] More than half the state's prewar military-age population, 76,000 males between the ages of eighteen and forty-five, eventually donned the blue uniform—among them 440 African Americans. Thirteen thousand would lose their lives.[3]

One of the new infantry regiments fell under the command of Thomas Hart Benton, Jr., who bore the name of his uncle, the legendary Thomas Hart Benton, Missouri's first U.S. senator. On August 10, Benton was commissioned a colonel and authorized to form a regiment from ten companies of volunteers. Assembling for training at Camp Dodge in Council Bluffs, August 15 through November 13, these companies were mustered in as the 29th Iowa Volunteer Infantry on December 1.

Company A was typical of the regiment. During the war, 139 men would serve in its ranks. The youngest was sixteen years old, the oldest forty-eight; the average age was under twenty-five—about that of the

Federal army as a whole. Ninety-two men declared Council Bluffs as their residence while one lived in Memphis, Tennessee. Only seven were native Iowans—not surprising, considering the immigrant character of the state's population. Thirty-three men listed Ohio as their place of birth. As was the case throughout the Union army, there was a foreign-born contingent: fifteen men represented England, Ireland, Germany, and Canada. Six company members claimed nativity in what were now Confederate states.[4]

Whatever their age or nationality, these men shared the experience of soldiering mostly in Arkansas, which with Missouri, western Louisiana, Texas, and the Indian Territory made up the Trans-Mississippi. This theater was an almost forgotten backwater, a dumping ground for underachieving generals, blue and gray. The Yankee invaders had more to fear from disease-carrying insects than Rebels shouldering muskets. While large-scale battles were rare (small-unit actions and hit-and-run raids being the order of the day), hard fighting and real dying did take place.

Whether called upon to fight a battle, conduct a march, or garrison a town, the 29th Iowa did its job. Adjutant Joseph Lyman wrote a fitting epitaph for the regiment: "It was unfortunate in being kept so long in the Department of the Arkansas, away from the more brilliant fields of action. It was one of the best disciplined regiments in the army, never shrank from any duty required of it, and only needed the opportunity to make a record equal to that of any Iowa regiment."[5]

Among those who responded to Governor Kirkwood's plea for volunteers was a twenty-year-old farm boy from Council Bluffs. On August 9, 1862, a mustering officer saw before him a youth five feet, six inches tall, with fair complexion, gray eyes, and brown hair. Charles Oliver Musser entered his name on the rolls as a private in Company A, 29th Iowa Volunteer Infantry.[6]

Because of the destruction of courthouse records in a fire, not much is known about Charles's early life. He was born in Millwood, Ohio, July 17, 1842, the second son of farmer John Musser and Caroline Souls Musser. Around 1845, John Musser uprooted his family from central Ohio's Knox County and moved to Iowa, probably in the expectation of finding better land. It was a time when Iowans were boasting that their soil was the best and there was plenty of it—a message that appealed to tillers of the Old Northwest's soil. In conse-

Charles O. Musser with wife, Emily, and unidentified infant. Courtesy of Joy Beatty, Melva Hughbanks, and Floyd Pierce.

Top row, left to right: Hester (sister), Charles O. Musser, and Martha (sister); bottom row, left to right: May (sister), Frances (sister), Caroline Souls Musser (mother), and Mary (sister). Courtesy of Joy Beatty, Melva Hughbanks, and Floyd Pierce.

quence, the second son would grow up working alongside his father on a farm near Council Bluffs.

Charles became an integral part of the Musser economy—a fact not lost on his parents when they learned of his intention to join the army. Their opposition indirectly sheds light on the son's motives for enlisting. Men who volunteered typically did so for an admixture of practical and philosophical reasons, a profile Charles fits. The timing suggests that he was moved to avoid the social stigma of being drafted—not to mention the bounty that would be his only if he volunteered. But another factor that led men to the recruiter was a sense of duty, which Charles certainly evinced in a July 1863 letter: "I done wrong in enlisting, but i thought it was my duty to Serve my country above all things." It was his patriotism, in a word, that overrode parental pressure to remain on the farm.[7]

Charles no doubt gladdened his parents' hearts upon returning to the family farm after his discharge in 1865. Two years later, however, he struck out on his own, marrying Emily Jane Triplett, also a Knox County native. The couple would produce ten children between 1868 and 1895, only six surviving into adulthood. Besides farming for a living, Charles became involved in veterans affairs as an active member of the Grand Army of the Republic (GAR). The Mussers remained at Council Bluffs until 1884, when the pioneering spirit took hold of the patriarch. Charles purchased land south of Miller, Nebraska, and entered the ranks of Buffalo County's first homesteaders. Early in the new century, he moved his family again, this time to a farm south of Sumner, Nebraska, becoming one of the original white settlers of Dawson County. In 1910, probably as a result of deteriorating health, Charles gave up farming and moved into town.

Sadly, army service exacted its toll. As early as age forty-two, he began complaining of severe rheumatism. It worsened to the extent that Charles was occasionally unable to leave his house for weeks at a time, and the family physician swore in an 1890 affidavit that he was 75 percent disabled. The following year, he successfully filed for a veteran's pension, claiming permanent disability because of rheumatism, heart and lung disease, hemorrhoids, and disease of the kidney and bladder. By January 1934 Charles's health had deteriorated so much that he was declared legally incompetent and placed in the care of a guardian.

The old soldier behind the wheel of a Model T. Courtesy of Joy Beatty, Melva Hughbanks, and Floyd Pierce.

Musser in later life. Courtesy of Joy Beatty, Melva Hughbanks, and Floyd Pierce.

Only a sketchy outline of Emily's life survives. It must have been
arduous, living as she did on the fringes of the western frontier, raising
a sizable family, and supporting the moves of a restless husband. Emily
evidently took an interest in Charles's GAR activities, one family photograph showing them in attendance at a postwar reunion. On March
10, 1933, she died, survived by her husband and five children. A brief
newspaper obituary observed that at Miller, Emily "suffered and en-
dured the hardships of pioneer motherhood." "She . . . knew of the de-
pressions following wars. . . . She knew about early settler happiness
and struggles." "She has lived many years seemingly on the brink. . . .
death was not unexpected."[8]

The old soldier himself faded away on March 10, 1938, at the age
of ninety-five—the last Civil War veteran in Dawson County and perhaps the last surviving member of the 29th Iowa. Old age and heart
and kidney failure were ruled the official causes of death. A local
newspaper reported, "Mr. Musser was quite active until a year ago,
and was frequently seen on the streets, and made daily trips to the post
office. . . . [But] for the past several months he has been confined to his
room and bed." With full military honors, Charles joined his wife at
the Odd Fellows Cemetery north of Sumner.[9]

*Charles and Emily at a postwar reunion of members of the Grand Army
of the Republic and the Women's Relief Corps. Courtesy of Joy Beatty,
Melva Hughbanks, and Floyd Pierce.*

Charles must have found it easy to call it the "Brothers' War," for his brother William soldiered in the Confederate army. A resident of Benton County, Missouri, William A. Musser enlisted September 20, 1862, as a private in Company D, Hunter's Missouri Infantry Regiment, for three years or the duration of the war. Hunter's regiment, organized five days earlier, was designated the 8th Missouri Infantry (subsequently redesignated the 11th Missouri) and assigned to the brigade of Colonel Mosby M. Parsons. William's usefulness to the Confederacy was short-lived, however. The day after enlisting, he was detached for duty as a government printer by order of the division commander, Major General Thomas C. Hindman. This duty came to an end on September 9, 1863, at Bolivar County, Mississippi, when Federal troops, probably cavalry, captured him.

William was imprisoned at Camp Morton, Indianapolis, Indiana, on September 22. Named after Indiana governor Oliver P. Morton, the compound occupied thirty-five acres on the site of the Indiana State Fairgrounds. At least 3,500 Rebels were interned here at any given time. During the war, 1,763 prisoners perished, a mortality figure lower than that of similar Northern POW compounds. Still, prisoners lived in overcrowded, drafty barracks with an open ditch to carry away sewage. When Colonel William Hoffman assumed command in 1863, he instituted certain reforms but also cut rations to save money.[10]

William was released March 14, 1865, after signing an oath to "faithfully support" both the Constitution of the United States and the wartime antislavery statutes enacted by Congress. He lingered in Indianapolis afterward, finding employment first as a printer for the *Herald*, then taking a position with the *Journal*. In 1867, twenty-seven-year-old William informed his father of his plans to marry an Iowa woman: "I am not as stout or healthy as I was six years ago. The sufferings and hardships of the war, and prison life, have left their effects upon me. I can never forget the treatment of prisoners at the hands of the Federal authorities." The estrangement from his family, no doubt originating with his service in the enemy army, continued after the war. William groused about receiving no reply to his letters: "I have been so anxious to hear from home. . . . I received a letter from no one [until a couple of days ago]. . . . It appeared you no longer cared to hear from me."[11]

None of the surviving correspondence indicates that William enjoyed a reconciliation with his family, nor does Musser oral history shed any light on the matter. He is next heard from in a letter to Charles, dated December 20, 1921. Then the trail runs cold. By this time, the elderly veteran was ensconced with his memories at the Union Printers Home in Colorado Springs, Colorado.[12]

Letter writing was one of the most popular amusements among Northern soldiers, and Charles was no exception. Besides penning at least 130 letters to his immediate family, he maintained an extensive correspondence with relatives and friends. The surviving letters constitute an exceptional firsthand account of a theater of operations largely overlooked by historians. In them, Charles, with a passion for trenchant observation, touches on a wide range of subjects: battles, marches, the Southern countryside, camp life, morale, contrabands, and Copperheads. Of course, there are the usual inquiries about the home front, news of Iowa boys in the service, and the time-honored soldier complaints.

What emerges from this correspondence is the saga of a boy soldier maturing in the crucible of war. Army life agreed with Charles (at least more so than the average "Billy Yank"), and he rose steadily through the ranks, gaining promotion to corporal May 2, 1863, and sergeant June 15, 1864.[13] Early on, though, as the inevitable winnowing process commenced (his company lost 30 percent of its strength in seven months), the excitement of the crusade wore off. In January 1865 it was a grim task that had to be finished: "another year will end the war at farthest, and I want to *see* it end before I go home."

Charles, like most of the North's men-at-arms, fought to restore the Union but learned that this could not be accomplished without a redefinition of freedom. Still, he accepted Lincoln's emancipation measures with reluctance: "we dont want the negroes among us. but as it is, they are here, and we . . . have to make the best of it." Here Charles joined a chorus of white Iowans anxious about the prospect of competing with freedmen in an integrated society. "I never did like the darky," he wrote, reflecting the sentiment of many comrades. At the same time, however, he participated with them in the hiring of runaway slaves as cooks, laundresses, and servants. Indeed, Charles became a model of the Yankee who resigned himself to abolition as a wartime necessity, endorsing the army's recruitment of fugitive slaves—"I know they will fight and like demons, too." He shared the experience of battle with them and expressed outrage at Confederate

8

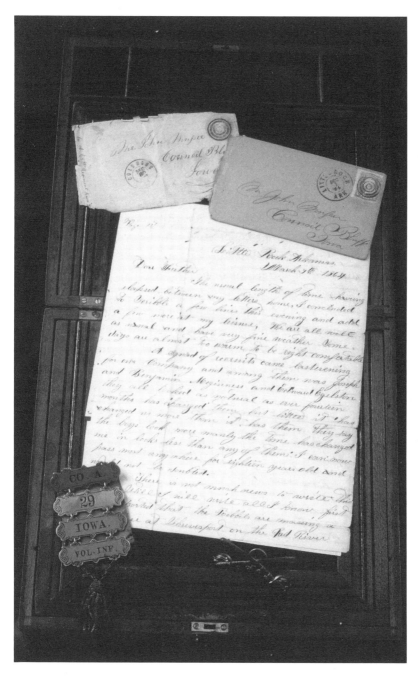

Memorabilia of a soldier boy: field desk, wartime letter and covers, and infantryman's badge. Courtesy of Joy Beatty, Melva Hughbanks, and Floyd Pierce.

atrocities committed against black prisoners. Yet he also embraced the everyday prejudice that African Americans could be good soldiers only under proper—that is, white—leadership.[14]

This is Charles Musser's story, and it has been my guiding principle to let him tell it. Therefore, all his surviving correspondence appears substantially as it was written. Charles was typically careless about paragraphing and punctuation, which I have supplied to make the reader's task less tedious. Aside from names of soldiers and civilians and important place-names, only gross spelling mistakes have been corrected for clarity's sake. The erratic capitalization remains. Due to space limitations, passages that are repetitive or obtuse, adding nothing to the narrative, have been omitted as indicated by ellipses. I have inserted some material enclosed in brackets as well as annotations and notes to complete or correct the historical record.

Soon after his baptism of fire at Helena, Charles instructed the family to "keep all of my letters untill i get home so that i can see what i wrote when in the army. it will be a terrible mixed up mess of Scribeling If you have not destroyed them." But the family, sharing his keen sense of history, did not destroy the "Scribeling." Consequently, we have a common soldier's first-rate chronicle of an uncommon time.

On December 5, 1862, 1,005 officers and men of the 29th Iowa left Council Bluffs to join the war.[1] After stops at Savannah and Saint Joseph, Missouri, the green regiment proceeded to Saint Louis, arriving December 20. A brief spell of guard duty followed. Christmas Day found the regiment aboard transports bound for Columbus, Kentucky, where a Federal outpost was threatened. The expected attack failed to materialize, however, and the Iowans were sent down the Mississippi to Helena, Arkansas, January 8.

Saint Joseph   Dec. 14/62

Dear father: . . . we arived here the eleventh. we came from Savannah, fifteen miles . . . by the [railroad] cars.

St. Jos is considerable of a town. it is three times as large as the bluffs. there is considerable business done here considering the times. nearly every man you meet is a Soldier. ther is a regiment of militia on duty all the time. no man is allowed on the streetes after ten oclock at night. we are quartered in ex governor Stewarts hall (Cos. A and C). the rest are quartered at diferent places in town.

the weather is quite warm here for the time of the year. it has not been cold enough to wear over coats yet.

the boys are all well but one. he is in the hospital. I never was stouter in my life than I am now.

the Seckond Ohio Cavalry came here the day before yesterday from fort Leavenworth, [Kansas] on their way back to ohio. they were from Columbus. they are going back to recruit [replacements for] their regiment. they were first in the three month service, then enlisted for the [duration of the] war. they Started out with about thirteen hundred men, and when they came through here, they numbered about six hundred. they looked lik they had seen servis.

the militia captured a rebel colonel a short time ago a few miles below here at platte bridge. he came home to see his family, and the guards found it out and went to his house. he was hid. they demanded his surender. his wife desired his being there. the guards told her to remove her things out of the house, for they would burn the house if she would not tell where he was conceiled. she finaly told. they raised the carpet in the parlor and found a square hole cut between the joist. they found him under the floor on the ground. he was brought here and confined in the county jail with a strong guard around it night and day. he will be tried tomorrow by court martial for burning the platte river bridge. it is the opinion of all that he will be shot.

we will leave with in ten days for Saint Louis. the whole regiment will be ready for marching by the eighteenth. where we will go from there is more than we know.

I will now end my poorly written letter. i wrote in a hurry—on my cap at that. . . . your Son, Charles O. Musser . . .

Saint Joseph   December 18th/62

Dear father: . . . we are all well and enjouing our selves hugely. the weather is fine here, with the ecseption of a shower now and then. we have plenty to live upon and good quarters. . . . we will leave here friday morning, nine oclock.

the people generaly profess to be loyal here. there are Some, however, that are open Seceshionists. there is one liveing close to our lines that has been in the rebel army and had his leg Shot off in a skirmish in south west missouri. he was captain of a company of [Major General Sterling] Prices M.S.Gs [Missouri State Guards]. he keeps very close within doors.

I went and Saw the rebel colonel . . . the other day at the jail. he is a fine looking man. he looks a good deal like our Lieutenant Colonel, only he is considerable taller. he says the war will never be ended by the bayonette or bulletts. his trial is comeing off now. it will take a good while to try his case. he has Some friends in this county. he wants to prove that he is a regular comissioned officer in the army and not a bushwhacker. if he does prove that, he will be exchanged for Some federal officer. the militia are all for hanging him. they sware that he Shall not leave the town alive.

Soldiering is a hard life, but it agrees with me and i with it. I think we will all be at home next fall at farthest. at any rate, I hope so.

we have some fun . . . sometimes a forageing. Sergeant [Craven V.] Gardner, [Sergeant Ira E.] Huffman, and some four or five of the boys just started out on an expedition of that kind with a citizen for a guide that knows the country. I was out once when we were at Savannah. in any other country . . . that would be called Stealing, but we don't in se-ceshia—especially in a secesh neighborhood.[2]

I am cooking for the orderlies mess yet. [I have] been cooking since I was at home all the time. I will cook a month yet if it suitz me.[3]

I had to pay my debts out of my months pay, or I would have sent more home. . . . next pay day, I will send all but a litle home. we will be paid the first of next month. . . . your Son, Charles O. Musser . . .

Columbus, Ky   Dec. 28/62

Dear father and mother: . . . we landed this morning early in sight of the old battlefield of Belmont, where the brave seventh [Iowa] fought so well.[4]

we are expecting an attack from the rebel [Brigadier] General [Nathan Bedford] Forrest of [General Braxton] Braggs division. they have been close up to our pickets. they captured about eight hundred prisoners on the railroad between here and Jackson, Tennessee, and tore up the track for several miles, and caryed off all they could find. we are making great preparation, throwing up breast works and dig-ing rifle pitts for the riflemen. the officers are confident we can hold the town against any force the rebels can fetch against it. there is Some heavy batteries on the hills around town; in all, about one hundred guns of large Calibre. there is one battery of six guns on the hill north of town that commands the country all around for two miles.

the Iowa 33rd, 40th, 35th, and 29th are here. . . . the boys are in good Spirits. one had very crouding times comeing down the river. the whole regmt . . . [was on] the Steamer. . . .

there is only one sick man in our company, that James Wilding.

we drew our tents to day. we are very comfortable. Situated for the time [being], we may be called away at a moments warning. we will in all probability go to Helena, Arkansas—So I heard our officers say today, but I expect they do not know any more about it than we do ourselves.

14

i have written Several letters but have not received any yet. gus Breese and I write a letter most every evening when we can. . . . Your Son, Chas. O. Musser . . .

Before long, the 29th Iowa encountered contrabands.

In May 1861 Major General Benjamin F. Butler learned that some fugitive slaves in his command had been employed in the construction of Confederate fortifications. Citing their value to the enemy (slaves also raised crops, fabricated ordnance, and transported supplies), Butler dubbed them "contraband of war." He put the able-bodied men to military work and issued rations to the women and children.[5]

Congress not only adopted but amplified Butler's policy, swelling the tide of black refugees; the president's Emancipation Proclamation had the same effect. As Yankees occupied more Southern territory, they increasingly came face to face with contrabands (the moniker for all runaway slaves). The historian of the 33rd Iowa recorded his regiment's reaction to a family of four that moved into the Iowans' camp: "The old man built himself a shanty . . . and busied himself at whatever work he could find to do; and his wife and the two girls officiated as washer-women for the regiment. . . . a mutual friendship between the regiment and 'Uncle Tony and Aunt Lucy' was firmly established."[6] Unfortunately, the relationship between soldiers and runaways could be an abusive one. A Federal chaplain at Helena reported instances of contrabands going unpaid for their labor and troops raping, robbing, even murdering them.

Many local commanders placed the contrabands in supervised camps, with guards providing a measure of security for some. Sadly, there was little protection against disease, which claimed numberless victims. Either the government or private charities supplied food and clothing—not always in sufficient quantity—to refugees unable to support themselves. (Fit men relieved white troops of noncombat duties or eventually joined the Union army. Women were less employable but could find work as laundresses, servants, or hospital attendants.) Housing, if available, ran the gamut from tents to abandoned houses. Some contraband camps featured schools or churches.

Contrabands also toiled on abandoned or seized cotton plantations leased by the government to Northern entrepreneurs. Lessees agreed to hire former slaves, pay them wages, and dispense food and clothing. But lessees did not always keep their end of the bargain, and worse, Rebels occasionally raided the plantations, killing or reenslaving the blacks.

Most contraband families managed to be self-supporting, some in their own settlements. In February 1864 180 runaways were living in a Helena shantytown, eking out an existence without army rations or medical care. Congress finally intervened to ease the transition from slavery to freedom, creating the Freedmen's Bureau in March 1865.

Columbus, Ky   January 3rd, 1863

Dear Father: . . . we are getting along very well—very few sick, considering the change of the climates. the water is very bad here. a great many of the boys have the diorhea. i have escaped it So far, but my turn may come Soon enough. some of the regiments here have lost a great many men by the typhus fever and measles. there is only one case of the measles in our camp and no fever. the 33rd Iowa, camped just over the rail road track, have lost a good many men.

one day a short time ago, I was busy cooking dinner when a man from the 33 Iowa Co. B came up to me, called me by my name, shook hands with me. who do you suppose it was? it was no other than John Gann. I did not know him at first. I knew his countenance. Leander is in the same co. with him. Lee is a great, tall man, about Six feet tall. John is about my weight but not so tall as Lee. Lee is the Same old boy he was when we seen him last time, [different] only in Size. he likes Soldiering as well as I do. John does not like it. he is not so Stout as Lee. it does not agree with him. he has not been on duty Since he enlisted. he is troubled with the dyspepsia.

I suppose you have heard of the great battle reported fought here. it was reported in the papers, but I did not hear any thing of it myself. we were once called out in line of battle, expecting an attack every moment. very Soon, a cavalry Soldier came cantering up. he reported it as a false allarm. the guards out on the rail road guarding bridges fired off their guns to try them, and the pickets supposed the enemy were fireing on the guards when there was not an enemy within ten miles of them. every man in our regiment that was able was in the

line, ready for a fight.

we have marching orders. they were read at drill parade this evening. we are to have three days cooked rations in our haversacks by monday morning early. we are bound for Vicksburg.

I have resigned my situation as cook in our mess to a contraband. the Camps are over run with the darkies. ther is about fifteen hundred here and comeing in every day by the dozens. they work very cheap. we pay our cook five dollars a month. . . . your dutyfull Son, Charles O. Musser . . .

Memphis, Tennessee   January 10th, 1863

Dear parents: I sit down once again to drop you a few lines—perhaps for the last time.

we arived here last evening about dark. it was raining all day yesterday. it was very disagreable, as crowded as we are on the boat. . . . [Major] General [Ulysses S.] Grant is expected here every hour with his army on his way to Vicksburg. every boat on the river is pressed in the service to transport the troops to the scene of action. we will probibly lay here till they get ready. ther is a considerable force here allready awaiting transportation.

we Started from columbus [on] the seventh [and] had quite a pleasant ride. . . . we stoped awhile at Island [Number] tenn. it is a rough looking place—very high banks. it is about a mile long and hardly a quarter wide. ther is only about one hundred men on the island and only two guns that is of any use. you have heard of the Spikeing of the rest of them some time ago by [Brigadier] Gen. [Thomas A.] Davies orders. it was a piece of folly. there was not the least danger of them being taken by the rebels. no land force could take the place without a regular siege if it had but one regiment there before the guns was destroyed. the men that is on the island said that they threw in the river twenty wagon loads of amunition. I counted 27 guns that was spiked on the north end of the island.[7]

the next place we stoped was new madrid, 25 miles below by the river. . . . I did not see much of the place.

the next point was fort Pillow. it is a very strong position. it is held by two regiments of infantry, a battalion of cavalry, one battery of two rifled field pieces. the day before we stoped ther, one company of Cavalry and one of infantry started out on a scout [and] came across a camp of bushwhackers, four hundred strong, while they were eating their breakfast. they charged on them, killed sixteen, and captured fourty five of them in a very short time. they brought them in to the fort. I seen some of them. they are hard looking fellows. there was one Major, three captains, and seven lieutenants. the officers were dressed very well in grey uniforms.

the fight at Vicksburg will be a hard one. the rebbels are desperate and determined to hold the place. we heard this morning that the gun boats had withdrew for reinforcements. one of our transports went down the river yesterday to reconoiter. as they were near a point about ten miles from helena, they were fired upon by a battery in a hollow not far from shore. the boat had to retreat back to this place. this morning, there was a gunboat sent down to shell them out. . . .

. . . Seven of the boys in our company has been unwell. . . . but they are getting better now.

the watter is so very bad. the river water is very muddy on account of the rise. it has rissen seven feet in the last tenn days. the largest boats can land close up to the Shore.

Memphis is the pretyest place I have Seen since I left home. the nicest residences I ever saw is in this town. fine gardens, evergreens growing. . . . pines, cytruses, and other Sothern trees for shade in front of the houses. they are mostly owned by rebbels. the wharf is lined with cotton bales and tobacco hogsheads, government property of different kinds.[8]

there is about fifty boats laying here. the guerrillas burnt a boat the other day above here a few miles. there was nobody aboard but the crew at the time. they let them go.

. . . all we have to eat is hard bread, meat, and coffee. i can get along very well on that. I have not been the least unwell Since I left home.

I wish you would send Some letter Stamps when you write. . . . they are very Scarce down here where there are so many Soldiers. some of the boys give five cents apiece for them. I had fifteen when we left camp Dodge. now they are nearly all gone and no chance to get more. I have not received a letter yet. . . . if we go on to Vicksburg, I may never write home again, so I will write all I can while I have time.

we are a going farther away from home every day. if we have to fight, we will fight. I do not think you will hear of the 29th runing. the 33rd just now started out for Vicksburg. I guess we will start out before long. the general of our brigade came down with us. his name is [Brigadier General Clinton B.] Fisk. our brigade is composed of the 29th, 33rd, 40th, 55th Iowa regiments, and the 35th Mo—all new regiments. . . . yours through all, Charles O. Musser . . .

The 29th Iowa was soon introduced to the harsh realities of a winter campaign. Upon reaching Helena on January 11, the regiment did not disembark but immediately joined a waterborne task force. Brigadier General Willis A. Gorman, commanding the District of Eastern Arkansas, planned to lead this force on a raid up the White River. A thirty-five-boat flotilla, including the ironclads Cincinnati *and* St. Louis, *got under way January 12, carrying infantry, cavalry, and artillery.*[9]

Gorman's force made Saint Charles the following day, only to discover that the Confederate garrison had fled. Amid a winter snowstorm, the Federals steamed upriver, taking Clarendon. Devall's Bluff, along with two heavy guns and twenty-five prisoners, was captured next, followed by Des Arc, with seventy Rebels, some government corn, and a quantity of ammunition. The Yankees destroyed anything of use to the enemy and seized a riverboat with its cargo of livestock.

On January 20 Gorman reported that all the Confederates in northeastern Arkansas had withdrawn: "They have driven their negroes and carried their property, supplies, and munitions . . . toward Arkadelphia."[10] *Nothing more could be accomplished, and the expedition was recalled to Helena.*

The 29th Iowa's first experience in the field was a grim one. Some 400 men were on the sick list when the demoralized regiment returned to Helena on January 26, having spent more than two weeks aboard a crowded transport. At least half of the sick eventually died or were discharged for disability, without firing a shot in anger.[11]

Camp of the 29th Iowa   Coahoma Co., Miss   Jan. 22/63

Dear father: . . . when we left Memphis, we supposed we were going direct to Vicksburg, but when we got as far down as the mouth of the white river, we turned in the direction of western Arkansas. I suppose you have heard of the expedition up white river, so there is no use of givein any details of the trip—only we had a prety hard time of it, generaly. we have been on board of the boat sixteen days.

a good many of the boys are sick owing to the change of climates we have gone through in so short a time. I have been unwell myself for a week, but I am getting well now. I can take care of my rations anyway, and that is a prety good sign. we are begining to see the realities of a Soldiers life: marching through mud and water, liveing on the roughest fare.

we are camped oposite Helena, Ark., in the State of Mississippi. we are here only temppirarily. we landed for our boat to take in supplies for the trip to Vicksburg—so we Suppose. we do not know for certain. a Soldier does not know where he is a going till he gets there, and then he dont know hardly. there is a large force concentrating at Napoleon, Ark., which is about one hundred miles . . . [from] here . . . , [awaiting] transportation to the Scene of Strife and blood shed at Vicksburg. if that point is taken, there will not be much more fighting done in these parts.

that was quite a little brawl we made at Arkansas Post. we got within hearing of the guns at the time of the fight. we were twelve miles from there on the White river the day after the fight. the guns could be distinctly heard fourtyfive miles [distant] on the river.[12]

when we was up in arkansas, we had quite a snow storm. it was about five inches deep, but when we got down here, it was all gone. . . .

I must end my poorly written letter, for it is getting dusk, and I am getting tired sitting on the poplar log. we will have to get aboard of the boat yet to night and perhaps Start down the river. . . . your dutifull Son, Charles O. Musser . . .

On board the Steamer *Henry Clay*
Helena, Arkansas   January 26th/1863

Dear Father: I received your leter . . . to day. was glad to hear from home, it being the first word I have heard, except by Some of the boys receiveing letters from home. . . .

I can not say this time that our boys are all well. confinement on the boats is what did the work for them. there is not out of our whole regiment four hundred men fit for duty. the measles got among them and Soon run through the regiment. there has not more than two or three died as yet, but there is a prospect for more. after we got ashore the other day in Mississippi, you ought to have Seen our fine new regiment, the pride of Iowa. So many sick, and the well looked more like corpses than well men, pale and thin from the liveing [conditions] and confinement. a Sicker Set of men of Soldiering you never Saw. if they had their dollar back again, they would not bet any more. for my part, I am not tired of it yet.

the way the war is caryed on down here, it will be a good while before it is ended. this slave work will never do. the men get discouraged and tired of the slow movements of our generals. I will give you an idea how we procede. in the first place, we are in camp, get marching orders one evening to be ready with our tents on a pile on the bank of the river in the morning at nine oclock, and wait untill the next morning in the mud and rain. get aboard of the boat at last, lay ther another night, and then go over to the other Side of the river. lay there another night, then go ashore with our bagage and mess chest. Stay there untill night, then get on the boat. this time we will go certain—so we think but we are mistaken again. Some more provisions and ammunition [are] to be loaded, and we lay here, still expecting to go every moment. Vicksburg is our certain destination, but how Soon we will go, we do not know.

I think the boys will get along better after awhile when they get over the measles. Jo. Shadden is very bad off. I think he will get well, though you may not be Surprised to hear that he does not. . . .

it rains nearly all the time here. the river is very high and still riseing. we expect to have a prety rough time going down the river. the country is very very flat and swampy here, easily overflowed by high water.

[Cousin] Henry may think hard of my not writeing to him, but if he considers the disadvantages of Soldiering he will not. tell him that I will write [at] the first opportunity. time is scarce with us. we have been knocked about here and there ever since we left Camp Dodge, and we expect to be as long as the war lasts. . . .

. . . there is so much confusion and bustle going on here that it is difficult to write, though I think I have done pretty well this time. . . . your Son, Charles O. Musser

. . . I have heard the marching orders have been countermanded, and we will go into camp here. . . . it may be a fals alarm. . . .

Disease cut a wide swath through the Federal army, accounting for the deaths of four men to every one killed in action. (For the 29th Iowa, the proportion was closer to six to one.) Measles usually struck first, but diarrhea/dysentery ("Arkansas Quickstep") was reported most frequently and caused more fatalities than any other malady. Malaria (ague or the shakes), pneumonia, and typhoid fever also ranked high on the list of deadly ailments.[13]

Twelve-and-a-half percent of Iowa soldiers died of disease, the highest such percentage of any Northern state. Some historians explain that the bulk of the state's troops served in the West, where they fell victim to the lower Mississippi Valley's inhospitable climate. More important, however, men from largely rural areas like Iowa were more vulnerable to disease than those from urban backgrounds. They were less exposed to contagion in civilian life and less fastidious about sanitary conditions in camp. Regardless of station or origin, though, units suffered from inadequate screening of recruits, contaminated water, insufficient fruits and vegetables, and surgeons unfamiliar with bacteriology.

Whatever the causes, Arkansas was the most unhealthful command in the Union army. In a given month, one-third of the men might be unfit for duty. Helena became "Hell-in-Arkansas," with its vicious heat in summer, continual rain, and mud in winter. One Yankee described it as "a low muddy place with numerous ponds of filthy green looking water"—a perfect breeding ground for disease-bearing insects.[14] In February 1863, as military hospitals rapidly filled to capacity, General Fisk, commanding the Thirteenth Division, wrote: "I am doing all I can to improve the sanitary condition of the army and the town.... I fear a pestilence, unless 'the powers that be' move vigorously in reform." They evidently did not, for eighteen months later an army inspector reported that "the health of the troops here is very bad." He bestowed upon Helena the dubious distinction of being the "most deadly place on the [Mississippi] river."[15]

Rampant illness in Arkansas and elsewhere, reported in soldier letters, touched a responsive chord on the home front. Iowa women were inspired to follow the example of Mrs. Annie Wittenmyer, a widow who joined the Keokuk Ladies' Soldiers' Aid Society at the start of the war. The society's purpose was to help relieve the sufferings of sick and wounded Iowa soldiers. Wittenmyer urged women in other towns to organize local relief efforts and send provisions—clothes, food, medicine, bandages, bedding, and the like— to Keokuk for distribution. (Charles's hometown, Council Bluffs, responded, *as Amelia Bloomer, the women's dress reformer, became the president of the local aid society.) Wittenmyer personally doled out these supplies to Iowa regiments in the field. Her initiative also led to the establishment of asylums for orphaned children of the state's soldiers and Special Diet Kitchens to improve patient fare in military hospitals, saving the lives of thousands of men.*[16]

Camp of Fisks Brigade   near Helena, Ark
Feb. 3rd, 1863

Dear Father: . . . today, we moved our camp from the old spot on the river bank about 1 1/2 miles back on a plantation formerly belonging to [Brigadier General Gideon J.] Pillow of the rebel army. we are camped on quite a healthy location next to the Bluffs. that was one reaon for our moveing quarters, and another reason was the rapid rise of the river. it is almost out of its banks. in another week it will be up to the levy, and if it should break through the levey, it will flood the whole country around.

there is a greatt deal of Sickness in our regiment, and . . . [it is] increasing. there are about 30 thousand troops encamped in and around Helena, and i can say without exagerating that there is buryed fourty men every day and some times more. we have buryed two of our company. I am Sorry to write home that we have lost one of our messmates and fellow Soldier, Joseph Shadden. he died the First of the month and was Buryed the Second, also Corporal H. P. McElroy, and we expect to hear every day of the death of Hiram Boyle. . . . Shadden and McElroy died with the measles.[17]

if the boys had the attention they needed, there would not be so many die. a Soldier down here is not So much thought of as a negro or even a good horse. we are furnished no hay or anything to lay on in our tents, and the army regulations alous So much to every man. the allowance is Small, but it would be a great help when we have to Sleep on the wet ground. the boys in our tent most always get Some by going in the night and take it away from the officers horses. it looks hard to rob the horses, but a man must look out for number one in the army or he will come out the Short row.

I have been nearly Sick for Some time back. John Boulden has been sick also. in fact, nearly all the boys are unwell and unfit for duty.

Area of operations, 29th Iowa, December 1862–February 1865. Map by Gaile Beatty.

there is but a few right harty men in the whole regt. yesterday evening at dressparade, there was about 230 men [present] out of 900 [in the regiment]. . . . all the regts i have seen are in the same fix. it is hard to See so many men away from home suffering and dieing more for the want of care and attention than anything else. the post hospital here is full, and Several Steamboats [are] ocupied for hospitals. there has been some of our Sick Sent up the river to St Louis, So i heard. if there is not a change in the state of the regiment in two months, there will not be 400 men all told in the regiment. . . . C. O. Musser

[undated—probably a continuation of the previous letter] . . . the mails came in this evening. I received a letter from you. . . . I was glad to hear that the folks were all well. Gus Breese got a letter at the same time. I tell you, he was a pleased man. he said that it was worth fifty dollars to hear of that fine boy of his.

was Sory to hear of the Holeman family haveing Sickness in it. the old man stands the rubs of the Company. george is hardy and tough. . . . they need not tell you that it takes the most hardy and robust men to Stand soldiering. the boys in our regiment Stands it generaly better than the men. Some of the Stoutest men in our company is the first to get Sick. Some men that never saw a day of sickness in their lives is down.

if we had officers that were officers, we would be better off. Colonel Benton has not been with the regiment Since we left St Louis. we do not know where he is now. we are like a flock of sheep without a leader. he is a good man but not a military man, or he would have not furnished us with such guns as we got at first. two Co.s have got better guns now. A and B have Enfield rifles for the present. the [new] arms for the regt is at Cairo [Illinois], we heard to day.

we had a very hard Shower of rain last night. to day, it cleared off warm and pleasant.

Some negroes here have comenced plowing up the ground ready for planting. nobody lives here but negroes and soldiers. the citizens have nearly all left. i would not live here if i owned the whole State of Arkansas. we have read of Helena [that] it is one of the dirtyest holes on the river. mud is knee deep there all the time. if yankees had owned the town in times of peace, they would make a city of it. there is a good chance to grade down the hills and fill up the flat, low Streets. what the nigger cannot do is not done.

i never did like the darky, and you may believe i do not now. there are hundreds of them around camp, wanting to work for little or nothing. we have nothing to pay for hired help.

In the last letter i wrote you, I Spoke of sending Some reading mater, also some letter Stamps. both are very Scarce articles with us here. Harvey Meginniss gets a *Nonpareil* once in a while, but it is soon read over by the whole company.[18]

there is Some hopes of being paid off Soon. now if we are, you may look for Some green backs about two weeks after. . . . your Affectionate Son, Chas. O. Musser . . .

[undated letter fragment, probably February 3, 1863]

I have been writeing what would be called the dark side of soldiering. it would not do to look at the dark side all the time. it would soon discourage a soldier. if a man gets homesick here, he will get along badly.

the boys are geting so that they do not care much for anything. they are all geting tired of the war. they are in for peace in any way or form. if there is not some great movements made between this [winter] and spring, i believe one half of the army will throw down their arms and go home. i have not seen one man but what thinks the same. the war party at home, if they had to undergo some of the hardships we have to, . . . would quickly cry for peace as well as the soldier in the field. as long as there is so many Speculators at the head of the armys, there will be war.

I never was so much disappointed in my life in a man as I was . . . Cap. [John P.] Williams. i thought he was grit to the back bone, but a sicker man of soldiering i never saw. he is talking of resigning. he has been sick for a long time. if he does resign, Gardner will be Capt in my opinion.

Col Benton joined the regt. the day be fore yesterday—the first time we Seen him Since we left St. Louis. he got to Helena when we were on the white river. he went on down to Vicksburg—was there Seven days. Said there was about 30000 troops there suffering the worst kind. he Said Helena was a Paradise . . . [compared to] that place. if so, we had better let the rebels keep the place than to keep the men there to die off like sheep with the rot.

I want you to send me some reading mater. i have not had a paper to read Since we left St Louis. we do not get any news here at all. i have seen but one *Nonpareil* Since i left home. i could read most any thing now, even old news papers. . . .

we have not received any pay yet. we will not get any before about the first of March. money is geting scarce in camp.

. . . there is nothing in the Vegetable line more than potatoes here. . . . beef is scarce. what we get is poor. it takes two men to hold them [the cattle] up while one knocks them down. . . .

the talk is now that we will stay here until Spring. if So, our regt will Soon . . . [regain] their health when the measles stop their course.

the country is nearly overrun with contrabands, and they are still coming in by dozens every day. a great many come from the Miss Side [of the river]. most of them lazey around and are an expense to government, liveing on the Soldiers rations. a great many are employed as teamsters. if the negro is wors off in Slavery than they are now, they needed pity. . . .

(Feb 4th) This morning, it is cold and frosty. the ground is frozen on the top. the boys gather around the camp fires. the large log fires feel very comfortable to Stamp around. the quartermaster isues rations of Whiskey: now one gill a day, half gill in the morning, and the same in the evening with quinine in it. it is isued by order of Col. Benton. . . .

. . . part of this letter is hard news to send home, but it is the truth. Some, when they write home, . . . flower things . . . , but i do not believe in such falsities. the truth must be told. the newspaper corespondents that are with the army magnify a small good and cover [up] anything bad. . . . your dutifull Son, Charles O. Musser

P.S. Do not forget to write Soon and give all the news. my best respects to all the neighbors and friends. . . .

Camp Near Helena, Ark   Feb 12th, 1863

Dear Father: . . . you stated in your letter that you had not received any word from me since you wrote last. I have written as many as 75 letters home since i left. I have received 4 letters from you . . . , and i more than doubly answered every one of them. . . . it is all in the neglect of the postmasters. if any of us get a letter in camp, every one . . . is asking the news from home.

time passes fast here in camp—So many things to See, and we are busy most all the time at Somthing or another that we do not notice the time as it passes swiftly by. I just came in from an inspection of arms.

we do not know how soon we may have a fight here. the rebels fire on our pickets every night or two. they fired on our boys last night and run. they may have the imprudence to come in on us, but if they do, i think some will stay within our lines, for they will have a pretty tough set to deal with.

I think there is not much of a rebel force in this part of the country—mostly guerrillas. I do not think there will be much fighting in this State any more and I hope no where [else], for there has been enough bloodshed already—not so much bloodshed as murder. i mean killed in battle and died of sickness. two thirds of the men that go out to fight for their country will never return to their homes. I know of three regts: the 14th and 13th Iowa and the 34th Ills, called the Union Brigade. when we were at columbus, the three regts together numbered 400 men, all told, out of . . . 3,000 that left their wives and familys to risk their lives in the cause of their country. a great many desert the army daily. they get discouraged, and homesick, and reckless. it is realy discouraging the way the war is a going on, but we all hope it will soon be over.

the boys in our comp'y are geting along very well—not a great many sick. they are geting well that were sick. there is 68 men of our co. in their quarters. the rest are in the hospital, sick and awaiting on the sick. Gus Breese is tough and harty. John and Moses Nixon and all the rest are very well. Co. D has lost 14 men, Co. C 5, Co. A 7, and other Co.'s in proportion eccept Co. E. they have lost none. the general health of the regt is improving. [letter incomplete]

Camp Near Helena, Ark   Feb the 17th

Dear father and mother: . . . funerals occur very often. I have witnessed five funerals to day. they are So frequent that we are a geting used to it. in my last [letter], i Spoke of the health of the regt as improving, but the deaths do not Seem to lessen much, if any.

it has been Cloudy all day, and it is raining now. it rains often here —every other day at least.

we have drill every day now. our Co. is geting very well drilled in the manual of arms. if we Stay here one month longer, there will be few regts ahead of us in the drill.

there is Some talk of our going to Vicksburg as Soon as the health of the regt is recruited Sufficient for the trip. [With] the fix we are in now, it would be wholeSale murder to crowd us on transports as they generaly do. that is the way we lose So many men on these river expeditions. the trip up the white river cost not less than 2000 lives indirectly out of 18.000 men, but government does not care for a few poor Soldiers. when this war first broke out, there was nothing good enough for a Soldier that would leave his home and friends to fight the battles of his country. but now the meanest nigger in the South is more thought of than a private Soldier in the army of his country.

There seems to be a poor prospect for the war to end Soon. you at home may think different. we are not very well posted in the movements of the head of our government. the news we get here is merely hearsay, for we get no papers worth speaking of down in this god and man forsaken country.

this country is not worth fighting three days for. i would not give forty acres of prairie in Iowa for the whole State of Arkansas. i have heard of the Arkansas traveler. if he traveled through this part of the State in the rainy Season of the year, he must have been very near done and gone up traveling through the mud. Six mule teams mire Sometimes in the Streets of Helena. it takes four mules to haul an empty ambulance in the Streets. we are Camped on tolerable good ground for this region. we are handy to the woods but the water is very poor here—not as good as the Mississippi water.

(Feb the 18th) The weather Still looks dark and cloudy—just Such weather as we want to give one the blues.

Some of the regts here are being payed off. Some of the boys, as Soon as they get their pay, . . . get the foolish notion in their heads that they want to go home and See their families. . . . they Start for the north with the intention of not coming back again and . . . , in most of the cases, Succeede. last night, three privates and a corporal tried to get through the chain pickets and were Stoped and Sent back to their regt. the gratest dissatisfaction prevails here that can be Seen anywhere among an army.

Capt. Williams has not been able for duty Since we left Columbus, Ky. he has to have his resignation accepted by the commanding officer here, General Gorman, and he has refused to sign his name to the resignation. So he will have to try and wear out his Sickness, or it will wear him out Soon. Gardner is just able to be out of his tent once in a while. [Jacob] Fulton is Stout and harty. John and Moses Nixon both are run down with the Camp dysintery badly. Reuben Barton is Sick with the mumps and dysintery. John Boulden has a very bad cold. So he is not able for duty. if it was not for Wall[ace] McFadden, we would all have the blues. he is all life and fun. When he is on duty, we miss him quickly. Harvey Meginniss is tough as a knot. Sam Underwood is the Same old Sam. Gus Breese is well. So is George Holeman. but i am Sorry to Say that his father is geting very poorly. he has applied for a discharge. Doc [Surgeon William S.] Grimes Said he would do his best for him. Curtis Burroughs is not very Stout. he has been troubled with the dysintery. also, the rest of the boys, as far as you know them, are geting along very well. I have Stood the rubs of the Campaign as well as most of them. So far, the boys all Stand it as well as the men.

we have had but one funeral to day. yet yesterday, we had two and the 33rd Mo. 2, the 28th Wis 1. that is about the average number daily. the loss in our regt So far is 64 men: Co A 3, B 4, C 11, D 14, E 1, F 7, G 12, H 2, I 8, K 2. this is the exact loss in each Company. where the officers do their duty in looking to the comforts of the men, there you will find the least number of deaths.

this morning, the picket guards were strengthened by nearly double their number. the detail from our regt is 72 men for chain guard or infantry pickets. they ocupy posts not more then 1/2 mile from camp, the cavalry pickets 1/2 mile farther. the 4th Iowa cavalry and the 5th Kansas are encamped close by, also the 2nd Wis cavalry and the 11th Ind Zouaves. they are a good Set of fellows and good Soldiers. the 33rd Iowa is still here, also. . . .

I am Still cooking for mess [illegible] Co A. it is a Small job to cook what we have to cook. baking bread is the gratest job.

I have just been out walking. Some co.'s of the 33rd Mo. [were] drilling in the bayonette exercise. it is worth Seeing.

I heard by a letter from a friend near home that little sister Julia was very Sick. i was Sory to hear Such news.

our letters come very irregular. Some of the boys get Some every mail and others once in two weeks. . . . you must write often. I write not less than two every week. . . . tell Jane and hester to write me a letter to let me know that they have not forgoton one that will never forget them—even on the battle field. I have written to henry once, and i will write again as soon as he answers that one. we away off down here in this wilderness think it a great treat to get a letter from friends and relatives at home. . . . your absent Son, Chas. O. Musser . . .

30   Dear Father: . . . at this time, we are geting along very well, considering all things. the boys begin to feel like themselves again.

we are going to leave here in a few days for the Yazoo pass, which is about eight miles below here. we are going to guard the canall and the contrabands that are at work there. the rebels are geting very Saucey there. our boys had a Skirmish there a few days ago with the rebs. they come in and fall timber in the ditch and bother the hands that are at work very much. So we go there to Strengthen the guards and aid in the construction of the canall. there will not be more than three hundred fit for that kind of duty out of our regiment. the rest will Stay here and keep the camp while we are there, for we will not Stay there over ten days at most.

to day, the paymaster happened around and payed the boys a little pile of Uncle Sams greenbacks. the amount was Small, but it came very good to us that had been Straped a good while. the pay we received was the back pay of the months of Aug and September. So you See, there was but one full month and some odd days. I drew $22.10 and had to pay for the clothing i got when we were at Sioux City out of the Small amount I received—besides a Small debt to the Sutler.[19] I will Send all I can Spare home in this letter. . . .

. . . i do not See why i get no letters from home lately. the rest of the boys get letters more frequent than I do. John Nixon and Harvey Meginniss get Some letters every mail. it is geting late, and i must Stop writeing, for tattoo has beat, and lights must be out Soon. . . . your Son, Chas. O. Musser

N.B. the amount of money i Send in this letter is ten dollars. . . .

Dear Parents: . . . i am well and harty again and hope when these few lines reach you, they may find you enjoying the Same blesings of life, for there is nothing so good as health in the army.

this evening on dress parade, we had marching orders read to us. we are to Strike tents and be ready to march by eight oclock in the morning to the river, where we take [a] boat for the Yazoo Pass (between Six and eight miles below here).

to day, Captain Williams, after a long delay, got his resignation signed by the head of our department. . . . he is going to Start home tomorrow or the next day. So i thought it a good opportunity to Send a letter home by him. i have got out of letter stamps, and there is none to be had in helena. and i cannot borrow any off the boys, for they will Soon run out also. i expected to get Some from home before now, for i have written Several times for them, but i know you do not get half of the letters i write home. . . . i do not get your letters, for it has been a good while since i received one from home. John Boulden has never got more than one. . . . he has begun to think that they care nothing about him. we will all have to quit writing home Soon, for we get no answers at all.

. . . only a part of our regt leave here tomorrow. about three hundred will go. the rest are nearly all Sick. two more of our Company died today. they make eight we have buryed and three discharged. Mr Holeman has got his discharge and is going home as soon as he is able to travle. George Holeman is not very well now.

the Captain will tell you just how things are here without flouring it over in [the] least. he will tell you what Soldiering is in this part of the country, for we have Seen the elephant [combat]. the truth will Satisfy any one that we do not play Soldier. . . . your affectionate Son, Charles O. Musser . . .

By January 1863 Ulysses S. Grant, as commander of the Department of the Tennessee, had made two unsuccessful attempts on the Confederate stronghold at Vicksburg. Grant now decided to approach Vicksburg from the north, which would allow him to bypass the garrison's powerful river batteries. The key to the northern approach was the Yazoo Pass. Located half a dozen miles below Helena on the east side of the Mississippi, this 14-mile-long channel led first to Moon Lake and then the Coldwater River. The Coldwater eventually joined the Tallahatchie, which in turn joined the Yazoo above Yazoo City. But the expedition would have to slice through a levee, 100 feet thick and 18 feet high, that sealed off the Yazoo Pass, then, once through, cover 700 miles of Mississippi's treacherous interior.[20]

A flotilla of gunboats under Lieutenant Commander Watson Smith escorted a dozen transports carrying 4,500 troops (including 401 men of the 29th Iowa) commanded by Brigadier General Leonard F. Ross. On February 2 and 3 the levee was breached, and Smith's flotilla passed through to the Yazoo Pass on a swift, turbulent current. But his travails had only just begun. As the channel narrowed, overhanging branches damaged superstruc-

tures, and Smith's sailors had to clear away fallen branches and trees and obstructions placed by the Rebels. More time was lost waiting for the troop transports to catch up. Consequently, Smith did not reach the Coldwater until February 28.

Meanwhile, 2,000 Southerners led by Major General William W. Loring took advantage of the delay, using cotton bales and earth to build Fort Pemberton. Mounting thirteen guns, the fort was sited on a neck of land between the Tallahatchie and the Yazoo, just above Greenwood, effectively standing in the way of Smith's gunboats. Surrounded as it was by swamps, bayous, and flooded ground, a land assault was out of the question. This would be a job for the Federal navy. On March 11, the Chillicothe *advanced with caution. The river was not wide enough to allow maneuvering, forcing the ironclad to approach straight on—an easy target for Confederate gunners. Indeed, after a half-hour exchange of gunfire with the fort, a thirty-two-pound shell struck the* Chillicothe, *killing and wounding sixteen men, and it promptly backed off. Two days later, joined by the ironclad* De Kalb, *a mortar boat, and a newly constructed land battery, the* Chillicothe *tried again—at a safer distance. Despite battering the Rebels all day, the Federal navy still had not achieved its objective. As there was no place to disembark infantry for a land assault, the gunboats made a final attempt March 16. Within fifteen minutes, however, the* Chillicothe *was knocked out of action, and the captain of the* De Kalb *decided that discretion was the better part of valor. The expedition put about on March 20.*

The reverse at Fort Pemberton was apparently too much for Lieutenant Commander Smith to bear. He suffered a nervous breakdown and was relieved of command. Grant canceled the operation, and the transports headed back up the Mississippi April 4, bound for Helena.

On board the Steamer *Emma*   Moon Lake, Miss.
Feb. the 25th, 1863

Dear Father: . . . we left Helena yesterday evening about Sundown, went as far down as the yazoo pass, and tied up for the night. this morning about daylight, we Started through the far famed pass from the Miss. River to the yazoo. it is very narrow and difficult for boats to pass through. about Sunup, we entered the Moon lake, run up about one mile, and tied up where we Still lay. we will not start from here untill morning.

i will try and give a short account of our expedition. our fleet consists of Six gunboats and fourteen transports loaded with troops.

(Feb the 26th) we are Still lying in moon lake. our boat was badly damaged a going through the Pass by the limbs of the trees, So we Stay here to reapare the damages. the rest of the fleet went on through to the little Sunflower lake. there they will wait for us. another gunboat came from Helena this evening to escort us through to the rest of the fleet.

the weather is the most disagreable i ever Saw. it rains continualy all the time and very hard at that. it Seems as if it rains the easyest here of any place i ever Saw.

the whole country is flooded Since the levee has been opened for the construction of the Pass. large plantations are entirely covered with water.

(Feb the 27th) the weather kleared up this morning, warm and pleasant.

in times of peace, no one ever would have thought of runing Steamboats through the State of Miss. by such Passes as this one. our boat, which is but a moderate Sized one, can hardly pass between the banks. the limbs of the trees touch on both Sides. our boat is badly damaged by the trees. . . . one of the Smoke Stacks is knocked down and the other leans. . . . in fact, the boat is ruined. the whole fleet is in the Same fix, except the gunboats and one new transport.

we will Soon get out of the pass—perhaps not before morning. the pass runs into the Coldwater river, a Small Stream that emptyes in the yazoo. where our destination is, we do not know. . . .

(Feb the 28th) we are Still Slowly working our way through the pass. we did not get more than five miles to day. we have tied up alongside of a large plantation we found here.

Some of our cavalry, belonging to the Fifth Ills. and 5th Kansas, . . . had a small fight a few days ago not far from here. they came upon a Small body of rebs numbering 180. our boys killed one, wounded seven, fifteen taken prisoners. there was only two of our boys slitely wounded. they will go back to Helena as soon as we get through the pass.

i expect our boat will have to be abandoned yet on account of being too large and badly damaged.

the pass is more difficult the farther we get in. it does not Seem to me that it is larger than our musquito creek when it is at its highest.

the boys are all well—except one or two, that is. . . . there is only

fourty of us. the Nixon boys, both the Holemans and John Boulden, James Robinson, Albert Rauschenberg, Reuben Barton, Al Mansfield . . . all stay in camp at Helena. Charles O. Musser

(March the 1st, 1863) The weather is delightful, and as we pass along by the large plantations, we see peach trees in full bloom. this is the nicest part of the country i have Seen since we came South. nearly all the plantations are deserted by the whites. the place we Stoped at last night was a plantation owned by a rebel general that had been parolled. there was a fine large dweling Surrounded by Shade trees of different kinds. the weeping Willow looked green and nice.

it will take part of another day to get through the pass. we go so very slow. we did not get more than four miles today. it is yet four miles [to get] through. there is so many Stopages on account of trees that are in the way.

(Cold Water River   March the 2nd/63) We run into the river about noon today and found the fleet all anchored at the mouth of the pass. we are making preparations to Start down the river in the morning. this evening, another iron ram joined the fleet. also, a mortar boat came down from helena. they say that there is an iron clad turtle gunboat ahead of the fleet.[21] So with that one and the Musquito gunboats, two rams, and transports, the fleet will number 22 in all. the opinion of all is that we will have hot work to do in a day or two.

the country is full of rebels about here. to day, two men belonging to one of the boats went ashore and was walking along not more than one forth of a mile from the boats when they were halted by two men armed with guns and pistols. they took them prisoners, but finding they were not Soldiers, they let them go without parolling them. the rebs took them to where there was a Small force to try and get Some information from them concerning our force. the head of the band Said we would get a warm reception down the river. we heard there was a fortified point between here and Yazoo City that will be hard to take. . . .

(March 3rd) we Still Stay at the mouth of the yazoo. our boat is so badly damaged that they would not risk her any further. so this evening, we removed on board the *Key West No 2*, a Small Stern wheeler.

we have the most beautyfull weather i ever Saw. the trees are begining to look green. Some canebrakes along the River are tenn feet high, but they are green all the year round. the more i see of this country, the better i like it. i Should like to live here if it was healthy. the country along the river, as far as i have Seen, is flat, low country, except some few plantations. they were kind of rolling past. . . .

(March the 4th) this morning, we left the mouth of the pass on our way down the Cold Water.

last night was quite frosty. we slept on the top of the boat—very comfortable with our India rubber blankets over us.

we have halted for a Short time to forage on a large plantation here. we learned that a force of rebels had left here Sunday last. this was a kind of rendesvous for them. So we thought we would Spoill it for them. we Set fire to the house and it was soon in ashes. we got Some hogs and cattle there, too.

the boys are all well. we have an easy time now. i have not done any duty worth Speaking of, except cooking, Since we left home. i have not ever been on picket duty yet and not very often camp duty.

our Captain is very good to us. he does all he can for our comfort. Captain C. V. Gardner is not Capt. Williams by considerable. we elected him capt. the day we left Helena. out of 63 votes he received 51, [First Lieutenant George A.] Haynes 8, [Second Lieutenant Robert R.] Kirkpatrick 4.[22] So you can See how the boys like him. Fulton is our orderly Sergeant now.

(March the 5th) . . . the weather is favorable for us. it will take us two days to get into the Tallahatchie River at the rate we have been runing.

the country is almost entirely deserted by the whites. there is a great many negroes. they will Soon have to evacuate the low land on account of the inundation of the plantations.

(March 6th) we are now within ten miles of the mouth of the [Tallahatchie] River. we Stoped early this evening to get Some forage. we got four or five beef cattle and Some molasses.

the negroes here Say that the rebels will give us fits below. there was, about Six months ago, a Small battle fought near the mouth of the Cold Water. our boys whiped the rebs then, and i think we can now.

(On board the Steamer *Key West No 2* Tallahatchie River, Mississippi March 7th) We came into the Tallahatchie about noon to day. it is not a very large Stream, not more than fifteen rods wide, but very deep. the water is still riseing. the country, in a few weeks, will be flooded for Several miles on each side of the River. it is now near twenty feet above low water mark.

there is Some very nice plantations along the river. we passed by one very fine one yesterday evening: a large White house and about a dozen log houses, all nicely white washed for the darkies. there was somewhere near fifty slaves, mostly women and children. the men had mostly all ran away.

the weather is very warm for the time of the year. the Holly tree is robed in her beautyfull robe of green. the woods will soon all be in full leaf.

(March the 8th) we started out this morning at day break. . . . as far as we have come to day, there is nothing but an unbroken wilderness to be seen and water, water every where and not a drop of good water to drink. nearly all of [the] land between here and the Mississippi river is overflowed. a great many of the people will Suffer by it, but Such is the consequences of rebellion.

Some talk of Starveing out the rebellious States, but i tell you, that is an utter imposibility, for as far as i have seen, the planters are abundantly Supplied with provisions. Several places i saw between three and four thousand bushels [of] corn in cribs and plenty of pork and beef, but where our armyes go through a portion of country, they are more Scarce.

(March the 9th) the weather is cool and cloudy and has the appearance of rain.

. . . plantations are more frequent and the land a very little higher. We are now about thirty miles from the yazoo River. the main portion of the fleet is in the yazoo now. our boat and a gunboat forms the rear guard of the expedition.[23]

· our Sergeant Major and Wall McFadden started yesterday from our boat with dispaches to head quarters, which is at the head of the fleet, and was to be back the Same evening and have not returned yet. last night, about two oclock, an officer from one of the gunboats came alongside with dispaches. he said that the dispach bearers had not been seen as yet. the probility is that they have been captured by the enemy.

(March the 10th) It rained all night and is still raining hard.

we came to the junction of the Tallahatchie and Yalobusha Rivers to day, about noon. the junction of those two Streams form the yazoo. . . .

Camp Near Greenwood
on the Tallahatchie River, Mississippi
March the 15th, 1863

Dear Father: we got here the 11th [and] found the fleet all here tied up, three miles from the rebel fort [Pemberton] at greenwood, a small vilage on the west side of the river on riseing ground. the fort is constructed of coton [bales] principaly and is supposed to be very Strong.

the evening before we arived, the gunboats *Chillicothe* and *Baron De Kalb* run down close to the fort to feel the strength of it. our boats fired three or four shots, and the rebels fired somewhere near thirty. one shot took effect on the *Chillicothe*, entering the port hole and killing four and wounding twelve. they then fell back out of range of the enemys guns.

that night, our regt was called out at midnight to aid in the construction of a battery within five hundred paces of the fort. all but our Co. went. by morning, they had it finished and masked without the knolege of the enemy. we was marched out in the morning, and [formed] a line of battle, and stacked our arms, ready to be called on at any moment. about the middle of the after noon, we was ordered to march down to relieve another regt that wer on the out posts to Support the battery. we Slept there that night—that only a part at a time. we could hear the rebels all night at work on the fortifycations and their boats runing up and down the river, loding and unloading Something all night. in the morning, we could hear their drums distinctly at revilee. all this time, our Side was not idle but wer making preparations for the coming engagement. the fighting all will have to be done by the cannon. between the battery and the fort is a large bayou with four feet of water in it.

about 10 1/2 oclock, the first gun was fired by the battery. it is a 32 pound rifled Parrott gun. and the gun boats then opened on the enemy. they fired Several Shots before the rebes returned the fire. the fireing then became general. the *Chillicothe* with her two hundred pound Dahlgrens talked for a while. it was a perfect roar, louder than any thunder for three hours. we wer close to the battery and gunboats, both right in the range of the rebel guns. the Shot and Shell whizzed over our heads rather too close to Suit us. Some Shot Struck So close they threw dirt all over us. prety Soon they got one of our mortars in position and comenced throwing Some thirteen inch Shell in the fort.

myself and a couple Indiana boys were siting under a tree by the river watching the Shell fall in the fort. just as a Shell exploded in the fort, the rebs fired a Shot from a Parrott gun, and the Shot Struck not more than fifteen feet over our heads, and completely Shattering the tree to pieces. the splinters fall down on us but hurt no one. we got up prety quick, i assure you, and as we were leaveing, another Shot came uncomfirtably near, cuting the limbs of the trees off. you better believe we left on the double quick [and] run back to our posts some distance off. the fireing continued till night, and an occasionall Shot was fired through the night. through the whole day, our loss was only two killed and three wounded. there has been no fireing done since on either side, but great preparations are being made. to night, we are building another battery, and perhaps tomorrow cannonading will begin again. we have not learned the damage done to the rebels, but one large gun was dismounted early in the engagement. the damage done the fort was soon mended.

the force of the rebels is estimated from ten to thirty thousand men. the place will be very hard to take, in my opinion, for this reason: there is no approaches by land to the fort. the water covers most all the land between here and the rebels. we are expecting reinforcements of both infantry and naval but do not know how Soon. Some Say [Major] General [Benjamin M.] Prentiss will lead our forces. if he does, we will *go through the enemyes country.* our force is but small but determined. we are now in camp, but how long we will remain here, good Shooting and Strategy will determine. . . . Charles O. Musser

On board the steamer *Key West No. 2*
Tallahatchie River, Miss   March the 20th/1863

Dear father: We are now between eighty and a hundred miles from the rebel fort Pemberton.

about Seven oclock yesterday evening, the order came to Strike tents immediately and carry them on board the boat. we were not very long in executing the order. the whole expedition was on the boats by nine oclock, and by five oclock in the morning, the whole Yankee fleet, bag and bagage, were on their way up the river as fast as Steamboats can go. the object of So precipitate a retreat is not known by us. . . . no doubt it is *military Strategy,* but we the high privates do not see it in that light. it will save the lives of a great many men, no doubt, for the present, but in the long run, will it save them I ask, giveing the enemy time to Strengthen their works and encourage their men by . . . driving the yankees from their country?

this part of the State is the most productive and richest portion of the rebel country lying along the Miss River. there has been more than ten Steamboat loads of coton burned by the enemy Since we entered the Yazoo Pass. three rebel Steamers came up the river a few days before we did . . . loaded with coton, and were on their way down when one of our rams overhauled them and chased them for twenty four hours. the ram got So close upon them that they abandoned one of them and fired her in the midle of the river. So our boat had to Stop on account of the flames from the burning coton. She had on board over five hundred bales.

we have several hundred bales of coton on the different boats used as breast works . . . [to] guard against guerrillas that lirk in the woods, awaiting for a chance to fire on our boats.

we Stop occasionaly to forage. we go out and drive a lot of cattle up to the cattle yard, and pick out the best ones, and Shoot them down, and dress them in short notice. hogs, chickens, and goats alike suffer the penalty of death for rebellion. our boats have nearly all run out of coal. So Sesesh [fence] rails has to answer the Same purpose as coal.

It Seems to me that if a rebel fleet was to com in to our rivers, for instance, the des moines, they would not pass through as we have done without molestation. for when it comes to destroying homes and leaveing wives and children Shelterless and without food to Sustain life, it raises the blood to Such a pitch that if there was a chance to revenge themselves on the destroyers of their homes and fire Sides, they would quickly do it. but we might do as they have done. . . .

I hope this unholy war will Soon end and Stop this horrible Slaughter of So many men. what will we gain if the war continues one year longer? the war does not Seem to be nearer to an end thane it was twelve months ago and look at the thousands that have fallen in the last year. the widows and orphans that are left to morn their loss—it is horrible to think of, but i hope it will all be right in the end. . . . Charles O. Musser . . .

On Board the Steamer *Key West.*   Shell Mound, Curtis Plantation.
Near Fort Pemberton, Tallahatchie River, Miss.
March the 24th, 1863

Dear Father: We are now back onto our old Stomping ground again. we got here yesterday evening Safe and sent a regiment out on scout. they came in about dark with one field piece and sixteen prisoners. they were captured near where our land battery was. the men were cuting logs to make a raft to go down to the fort on. they were not expecting our return so soon, or they would have left before we arived.[24]

our regiment is now out on picket duty. I was not very well this morning, and I was excused from duty. I have a slight billious attack but will be well in a day or two.

. . . it has been raining over twenty four hours. . . . the planters here Say that this has been the most backwards Spring known for many years. I have seen corn here allready four inches high. . . . in a few weeks, we will have plenty of vegetables. . . .

we have plenty of provisions, Such as they are, though we cannot complain, for we know what we had to live upon before we Sold ourselves to uncle Sam.

the general health of the boys here are very good. of those that were left at Helena, the greater part of them were sent up the River either to Memphis or St Louis general Hospitals. of our company, I do not know who were Sent up or who was not. . . . (I hardly know what to write. the weather is dull and disagreeable, and one gets low spirited Such days.) Sheridan Street is a going to Start home on the first boat that goes up the river. he has been unwell for sometimes, and he thinks he cant Stand the climate of the South. . . . I will Send Some letters by him when he goes. he can tell you how things go here plainer than i can write it.

when you receive this letter, we will, no doubt, be farther down the river, working our way Slowly toward Yazoo City or back to Helena on a retreat. . . . your Son, Charles O. Musser

P.S. Write soon and give all the news, and how they are geting along in the political world, and the opinions of the people generaly about the war. . . .

Camp Shell Mound   Near Fort Pemberton, Tallahatchie River
State of Mississippi   March the 26th, 1863

Dear Father: . . . we are now in camp again on the old Spot, a going through the Same old routine of camp duty. we are busy all the time, and it is doing us good. a man is more healthy here with daily exercise than without. our regiment is in prety good Spirits now. the convalescents that were left at helena are on their way down here. they are expected this evening. Company F arived last evening. they had bad luck on their way down here. as they were coming through the pass with Some other boats, they were run in to by another boat, and was Stoved in, and went down in a few minites. the boys lost all their clothing and arms, but no lives were lost.[25]

as we were enjoying ourselves over our bountifull breakfast this morning, orders came to be ready for a march in half an hour with twenty four hours rations in our haversacks. we were ready in due time and were Soon on our way—as we Supposed, to releive other regiments on picket duty. but when we got to the lines, instead of stoping to releive, we passed on out, then we knew that we were on a scout.

we went on untill we came near the rebel lines. there we left a reserve of about three comp's. the rest went on, waiding through the swamp—from four inches to four feet of water and mud. our Company went across the bayou and pretty Soon came across Some rebel pickets—within gunshot of them. the rebels were watching our boys on the other Side and did not See our Co. there were ten rebels and eleven of our company. So they were nearly equal. the rebs took to the trees, and our boys got behind a large white oak log. the rebs fired at the boys on the other side. . . . our boys got around [the log] So as to bring the rebs between them and the bayou. so when the rebs fired, our co. fired, and seven of the rebs took to the canebreaks, and the other three raised the white flag and . . . give them Selves up as prisoners. . . . [they] seemed to be very willing prisoners. they belonged to the 40th Miss regt. they were armed with old U.S. pieces. they were Stout and hearty looking men.

well, after the Small Skirmish, we retreated back to camp. the principal object of the Scout was to learn the approaches to the fort, and all was Satisfactory at head quarters. Co. A has done So much for our country. . . . your affectionate Son, Charles O. Musser . . .

On Board the Steamer *Key West No. 2*
Helena, Arkansas   April 8th, 1863

Dear Father: . . . You may be Surprised to have a letter addressed to you
from Helena at this time, for but a few days ago we were away down in
the very heart of rebeldom—even under the fire of the rebel guns.
The morning we left Camp Shell Mound, we were Sent out to the out
posts near the rebel Fort. was there not more then three hours when
an order came to fall back on the grand guard line, and form [a col-
umn], and march back to camp. when we arived there, our whole
camp was torn up and the tents and camp furniture all on the boats,
ready for going up river. (our brigade consisted of the 29th, 33rd, 36th
Iowa regts, and the 33rd Mo., and the 28th Wisconsin regiment.) as
Soon as we could get on board of the steamers, we Started up the river.

the object of removeing So Soon, the Generals only know. we have
heard that the whole expedition was coming, but we do not know how
true it is. everything and every movement in the army is mysteriously
done, though it is all for the best, i hope. when we first Started out, we
expected that we would know every movement and hear all the news,
but we have found out Since that we do not know anything at all.

We have one of the best commanders of our regt there is in the
field. I mean [Lieutenant] Col. [Robert F.] Patterson. there is fight in
him. if he had command of a brigade of troops of his choise, he would
take us through thick and thin. Colonel Benton is Still Sick, though
not confined to his bed.

there is less complaining in our regt every day. . . . most of the convalescents have joined the regt.

I am Sorry to write you that we lost one of our comp'y a few days
ago by drowning. he was on his way down to join the comp'y in the
night. Some loose coton that was on board the boat caught fire, and
the alarm was Soon raised. [Erastus] Clark was sleeping on Some coton bales on the Steerage guard and was aroused So Sudden that it
scared him, and he Sliped over board and was drowned. . . . he leaves
two Sons to mourn his loss. he makes the twelvthe man we have lost
by death.[26]

. . . Some of the convalescents were coming down through the
pass on an old rickety boat when She run against a Snag and tore a
hole in her, and She Soon began to Sink. Some of the boys, being badly
Scared, . . . jumped off in to the water among the boxes and barrels

that constituted the cargo. . . . among them . . . was George Holeman. he hurt himself So that he had to be Sent back to Helena. I have not heard from him since.

Father, you Spoke of Capt Williams recovering *from his illness* so Soon. I do not like to Speak of an old friend and fellow Soldier any ways disrespectfull, but all the harm i wish ex Capt Williams is the conscript act will take him in its care. he was no more Sick when he left us than I am now, and there are very few heartyer boys than your own *Soldier boy*. he played his part well *and deserves praise for it*.

I have heard that the Copperheads are geting very Saucey about the Bluffs.²⁷ I do, from the botom of my hart, wish that the *twentyninth regiment* was there only one month. there would be a great change at the end of that time in the political opinions of the people. I mean the troublesome party or, Speaking more plainly, the black harted traitors that are trying with all their might to bring the war even to the very homes of those that are here fighting to end the war.

You Spoke of Some of the boys expressing their opinions too freely and Violateing their oath in So Speaking. It is just as you Say. they are home Sick and would give their all to be free from the army. You may depend upon it, i will be one of the last to desert my country in its darkest hour of danger. I came into the army honerably, and by the help of the maker, i will leave it the Same way. I knew the hardships we had to undergo and was pursuaded and coaxed not to enlist. but i thought it my duty to Serve my country in that way, and so far i have done my duty, and no one in my company will Say otherwise. but here, this will not do—too much Selfpraise.

By the way, i almost forgot to tell you that i am cooking for Capt Gardner and the Lieuts—a very easy posishion and but litle to do.

I have received no papers as yet from any one. (i have received from you letter Stamps at two different times and was very much pleased to get them.) you Speak of the military authorities at Vicksburg . . . keeping all newspapers out of the line. but it is only certain papers, such as the *Chicago Times* and other papers of like principal. that is perfectly right, in my opinion. . . . Your faithfull and loveing Son, Charles O. Musser

Northeastern Arkansas was mostly quiet when the 29th Iowa disembarked at Helena on April 8, 1863. Major General Ulysses S. Grant, in need of reinforcements for his drive on Vicksburg, had stripped the town of all but 5,000 troops. Consequently, Major General Benjamin M. Prentiss, commanding the District of Eastern Arkansas from Helena, was exercising caution. Prentiss ordered earthworks strengthened and regular patrols sent out. Small bodies of Confederates were harassing the garrison, and he feared that these firefights could be the prelude to an all-out offensive. But the big Rebel push was three months off.

Helena, Arkansas   April 14th/63

Dear Father: . . . the newspapers have all published the account of our doings: the doings of our famous Yazoo Pass expedition, composed of the two divisions of [Brigadier Generals Isaac F.] Quinby and [Leonard F.] Ross. I read a Short time ago in a certain newspaper of the capture of the yazoo City and a large force of rebels by the expedition from Helena. It is Strange that Such glorious Victories are won, and the Victors know nothing about it—even at the time it is done. you Speak in your letter of the reported Success of our expedition and the capture of Steamers. well, i Suppose all that report . . . [came] from the captureing of a rebel Steamer loaded with coton . . . [and] a few priseners while on our way down the river. where Such Scandulous lies originate we would like to know, for they only create fals impresions in the north.

If you had only one acre of timber Such as I have Seen down here, you would not want for fenceing for many years. but it would not do to have all good things together. I Suppose Mr. Peterson is geting quite aristocratic Since he has got a new house. he will feel above Speaking to a poor Soldier when he comes home from the war. . . .

I would like to know how the people like the conscription act . . . [at] the Bluffs.[1] I hope it will take Some of them milk and water men. we would like to see some of them down here toteing the musket in the hot sun all day. then they would have some cause to cry for peace.

I want to know how Cap. Williams talks and his opinion of the war Since he left us. i hear that he Says the rebs can never be whiped out. If the whole army was like him, then he might well Say that without missing the truth much. well, it is too bad to talk thus about one that has been our leader for a long time.[2] . . . your Son, Charles O. Musser . . .

N.B. we are going to be payed off tomorrow. we will receive four months pay. i will send Some home by express Soon as i can. . . .

Camp of 29th Iowa   Helena, Ark   Apr. 18th/63

Dear Father: we are Still all well and as hapy as Soldiers can be. . . .

. . . we received four months wages to day.[3] i send you $25 (twenty five) dollars by Express. . . . there is a considerable amount Sent by the boys by the Same trip. i thought i would Send the above named amount this time and await an answer from you to know that you received it. if it goes safe through, i will send all i can spare of the balance. but the probibility is that we will not be payed again for four months, so i will have to keep more than i would otherwise. If a person gets Sick here and has no money, he gets along poorly, for nicknacks and dainties are scarce in the Sanitary department here.[4]

. . . the Scorching rays of the Sun comes right Strait down in earnest. we have to retreat to our tents in the heat of the day.

the health of our regiment is very good. we have become hardened to the climate of the South, but we have had a Sorrowful time in becomeing So climated. it has cost us over one hundred and twentyfive valuable lives. the widows and orphans they have left almost makes a person Shudder to think. . . .

. . . the greater part of the troops that were here have gone down the river to the Scene of action [Vicksburg].

. . . we have the nicest camp in the outfit—the best aranged and the most orderly. everything is in complete order. we have it layed off in Streets and Squares. the Streets are graded smoothe as a floor. there is to be a premium awarded to the company that has the neatest quarters, . . . Keep themselves the cleanest, . . . has the most Soldierly [appearance], . . . and are the best drilled in the manual of arms. the premium is twenty dollars and Shall be awarded in a month. Company A will do its best. . . .

The newspapers have all been repulsed from the lines here, So i have heard. i have received three of them Cincinnati papers, but i do not expect to get any more Soon. . . .

Harvey Meginniss writes very often but gets no answers. . . . Some of his comunications with the *Nonpareil* have been intercepted and opened before it left the regiment. i saw one opened myself by Colonel Benton. he may have been justifyed in so doing, but it looks too much like medling with other peoples business. he found no contraband in it, but i do not know wether he sent it on or not. the probibility is he did not. Harvey thinks all his letters are served the same way [and] says that accounts for Sarah not receiveing any letters of late. such work does not gain him [Benton] much good will among his own command, for all he may have the right to do such things.

Adjutant Lyman is very Sick. Col Benton is geting well again, but Lieut Col Patterson is in command of the regiment—just where he ought to be allways. he is the man for that position and even competent of a higher one. . . .

it looks more like [we are] Staying here every day—Should not wonder if we Stayed two months at this place. . . . your affectionate boy, Charles O. Musser . . .

On Guard at Head Quarters, Fisks Brigade
Helena, Arkansas   April 24th, 1863

Dear Sister Hester: it has been a good while now Since i got a letter from home, and i have written So many. it is all on account of the delay of the mail. . . . there has been but very little mail matter for over two weeks. i have not had more than one Since we came back from the Yazoo Pass expedition.

I received one *Western Christian Advocate* yesterday. that makes the fourth one received by me. i tell you, they come good when a person has nothing to do. he can Sit in his tent and enjoy himself reading. it is but little time that we have to read. when not on guard, we are drilling, or policeing, or sweeping and cleaning up around our quarters.

It is reported that there is a large body of rebels advanceing onto this town, but as to the truth of the report, we cannot Vouch. we are building batteries here for their reception. in case they Should give us a visit, we will be prepared for them. at any rate, our cavalry Scouts came across a body of rebel cavalry up toward the Saint Francis River the other day. [Our scouts] had a Skirmish with them, routing them, killing two and wounded Several, and captured the horses of the fallen rebels.

the rebels fire on our pickets often, once in awhile killing one. a few days ago, they fired on some and Shot one poor fellow through both thighs, dangerously wounding him. i have not heard Since wether he is dead or not, but most likely he is. a person that is any ways dangerously wounded down here is almost sure to die. the climate is Such that a wound does not heal quick. of those that were wounded at the fight at fort pemberton, very few live now. i seen a good many that had only flesh wounds in the leggs and arms, and they would have to be amputated, and they died after all. one poor fellow . . . had his left arm Shot off by a cannon ball just below the elbow. he had it taken off first at the elbow, and in a short time inflammation took place, and the arm had to be cut off again, close up to the Shoulder. . . . in a couple of days, he died. i saw several cases where the wounds were only Slight in the first place, and they would die of them. there is but little hopes where a person is struck by the fragments of Shell. they Scarcely ever recover.[5]

The weather is Still warm and pleasant. it looks very much like rain now. the Mississippi River has fallen six or seven feet in the last ten days. it will soon be down to its usual hight. . . . your affectionate Brother, Charles . . .

Camp of the twenty-ninth Iowa
Helena, Arkansas   April 29th, 1863

My Dear Father & Mother: . . . we have news quite cheering from our forces around vicksburg. they have completely Surrounded the place and have Stoped all communication with other points held by the rebs. all is going on to the Satisfaction of our leaders.

the day before yesterday, a large ironclad gunboat of a new pattern came here on the way to the scene of action. it mounts ten heavy guns. it is the Strongest one i have seen as yet. it has a revolving turrett in front with two 190 pdrs. [pounders] mounted in it. the rest of the guns are mounted back of the turett and are of less calibre. I tell you, She is a powerful looking boat. She is painted red, while all other gunboats are of a mouse color or drab. if that boat does not Stand the Shot from the rebel batteries, we had better give it up and go home.

. . . I think we are doomed to Stay at this miserable town of graves and Sutler Shops all Summer. i would rather run the risk of one battle than Stay here through the hot months of august and september.

If the capture of the Vicksburg fortifycations will [in] any way have a tending to end this war soon, I think the rebels, if they looked ahead, could See [it] dimly in the distance [as] their "last ditch." If our armies in the east gained even no more than we in the west, the war would soon end. this lying befor an enemy for months and nearly years will never restore the union or end the war.

we are in for fighting to the last rather than give way to traitors and rebels. we will kill, "burn," and destroy every thing before us to gain our end. I never want to come home untill the war is ended. the rebel conscripts ar deserting by hundreds. they come into our lines everywhere. they begin to see that the old dog is dieing, and they want to come away and let him kick his last alone.

we are glad to hear of the change that is taking place in the opinions of the people, that is, the Democratic part. I did not think they were entirely lost to all reason. If the people were united, this war would last but a few months longer.

How the report of the death of the three persons, Moses Nixon, George Holeman, and his father Started i would like to know. what good can it do a person to write Such news home, when it causes Sorrow and distress among the friends of the Supposed dead? Such persons deserve punishment of somekind. I will tell you the true State of affairs as concerning the three persons mourned. in the first place, Moses Nixon is here in camp geting well and Stout. George Holeman is at the Hindman hospital in this town. he has been very Sick, but i went to see him the other day. he was geting Stout [and] will be in camp in a few days. The old man Holeman is now at St. Louis and will, if he lives, be at home befor long.[6]

Much obliged for those stamps Sent me. i have now enough to last me some time. i was fortunate enough to by a dollars worth. . . .

. . . tell Jane [one of Charles's sisters] i have sent her my picture. . . . I would like to have the pictures . . . [for] you all, but it costs too much to Send so many unless taken in groups of four or five. i had two taken just on plates to be sent in letters. one stamp will take them through in that way, but the pictures cost one dollar a piece.[7] . . . your Affectionate Son, Charles

Camp Curtis Helena, Arkansas May 8th, 1863

My Dear Parents: . . . I am now on duty in town guarding government property. we are a standing detail—thirty of us in all—a detail from each company of three men. we quarter in a very good house [and] have easy times on duty: four hours out of twentyfour. so, you see, we have very light duty for the present. it may be harder at any time for this reason: if any boats come down the river loaded, we have to guard it until [the cargo is] Stored away in Storehouses.

the health of the regiment is very good. Some deaths occurr occasionaly from chronic diseases. We buryed Sergeant [Curtis] Burroughs the other day.[8] he died of the Camp Dysentery. he was worn down to a mere skeleton. he looked very bad for some time back. if he had been sent up the river one month ago, he would have got well, but poor fellow, he is gone now and leaves a widow and orphans to mourn his loss. there are too many that go the Same way, to the Shame of the army Surgeons.[9]

there was quite an excitement created here a few days ago, caused by the rout of our cavalry by guerrillas. . . . about one hundred and eighty of the third Iowa cavalry Started out on a scout, intending to go as far as the town of La Grange, fifteen miles from here on the St. Francis river. well, the boys went on within a Short distance of the town, when they run into an ambushcade of guerrillas. as they fired on our boys, Scattering them some, they [the Federals] soon closed up and made a charge. but the rebs were too many for them, and they wheeled about and fell back prety briskly some distance and then wheeled and charged on the enemy again. but again they were forced to flee, this time in a complete panic, Scattered by thrice their number. the guerrillas chaced our fleeing cavalry over three miles as hard as their horses could go. but the greater part of our Squadron out ran the rebels and came into town, their horses all covered with Sweat and dust. Some of the men had lost their hats, others their Sabres and Carbines. Some [returned] with their heads tied up that had been thrown from their horses and struck the ground head foremost. there is about thirty killed, wounded, and missing.[10]

the same day, the 33rd Iowa . . . , about 300 cavalry, and two pieces of artilery . . . went out to where the Skirmish first began. but the birds had flown. they were gone all night [and] came in in the morning.

the next day, three regts. Infantry, two of cavalry, and a section of artilery [went out]. heard today that they had come up with the enemy and had driven them. our forces are determined to rid the country of them pests, the guerrilla bands that loiter in the vicinity of our armies. they took ten days rations with them.

It is not known how strong the enemys force is. we have been expecting an attack for Some time. but now we do not fear any force that the enemy can bring against us. the town is now strongly fortifyed. there are several distinct forts all connected by rifle pits. fifty thousand men could not take this town by attacking it. in the rear, the batteries command the whole country around. the country is very rough and hilly in the rear of the town, and no artilery can be brought against it.

The weather is geting very warm. the river is begining to rise again slowly.

. . . I have had no letters for so long that i have almost quit writing. . . . your affectionate Son, Charles

Camp Curtis   Helena, Ark   May 25th, 1863

Dear Father: . . . [Your letter] found us all well as usual. glad that the money got safe through, allso the likeness i sent to Jane. . . . I received a letter from henry along with the package of ambrotypes.

Curtis Burroughs died in camp at the regimental hospital. George Holeman died at the Post Hospital, Helena. we have not heard from Joseph Holeman for a long time. i expect he will be at home by the time this reaches you.

Sorry to hear of the Sickness of Doc Philips. why need a person be so fearfull of the Small Pox? I have been in small Pox Hospitals and among it many a time since i come in the army, and we have never lost one man out of our regiment by that disease. i was vaccinated while at Schofield Barracks, St. Louis. our whole regiment was at the same time Vaccinated.

the old rebel [Brigadier General John S.] Marmaduke is trying his hand again near town. five men of the 5th Kansas [Cavalry] came in wounded a while ago. they reported the rebels within five miles of town in force. ther was soon a sufficient force sent out to [illegible] them. how the fight will turn out we cannot tell yet. Should not wonder if we would have to stay in the rifle pits all night.

there was a general review of all the troops at this Post [on] the 23rd by the commanders of the different divisions and Brigades. . . .

I just now heard that there is a prety serious fighting going on near our old camp on the Coton plantation, where we camped before we went down on the Yazoo Pass expedition. . . . your affectionate son, Charles

Camp Curtis   Helena, Arkansas   May the 26th, 1863

Dear Sister [Hester]: . . . i have written a great many letters home lately, and ther is no news of any importance here now. . . . I am not very well this morning and feel but little like writing. my nerves are rather unsteady. . . . your Affectionate Brother, Charles

To Sister Martha: Hester said you wanted me to write you a letter, so here you have it. . . . you must learn to write so that you can write me one. be a good little sister and mind mother, and some of these days i will send you a present of some kind. wont this do you for a letter this time? i will write you a longer one some of thes days. . . . be a good girl. from your Brother, Charles

now i expect i will have to write May one, or she will be jealous of Martha.

My Dear little Sister May: I wrote a letter for Martha and thought you wanted one, too. be a good girl. mind mother, and i will come home some time and fetch you something prety—and maybe send one before i come home. this will do for this time, wont it, May? i will write some to you again some time. take good care of Julia for Brother Charles.

I must not slight Mary either, so . . . i will write a little for her.

Dear Sister Mary: As i have never written you anything, i will scribble a few lines in this one to hester and the rest. you must learn to write me a letter before i get home. i will expect to see a nice young woman of you when i get home. be industrious, and study hard, and make . . . [good use of your] time. you will yet make a good schollar—

even better than your brother—if you only improve your time. be a good girl. mind father and mother, and you will get along well. . . . your loving Brother, Charles

Well, Father, . . . ther was over two bushels of back mail came to one regiment yesterday from down the river. . . . [Our mail] went to the 29th Wisconsin, and their mail was detained here, so that explains the mystery of [my] not receiveing any letters for so long. . . .

the weather is still very warm. . . . yours as ever, Charles

[undated letter fragment, probably June 1863]

. . . many a poor miserable guerrilla has looked up a rope around this town. not long since, a Squad of the 3rd Iowa Cavalry captured 17 guerrillas out on the Saint Francis at a little town called La Grange. well, they brought them in within Six miles of town and there gave them into the hands of forty Infantry scouts that were out for the same purpose. they started towards town with them. . . . going through some thick timber, they [the infantry scouts] misteriously disappeared one by one, and when they got to the lines there was no prisoners with them. about that time, the cavalry scouts came up and asked where their butternuts was. they [the infantry scouts] replyed, "they got away in the brush just after you left us," and winked to the cavalry. they all had a good laugh over the fun, as they called it, [and] said that no guerrillas should ever enter our lines alive. *So you can guess the way the guerrillas escaped* that time.

and i will give you another instance of nearly the same kind. in a skirmish not long since, several miles from this place, eight guerrillas were taken by the 5th Kansas Cavalry and wer sent toward town by order of Colonel Powell Clayton, with an escort of ten men. . . . on the road they had to ford the St Francis, and in crossing, all the prisoners disappeared very suden by some meanes. when they [the escort] arived at camp, the Col sent for the prisoners. the boys walked boldly up to him. "where are those prisoners i sent to camp with you?" "well Col., they tried to escape from us when we were crossing the St Francis, and they were drowned among our horses feet in the middle of the river." the Colonel looked pretty hard at them and said he would have the matter looked into, but there was no more ever said of the affair. the name of the 5th Kansas grates harshly on the ears of the butternuts in

Ark. and Missouri [and] well it may, for the Sabre, and Carbine, and Revolver has brought down many a one. . . .

I have no pity, no mercy for the cowardly Scoundrels. i would rather put a minne Ball through the brain of one of them renegades than the . . . [regular army] rebel down here. I want nothing to do with them. they are my deadly enemyes.

I received a letter from a person a short time ago that i thought was a friend, but i found his toung was all on peace, peace, peace. I wrote him such a letter that he will never forget me the longest day he lives—and will no doubt forget to answer my letter. i hope so at any rate, for i do not want to correspond with a traitor. oh, how i wish that our regiment was at our old quarters at camp Dodge. i think some of the citizens would become acquainted with the tight rope. . . .

There are some large buildings being put up in town for government purposes. there is a great improvement in the looks of the town in the last two months. the streets has been filled up and side walks made. . . .

There is some talk of our going up the river before long, but i think we will stay here most of the summer.

The general health of our regiment is not so good as it has been. . . . the sick list is daily increasing. the disease most prevalent here among the troops is the camp Dysintery, more comonly Known among the boys as the *Arkansas quick step*. It causes the death of many a poor fellow. the water is so very bad here. . . . your Affectionate Son, Charles O. Musser

P.S. I will Send you a [Memphis] *Bulletin* occasionaly, so you can read a sothern paper. . . .

Camp Curtis   Helena, Ark   June 6th/63

Dear Sister Hester: . . . I write from one to three letters home every week and sometimes more. I write more letters than any other one in our Company. . . .

the weather is still very warm. the night before last, we had a very hard Storm. it rained harder than i ever Saw it rain up in Iowa. it blew a perfect gale for a while, and then the rain came down in torrents— perfect Sheets of watter. i was Corporal of the guard that night and got as wet as i could be, but geting wet does not hurt me any more. i have become used to it Since i have been in the Service.

. . . the sick list is growing rapidly. we are prepairing to move our camp on the riverbank [to] where we will have fresh air all the time and better water. the Mississippi water is the best watter we can get down here, and that is bad enough at best.

Why did not Hiram Boyles folkes have his funeral Sermon preached Sooner? it has been nearly five months since he died. he died the first of february. I wrote a letter to the old man a few days after he died. he must have got it in time.

We have preaching once in a while, Say once or twice in three months. Our Chaplains name is [John M.] Conrad. he is sick now and is going home. he is little better than no chaplain. he tends to our mail matter. that is all the good he does us or has done us so far. we would like to have a good Chaplain, but a poor one is a nuisance in a regiment.[11] . . . your brother, Charles

Helena, Arkansas   June the 12th/63

Dear Father: . . . glad to hear from home again. it has been some time since i got a letter from you. I began to think you had all forgoten me. i have come to the conclusion lately to answer all the letters i get and no more. the way i have been writing in the last four months, it will take all my wages to keep me in writing materials. i do not get an answer from half of my letters, and i will stop writing to those that are so slack in answering. *it does not pay a poor soldier that gets only his 13 [dollars] a month. . . .*

I was very glad to hear that David Breese had got home. he has by this time had enough of Soldiering. i think he has done his share. Sorry too that Victor Keller is Sick—had not heard from him Since before we went down the Yazoo Pass. but he will get his discharge, for his Father has money. more will get anyone a discharge. *Greenbacks are too much mixed up with this war to get along well.*

the news is very good. all promises to go on well down below. Vicksburg and Port Hudson will Soon be in the hand of [Federal] troops.[12] i have no fears of the results.

there is nothing going on around here, only the fortyfying of the place. it would take a large number of troops to take this place. we have a line of batteries and rifle pits all round town, and all the roads are blocked up by the falling of heavy timber.

I was very much Surprised to hear that one of our neighbors that allways appeared to be among the first circles had met with such an accident. for, of course, it was not intentional on her part. oh, no. guess not.

I would like to beat home and help to gather some of them Straw-bereyies. there is a few here or has been. they are all gone long ago. glad you have an increase in your horseflesh [and] hope you will have good luck with them, for i want a colt to ride when i get home. i will have to learn to ride horseback again. i have not mounted a horse since i came South. I expect [I] will be so lazy when i get home that [I] will never be able to work again. [I will] have to import Some darkies. they are a very good Substitute for work hands. . . . your Son, Chas. O. Musser . . .

Camp of the 29th Iowa Infantry   Helena, Arkansas   June 24th/63

Dear Father: I received your letter. . . . I am equaly anxious to know the cause of the delay of the mails. I have not written much in the two past weeks, for i got no letters and did not feel much like writing. besides, we have been very busy and but little time to spare in writing. . . .

It is raining to day, and it is very warm. we have showers very frequently. it does not take much rain here to make the water Stand on top of the ground.

News is very meager. all is stoped from coming up the river by order of General Grant. . . .

all is quiet around here. we have Scouting parties out every day. we were out yesterday. Started out at twelve o.clock night before last. marched down to the wharf [and] got on board of a steamer (*Bill Hamilton*), 250 of us, Colonel Patterson comanding the party. Shoved off down the river [and] went down about twentyfive miles to a vilage called Old Town. ther we landed (or rather below) about an hour befor daylight. we had four Negroes for guides. they Said there was a band of guerrillas hid in that vicinity some where. our Company and a part of company F were deployed as Skirmishers or flankers to prevent Surprise by the enemy. we marched ahead through the bush and canebrakes for nearly five miles, then come to a large plantation. then in the dim light of the morning, the boys fired on Some negroes that we saw runing, thinking they were rebels. fortunately, none were killed and but one wounded. the surgeon dressed the wound and left him in care of the women. the rest we brought along as recruits for our black regiment.[13] went to another farm. on our way we came across two rebs that were asleep in the bushes. Sent them back to the main body and then Shoved ahead again. next place we found the owner of the farm, a rank rebel, took him prisoner and Sent him also to the rear. here we found about fifty head of fine beef Cattle, drove them with us untill we met some of our cavalry that was out scouting, turned the cattle over to them, and went back to our boat. got here about noon, Satisfied with our one days work.

. . . Lieut George. A. Haynes has resigned and gone home. also, Doctor Wm S Grimes has gone home.[14] we are well rid of both, for they were regular Swill Tubs or Whiskey Bloats. . . . your Son, Charles O. Musser

Helena, Arkansas   June 24th, 1863

Dear Sister [Hester]: . . . glad to hear from home again after so long a time. . . . I was just going to write to see if you were all dead or not. just when the mail came, i had began to think that i had outlived all my relatives and friends.

I am Still well and harty as ever. we are now encamped on the river bank about one mile from our old camp. here we have quite a pleasant camp—allways a cool breaze from the river.

. . . we hear nothing from Vicksburg. news is stoped by order of General Grant.

I would like to be at home to eat some of them Strawberries. there was a few here, but they are gone long ago (nearly six weeks). wild fruit is not very plenty here. there is some Black berries and Dew Berries, but we have but little time to look for such things.

I am Sorry to hear that Mrs Holeman feels so bad over the death of George. he died in a good cause and deserves praises.

It is raining to day. it is very warm, though.

. . . nothing going on more than the usual routine of camp duty.

I got a letter from Douglass Harl to day, and not long since i got one from Watson Cooper from Vicksburg. the boys were both well and harty. [They] had been in Several fights down there. . . . your brother, Charles. O. Musser . . .

Helena, Arkansas   June 29th, 1863

Dear Father: . . . your letter found the 29th in tolerable good health. the Sick list is, i hear from the last morning report, increasing a little. but in our company there is more men reported for duty than usual. two men of our company that have been from the company for three months have just returned. they were on the gunboat *Prairie Bird* as sharp shooters, and another [has returned] that has been up to memphis, attached to an Illinois battery.

We have good news from below. Port Hudson is taken and ten thousand prisoners captured with it.[15] they are expected to pass here Soon on their way north, and the Shelling of Vicksburg is going on more furious than ever. a continual Shower of Shells fall day and night in to the doomed Garrison of the Gibraltar of America. General Grant has promised his men a fourth of july celebration inside of the fortifications of Vicksburg, and he will do it or Spill rivers of rebel and federal blood. if that stronghold is taken before the fourth of July, there will be Some of the lustyest cheering you ever heard on that memoriable day echo and reecho through the hollers and over the hills of old Arkansas. Such cheering will never be heard after that in this miserable grave yard of Soldiers.

I hope when we leave this place, it will . . . Sink down and the Waters of the Old Mississippi cover it so deep that no lead can Sound the bottom. you may think I am down on this town too much, but if you Saw the graves of our brave boys, you would Say may you have the fate of Sodom. On a small piece of ground not exceeding one half of an acre a short distance from town, I *counted two hundred and Eighty graves, and some of them had as high [as] three corpses in them.* If there is not ten thousand men buryed in and around this town, there is *not one*, and how long has our forces ocupyed this place? why, only one year. what do you think of that? It is the truth, the whole truth, and nothing but the truth. . . .

The armying of Negroes for Soldiers is now considered by all or a large majority of the boys as a necesity, and they go in Strong for it. for my part, i say arm every nigger of them and let them fight, for they need no force . . . to make them fight. I know they will fight and like demons, too. they know their fate if taken as prisoners.[16]

We have been out on several recruiting excursions since [we] have been here. at one time, [we] brought in nearly a hundred stout darkies for the ranks. there is one regiment of blacks here now. one went down to Lake Providence [Louisiana] from here some time ago. It was them that had such a desperate fight not long since down there. they fought like heroes. after the first fire, they went right in with the bayonette and clubed musket. a surgeon that helped to dress the wounds of the rebels left on the field Said that he never in his life saw such a mangled up set of soldiers: some bruised, and arms and leggs broken by blows from the clubed musket and thrusts from the bayonette. . . . Some of the most desperate hand to hand encounters were fought there that has been seen since the war began. The Colonel of that regt, the 1st Arkansas Volunteers [African Descent], is a perfect tiger to fight. if there is fight in them, he will bring it out. he was Col. of the 43rd Indiana Infantry. . . .

The 33rd Iowa is still here and encamps close to us. the Gann boys are Still here, well and harty. I see them nearly every day. Lee is perfectly at home, but John is sick of So much guard mounting and Parades. he is out of his Sphere. they are both prety rough boys. Lee does not stutter any now. he is a great, tall, crane-legged Six feet two in his shoes—John not quite so tall.

Glad to hear that David Breese is geting . . . well again. [I] would like to see him [and] will if i live next winter. Gus Breese got a letter from Mary Breese this morning. she says Dave is geting well. . . . I am afraid that Mr Holeman will never see his family again. I pity his family. they need all the services he could do for them and more, too. i dont think the neighbors will see them suffer if they can help it. where is the man that would see the family of a soldier suffer while he is serving his country? if there are any sick men in our neighborhood, I hop his maker will have some mercy on them, for *no soldier will.*

I would like to be at home a while and help you with your work but dont want to go home untill [I] can go home to stay—would not have a furlough if it was offered to me.[17] glad the crops look so well. [I] have seen no wheat or corn growing since last season. I want to break "Doll" to ride next winter when i get home.

Colonel R F Patterson Says that he will bet any man any amount under three thousand dollars that we will be discharged by the last of September next. no body feels inclind to take the bet as i have heard yet. hope he guesses right but am a little fearfull that he will be disappointed. christmas is my set time for the declaration of peace but will not be sorry if sooner declared. [letter incomplete]

60

The Confederacy had good reason to covet Helena. The enemy-occupied town served as a supply base for Grant's Vicksburg campaign and made an ideal springboard for an offensive against Little Rock. Moreover, Rebel Secretary of War James A. Seddon wanted action to relieve the pressure on Vicksburg. Recapturing Helena would crimp Grant's supply line and possibly siphon some of his troops to Arkansas. In Seddon's view, if Vicksburg fell anyway, Confederate forces in Helena could interdict traffic on the Mississippi. Lieutenant General Theophilus H. Holmes, in command of the District of Arkansas, became receptive to the idea upon receiving intelligence—remarkably accurate—that Helena's garrison had shrunk to fewer than 5,000 men. By July 3, Holmes's army was assembled at a staging area five miles west of the town.[18]

From his headquarters at Helena, General Prentiss sensed that some-

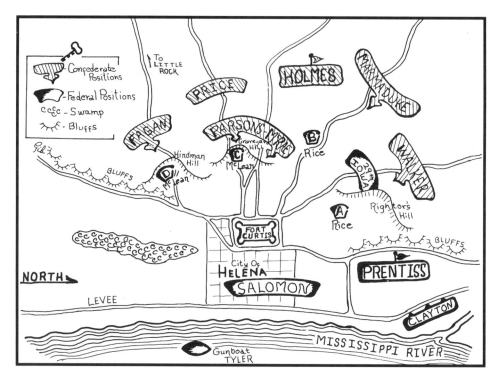

Battle of Helena, July 4, 1863. Map by Gaile Beatty.

thing was in the wind—for one thing, Rebel cavalry patrols had become more aggressive, tightening their cordon around the town. He acted with dispatch, placing four batteries on Crowley's Ridge, a range of steep hills to the west. Each battery, designated north to south, A, B, C, and D, included two field guns protected in a redoubt. Felled trees obstructed passage on the half-dozen roads leading into town. Between the line of works and the town stood the formidable Fort Curtis, bristling with thirty-pound Parrott rifles. Even more impressive were the eight-inch cannon of the gunboat Tyler, *which moved into position on the waterfront. Prentiss had the garrison— 4,100 men—sleep under arms, ordered reveille sounded at 2:30 each morning, and canceled an Independence Day celebration.*

Helena became a tragicomedy of errors for the Confederate side. On the eve of battle, Holmes conceded that the Federal defenses were much stronger than he had supposed—the result of poor reconnaissance. According to his orders, the attack was to be made "at daylight"—a vague term subject to each officer's interpretation—on a broad front.[19] Such an attack would be extremely difficult to coordinate, and the Southern army, 7,650 strong, was too small to carry it out. Still, Holmes expected to plant his headquarters flag in Helena after the commanding high ground was taken.

Holmes had his army on the move by midnight, July 3, but units searching in the dark for attack positions lost their way. Sunrise brought them no relief, for a heavy early morning fog had descended. Hundreds of men straggled into the assembly area, ill and exhausted from what had been a hard march. Brigadier General James F. Fagan, unaware of the roadblocks, had not ordered that axes be brought along, and as a result his artillery could not move forward. Major General Sterling Price's column also encountered roadblocks and rugged terrain, forcing the artillery to stay behind. As if this were not enough, Price misconstrued Holmes's orders and attacked hours late. To the north, roadblocks forced Brigadier General John S. Marmaduke's dismounted cavalrymen to detour. Crossing the rough ground was difficult and their guides got lost, retarding progress.

About 3:00 A.M. on what was promising to be an intensely hot day, picket firing broke out, and the long roll sounded in the Union camps. Within an hour, as Prentiss recalled, "the enemy covered every hill-top, swarmed in every ravine."[20] Complying with Holmes's instructions, Fagan had his infantrymen charge their objective, Hindman Hill, just after daybreak (4:00 A.M.). Having gone into action without waiting for Price, they suffered a terrible enfilade fire from Graveyard Hill. Still, though it took three hours, Fagan's men overran four lines of Union rifle pits before exhaustion brought them to a halt.

On Fagan's left, a breakdown in communication between Price's brigade commanders, Brigadier Generals Dandridge McRae and Mosby M. Parsons, further delayed his planned assault on Graveyard Hill. Finally unleashed at 8:00 A.M., Price's foot soldiers swept up the hill, planting their colors on the summit.

North of Helena, Marmaduke's column, assigned the task of neutralizing Batteries A and B, continued its struggle to get into position. At length, Colonel Joseph O. Shelby's brigade, leading the advance, drove in Yankee pickets—Charles Musser among them—just north of Rightor's Hill, killing several and capturing five. But the 29th Iowa halted Shelby's brigade near the crest of the hill with a thunderous volley. By the time Marmaduke got his advance unsnarled, Colonel Powell Clayton's Federal cavalry brigade, with four field guns, had taken cover behind a levee to Marmaduke's left and rear. Clayton's enfilading fire destroyed Marmaduke's intention to turn the flank of Battery A.

Meanwhile, Price, whose infantrymen had broken through the center of the Union defensive perimeter, had cause for optimism. If he could get cannon to the top of Graveyard Hill (the Yankees had disabled Battery C's guns before retreating), they would command both Helena and Fort Curtis. A staff officer was sent to bring up artillery, but the roadblocks made it impossible.

While the Confederates scrambled to exploit their breakthrough, Prentiss did not stand idle. He cobbled together a new defensive line to the east and concentrated artillery fire—including that of the Tyler—on Price's position. Holmes countered with a foolish attack on the thirty-pound Parrotts at Fort Curtis, an attack that was easily repulsed with the help of the Tyler's huge guns. The gunboat's eight-inch projectiles literally blew charging Rebels to bits, and their comrades, demoralized at the sight, either fled in panic or surrendered meekly.

About 9:00 A.M., McRae, one of Price's brigadiers, scraped together 200 men to help Fagan, now pinned down on Hindman Hill. He launched an abortive assault that accomplished nothing more than to briefly distract the Federals. But Fagan took advantage of this opening and moved forward. His exhausted men seized the last line of rifle pits before their attack ran out of momentum—short of Battery D's guns.

To the north, Marmaduke's artillerymen managed to bring up two fieldpieces. Under cover of their brisk fire, his dismounted troopers ad-

vanced—at least until they encountered the fire of the 29th Iowa. The Iowans then moved up to a ridge from which their sharpshooters could harass the Rebel gunners. This, combined with Clayton's artillery fire from the levee, forced Marmaduke to withdraw his guns. A stalemate now prevailed in this sector.

On Graveyard Hill, Holmes later reported, "everything was in confusion, regiments and brigades mixed up."[21] Price's men, pounded relentlessly by Union cannon, had none of their own with which to reply. By 10:00 A.M., Fagan was driven back on their right, and Federal infantry was advancing to reclaim the hill. Some 350 Rebels laid down their arms and surrendered rather than retreat through the deadly gauntlet of artillery fire.

Holmes conceded the hopelessness of the situation and called for a general withdrawal at 10:30 A.M. Most of Fagan's command was able to pull back in good order, and Marmaduke extricated his troops without incident. At 2:00 P.M., the battlefield at last fell silent.

The Confederate army, its ranks thinned by 1,636 casualties, reassembled at the staging area. Holmes reported—"with a deep pain"—the loss of a pair of battle flags and almost 2,000 stand of small arms.[22] His men were on the road next morning, heading for either Little Rock or Des Arc. Heavy straggling further reduced their numbers. On July 23, with the state legislature preparing to evacuate Little Rock, a humbled Holmes turned over what was left of his command to Price and took to a sickbed.

That evening, Prentiss wrote that the enemy's "dead and wounded strewed the bluffs in every direction."[23] Believing that the Confederates, although badly beaten, were still present in overwhelming numbers, regrouping for another attack, he did not pursue but appealed for reinforcements. In fact, Prentiss did not stir at all until July 6, when he finally ordered a cavalry patrol to investigate reports of a Rebel withdrawal. These reports were confirmed, but it was now too late to mount a full-scale pursuit.

As the sun set on the third Fourth of July of the war, the Stars and Bars no longer flew over Crowley's Ridge. Indeed, to paraphrase Lincoln, the Mississippi would flow to the sea, unvexed at either Helena or Vicksburg, the latter having fallen about the time Holmes's offensive fizzled. It was not, of course, a victory without cost, as the casualty figures of the 29th Iowa showed: seven killed and twenty-four wounded, all enlisted men, representing 13 percent of total Union losses.[24] In front of their position, the surviving Iowans buried fourteen Confederate dead and counted the graves of seventeen others.

64   Dear Father: . . . We have had a desperate and bloody battle. it was
fought on the 4th day of July, the day of american independence. We
have won a great victory and have lost but few men on our side. rebel
loss is, as near as i can learn, killed 650, Wounded 900, prisoners 1,000.
the attack was comenced on the town at 4 O.Clock in the Morning and
continued untill 10 1/2 O.Clock. it was a Sharp and bloody battle. . . .

I will now give you some particulars of the battle. we had been expecting an attack in the town for some time. I was on picket the third
of July. we was told to Keep a watchfull eye, for the enemy was within
a Short distance of town, and we would be attacked early in this morning. about two o'clock in this morning, we heard a few Shots fired on
our picket line, and in about an hour it was increased considerable all
along the line, except at one place where our batteries had the complete range. all of the available force at the port was brought out Just at
daylight, and about that time a very heavy fog rose and all was dark.
the rebs took advantage of the time and posted their troops to the best
advantage all along our lines.

we had not long to wait for the ball to open. as Soon as the fog began to clear away, the rebs came on with a yell and charged on to battery C, the middle of our line, and was repulsed with great loss. again
they charged on the battery, and again they were driven back with
great loss. [They were repulsed] the third time also. . . . the fourth
time, they were more successfull. they drove our boys out of the battery and took posession of it, but their Stay was but Short. the rest of
the batteries got range of them, and the gunboats also began to shell
them. Oh, what Slaughter and bloodshed. they were mowed down by
hundreds by the grape Shot and Shell. It makes the cold chills run
over me as i think of the dreadfull Scene i witnessed on the battlefield:
men lying in heaps in some of the ravines, four and five deep.

. . . while this was going on at that battery, Marmaduke tried our
right wing. our regiment was in the lead there all the time and fought
like veterans but not without loss. it was a Sharp contest, but our boys
drove the rebels before them and made many a poor rebel bite the
dust. pretty Soon there was a great cheer arose all round the line. the
enemy was . . . retreating. while the fighting was going on, there was a
continuos roar of artillery and musketry. when we were down at Fort
Pemberton, i thought there was heavy fireing, but it did not come any

ways near to the present canonading. We just mowed them down like grass. the hillsides were swarming with them. they had three times our number but all of no avail.

I was not with our regiment; when i retreated from the picket-line, i joined the 28th wisconsin untill the battle was over. we were in the rifle pits and within good gunshot of the enemy. I will not say that i Killed any, but i saw many a reb fall headlong down the hills by the fire of our small party that was posted at the nearest point to the enemy. two of the Wisconsin boys and myself were each ocupying a stump all the time while the battle raged near the rifle pits. . . . the rest of the Wisconsin boys were in the pits close by. we had fired all of our Cartridges away, and one of the boys Started for summore, when a rebel bullet Struck the poor fellow, and he fell pierced to the brain. the other one thus Started on the same errand, and a ball Struck him on the top of the head, stunning him Slightly. he got up and got the amunition, and we kept up the fire untill the rebs began to retreat then.

you ought to have seen and heard the cannonading. it was awfull to hear. then is when the Slaughter was the greatest. Our regiment had driven the enemy off on our right, and we had in our front . . . Killed, and Wounded, and taken prisoners half of the rebel force.

I have Spent Several fourths of July but never celebrated it with so much fire works before. I would not have missed that day for Six months wages. i have escaped with out a scratch.

The rebels, when they charged, . . . gave some of the most unearthly yells i ever heard, and when they were repulsed, our boys cheered, yess, real genuine yankee cheers—none of your rebel yells. I saw three rebel Officers ride along their lines, waive their swords, and order their men to "form [and] Charge on that battery, you cowardly h———l hounds." but they never all left their tracks.

lead rained around us like hail, but we lost but few. but the enemy lost half as many men as we had in our whole command. in the afternoon after the battle, thirty of us was four hours burying the rebels that our regiment Killed, and there was over one hundred men detailed to bury the rebel dead yesterday, all day. and there has been over one hundred more found in the woods around town. Some were Killed three miles from town by the shells from the old gunboat *Tyler.* five companies of the 43rd Indiana captured one whole rebel regiment, and about twenty five of the 33rd Iowa captured 60 of the rebs. and at another time Some rebs, two or three hundred in number, blundered into a ravine, and before they knew it, they were flanked and had to come right out to the battery and Surrender. our boys are still finding dead and wounded in the bushes. they left all of their wounded and sent a flag of truce to Surrender them into our hands, for they could not take care of them. *Our regiment did not take more than two prisoners, and none of us were taken.* we were detailed as SharpShooters and had no chance to take prisoners, but nearly all of the rebs that they shot were shot in the head and breast—all mortal wounds.

I will now give you an estimate of the loss in our regiment. I have not heard the true report, but as near as i can guess, there is ten Killed and twenty wounded. in our company, [there are] two Killed and two wounded. their names are as follows: Sergeant Isaac T. Lucas, Killed; private Edward Harl, Killed; Daniel D. Johnson, Severely wounded in the thigh; Moses Nixon, right arm amputated below the elbow, doing well.[25] poor Moses. he fought bravely and deserves praise. it is a great misfortune to loose an arm and right arm the worst of the two, but if you Saw what i have seen On the battlefield of Helena, you would think he was very fortunate in escaping so well.

. . . it was a very exciting fourth of July celebration we had here. And the news came today that Vicksburg is in our posession and 22.000 prisoners taken. it is sayed that the rebs offered to give up on the 3rd, but General Grant wanted to take it on the fourth, and he refused to take it untill the next day, which was the fourth. Rebellion is Knocked in a Cocked hat in the west. . . .

There was no commander, no officer here that day. every man fought. every man was as good as a Brigadier General. When the news of the capture of Vicksburg came to town, there was the loudest cheering you ever heard. everbody was wild with excitement. if the rebs had a come in then, we would have fought to the last Hurrah for the fourth of July celebration at Vicksburg and Helena. It was worth all the Suffering i have seen. [I] would go into it again with a good will. I was 76 hours from camp and never had my accouterments off while out two days on picket and one days fighting and lying in the rifle pits and behind Stumps.

Some persons can say that the rebs wont fight, but i will give them my word for it that they will fight and that bravely. no man here can dispute that.

I will now bring my rather wild letter to a close for this time. . . . Yours as ever, Charles O. Musser . . .

Helena, Arkansas   July the 9th, 63

Dear Father, Mother and Sisters: . . . Since i last wrote, we have been
finding dead and wounded, and captureing straglers from the rebel
army. yesterday our scouts had a little Skirmish with the rebs. we lost
one Killed. dont know what the enemy lost, but they run like fun.[26]
Oh, the 4th was a glorious day to the Federal Armys of the Southwest.
How the report got home that we were going to Vicks'g is a mystery.
well, we are here now and will probibly stay here some time yet—at
all events, untill there is no more danger of an attack from the rebels.
we have not forces enough to follow them, or we would have had another Battle or a big run on one side or another.

I talked to Several of the rebels we took, and they said they were
deceived in us. they expected to find but a slight resistance at the attack of helena. (. . . in the hottest of the fight, Some of the rebs yelled
out, "by . . . g——d, them must be Iowa boys." and then we yelled out,
"Iowa, Iowa for ever.") they said that "if it had not been for that regiment of Sharpshooters that wore caps, we would have whipped you,"
and that regiment was the 29th, the only ones at the post that wears
caps.[27] we put in our minnie balls prety close, they said. they expected
to find only convelescents in helena, but they were badly mistaken. . . .

I will now have to quit for a while. we have target practice every
day, and the drum has beat to fall in, so no more just now—Just came
in from targot Shooting. Co. A came out best: three best Shots. John
Boulden, Thomas Hutton, and Myself were the best three line Shots.
one of Co K Made the best center Shot. the distance [was] 150 paces off
hand.[28] . . .

I hope Soon to hear of the capture of [General Robert E.] Lees
whole army. then i will think rebellion is about gone up. it is in this
part of rebeldom. Some of the rebel prisoners from Vicksburg passed
here this morning up river. you will be overrun with live rebs up north
Soon if we Still Send them. we Sent 1,240 up the river [on] the 5th. on
their way [they were] rejoising.

the day of the Battle, Some of the ladies of Helena wore the Con-
federate colors publicly in the streets. Some of the boys told General
Prentiss about it, and in less than no time 14 of them were going up to
Memphis.

I do not know as there is any use of my writing anymore this time,
but i must Pass time away to the best advantage and writing when i

take pains will do some good. but i cannot write as good as i could Six years ago.

The weather is almost too hot for a white man to live here. i never felt Such hot Sun before. we lay in our tents almost panting for breath. it [is] awful Sultry. I will never complain of the hot sun in Iowa again if i get there.

The river is riseing very fast [and is] in a good Stage for boating. we have one of the best bathing places in the land. we bathe once a day regular, and since we have comenced it, the health of the regt is improveing. but our 29th is not [a] very large reg't—about half as many men [fit] for duty as we had when we left Camp Dodge—but it is more effective and will do more real good fighting now than when we numbered 950 men.

. . . I want you to write and tell me what kind of a time you will have on the 4th of July and if it has been as good as the one we had at Helena. I was playing Soldier last fourth, but this time it was a reality and a fearfull one, too, to Some. Mother, I want you to write me a letter. it will seem So good to get one from you, as i never have yet. all of the rest that can write has written to me, and you must write one once in a while.

It is Just eleven months today Since i enlisted, and the twelvth will Soon roll round, and when one year is passed, it will pass away quick. a few more days and i will no longer be a minor. I am the youngest looking boy of my age in the regiment. i can pass any where for eighteen years old, and it would not be doubted. The Adjutant Says i am a "gay little Soldier." that is what he told Cap Gardner. I told Cap the other evening that i guess he had forgoten his old friends up in old Pottawattamie [County]. he did not say much, only that he must write some of these times to you (father). . . .

. . . you must keep all of my letters untill i get home so that i can see what i wrote when in the army. it will be a terrible mixed up mess of Scribeling If you have not destroyed them. save them any way, for i have destroyed all of mine. they are so unhandy to take care of when not at home. My love to all, Charles O. Musser . . .

Camp Helena, Arkansas   July the 19th/63

Dear Father: . . . I am not very well. the day before yesterday, i had a very hard Shake of the ague, and a violent fever followed. i have had a fever off and on ever since, untill this evening. it has left me, and i feel tolerable well, only very weak. I have not been right well since the day of the battle. i was so completely out done. i have been tired before, but that day was the hardest day on me i ever saw. it was very hot, and [there was] the excitement of the battle, and lying on the hillside in the rifle pits, where not a particle of air stired to cool us, and the water we had was very warm. the next day after the battle, i was broke out all over with the heat. i was as speckled as a turkey egg, and whenever i exerted myself enough to sweat, it allmost set me crazy.

glad to hear that Cyrus Street is geting better. he was about right in his conjectures about Doc Grimes. the 29th is about as well off without him as with him, and we would be well rid of summore if they would go. likewise, for instance, [Assistant Surgeon William L.] Nicholson. he is worth about five cents in "sutler checks." W. W. Dried Apple Wilson has come back to the regiment again. I was in hopes he would never get back again, but a bad penny will return. he has Swindled the 29th out of enough of rations allready, and if he does not do better now, Dried Apples will have a hard row to hoe among the boys. when we were down on the Tallahatchie last spring, we had to live on half rations for ten days, just on his account, and the boys have sworn vengeance against him. . . . he had better keep a steady front or he will come up missing, for the boys do not stand on small matters now.[29] Orderlie Fulton has been promoted to the Seckond Lieutenancy [Company A] and [Second Lieutenant] R. R. Kirkpatrick to the first Lieutenancy [Company A].

Lieutenant Colonel Patterson has left the regiment on a furlough. . . . if it had not been for Patterson, the 29th Iowa would have been among the things of the past after the battle on the fourth.[30] our regiment fought against a whole brigade of rebels all the time. they were formed in line of battle just over the brow of the hills, far enough to be out of range of our fire. they had a force of sharpshooters equal to one whole reg't scattered all over the hills. at the time of the hottest part of the battle, Colonel Benton wanted to call the boys in . . . , form [a battle line], and charge onto the rebels. we, the 29th, was scattered all over the hillside sharpshooting, and Col. Benton was about to order us to retreat and form, when Patterson rode up and said that we should not, for it would be rashness and murder to order such a dareing movement. we would have been fools enough to go right into the Jaws of death then. If we had a charged onto the rebels, then there would not [be] enough of us got out of it to tell the tale. three thousand rifles would have been emptied among us many times before we could have gained the brow of the hill, and the rebels would have lost comparatively few. but as we were, we could lie behind stumps, logs, and in riflepits, and every shot we fired told on the rebels, for we were deliberate, and our Enfield rifles made many a rebel bite the dust. if a reb but showed a mark the size of a mans hand, a dozen minnie balls would take their deadly flight for it and was prety certain to hit. I helped to bury one dead rebel that had four ball holes through him: two through the head, and one through the breast, and one through the hand, all having struck him at the same time. three of the wounds were mortal.

I am sorry to hear that you are geting so that you cannot do your work. I ought to have stayed at home on your account, but I thought i was doing my duty to enlist in my countrys cause. I am not now tired of the service, but i do, from the bottom of my heart, wish that this war would end that we might all go home and live in peace. but as long as this war lasts, if that is ten years, i will give Uncle sam my service—if i keep well as i have heretofore. for what is life to a man without a country? there are a great many ties to bind a mans mind to home, but my countrys ties are stronger. hardship and suffering does not discourage me in the least. a great many of the boys are geting very tired and sick of the war and talk of home and peace. I cannot blame those men that have familie that need their support and protection for wanting to get home, but there are men here that are young and without families, and they are fretting and grumbling all the time and play off sick to keep from doing duty. Such men as them are not fit for anything anywhere. I would not give five cents a dozen for them to make soldiers of. they eat Uncle sams grub and are an expense, a useless expense to him. If I get home anyways soon, i want to go to school about a year or eighteen months—if i can raise the means to back me, and i think ther will be no trouble about that. . . . your affectionate Son etc., Charles O. Musser

3 ← ARMY OF OCCUPATION

July–December 1863

After the fall of Vicksburg, Grant returned troops to Arkansas, making active campaigning there possible. Little Rock, the capital and largest city in the state, was an obvious objective. Possession of it would give the Federals control of the Arkansas valley and a base for operations in the southern part of the state. So on July 31, 1863, Major General Frederick Steele came to Helena to organize an expedition.[1] Steele would join forces with the cavalry division of Brigadier General John W. Davidson, then stationed in southeastern Missouri.[2]

In the aftermath of Helena, the Confederates were on the defensive. Arriving in Little Rock July 24, "Pap" Price took charge of the District of Arkansas. Anticipating a Union offensive, Price moved to concentrate all available units to defend the capital. Fagan's infantry division would dig in at a point where the Memphis & Little Rock Railroad crossed Bayou Meto, twelve miles northeast of the city. Marmaduke's cavalry division, reinforced at Clarendon by a mounted brigade under Brigadier General Marsh Walker, was to delay the Yankee cavalry as much as possible.

Meanwhile, Price had defensive works erected behind Ink Bayou, north of the Arkansas River, opposite Little Rock. But this was merely a fallback position. Price knew that the river, low at this time of year, was fordable at a dozen points near the city, and he lacked the forces to cover all of them. Once the Federals got past Bayou Meto, they could easily cross the Arkansas River southeast of Little Rock, flanking the Ink Bayou line.

Camp Helena, Arkansas   Friday, July the 31st, 1863

Dear Father: . . . Our regt, and the 36th Iowa, and 43rd Ind, and the 5th Kansas was out on a scout of two days—Started early Tuesday morning.

the evening before we started, two companies of the 1st Iowa Cavalry, forming the advanceguard of . . . Davidsons army, from Missouri, cut their way through the rebel lines and came into Helena. they reported Davidsons cavalry sixty miles from here. [They were] on their way to cross the white River and wanted supplies for the army, numbering about ten thousand, all cavalry or mounted Infantry. So about ten Oclock Monday Night, two Companies of our regiment (B and G) were ordered to prepare five days rations and be ready to go on board of a Supply Boat as a guard up White River to St Charles. there they would find the army, and the rest of the regiment was to have two days rations in their haversacks and be ready to march at five in the morning.

. . . we were ready and waiting for the word to fall in. . . . at the time the bugle Sounded, . . . every man was at his post. Soon the comand "forward" was heard, and off we marched at a Slow and Steady tramp, tramp. we marched to Fort Curtis and there waited for the rest of the forces. Soon a long line of Cavalry was seen coming in our rear. it was the famous 5th Kansas. there seemed to be no end to them. tough and hardy looking fellows, they passed on, and about the middle of the column, there was them savage looking little Mountain Howitzers, four in number, belonging to the 1st Indiana Cavalry. they do terrible execution when they are set to work—all rifled pieces. Our regiment came next in the column, then the 36th [Iowa], and next the 43rd Ind, then the 3rd Iowa Battery, then one Baggage train, and ambulance Corps, and last of all, the rearguard (fifty of the cavalry).

The weather being very warm, we marched slow, halting often near the Orchards along the route. at noon, we halted near a large plantation (9 miles from town). the mansion House is used as a hospital for the wounded rebels that were caryed from here on [July] the 4th. there was nearly twentyfive patients when we were there, and a great many have died lately. our Surgeons visit them often with a flag of truce. We stoped there about two hours, and took our dinner, and had all the fruit we wanted.

"Forward" was the word, and again we were "marching on."

Colonel Clayton said that we must reach La Grange by evening.[3] We arived at La Grange about sundown, formed Stacked arms, and went to geting supper. Quartermaster Wilson went and hunted up some cattle and Hogs, and we soon had plenty of beef and pork cooking for our suppers. apples, peaches, green corn, chicken, turkeys, milk, potatoes, onions &c. formed our meal. soon the order came that we would stay there untill we heard from the 5th Kansas that had went on ahead of us and passed through La Grange about noon.

La Grange is a town only in name. there is now only about one dozen houses there. several has been burned down. the citizens are all Secesh, though they claim protection from our side.

We had more fun in them two days than we have had in a month before. . . . There is a maiden lady liveing there in a very fine House. [She] owns lots of poultry and Hogs, Cattle &c., and some of the boys concluded to have some "chicken fixens." soon the birds could be heard Squalling out their death cries all round. pigs also runing for dear life and many a one uttered his last cry. the Lady concluded She was going to be stripped of her all, and got quite Feisty at the "yankee thieves," and drew a revolver on them. threatened to Shoot them if they did not stop their Stealing. the boys cared no more for the pistol than for a musquito. Some of the boys yelled out, "Shoot Old gal," "bully for you," "give 'em h———l." she found that they would not Scare worth a cent, and she put up the pistol and went into the house.

I was on picket that night at one end of a lane leading from town (20 of us), and at the other end, not over four hundred paces off, was the rebel "Vedette" and the reserve not far in the rear of him. Our Vidette could see the reb all the time, and about daylight he left, and we saw no more of him.

About ten Oclock, Some of the cavalry came in and Said that the whole force would be in in a few minutes and we would start for Helena again. they had met some of Davidsons cavalry, and two thousands of them would be at La Grange that evening and await supplies from helena. So back we Started for "grave town," halted several times on the way, [and] met a large train of wagons going to La Grange under escort of the 10th Illinois Cavalry. . . . We got into town 8 1/2 Oclock at night, tired and hungry. next morning, we were all so sore that we could hardly walk at first but soon warmed up and have felt better ever Since. . . .

Furloughs are being granted to five percent of our regiment. three men will leave our company. James Wilding is one of them. . . . as for my part, i don't want one. when i go home, i will go to Stay. Rebellion is about played out in this section of the country. [There are] only a few Independent Battalions of Cavalry, the largest force under Col. [Archibald] Dobbin (900 men, all mounted). they are the ones we saw at La Grange.

there has a large force come here lately from below. we are going to move from here soon but don't know the direction. General Prentiss has returned from St Louis where he went soon after the Battle [of Helena]. Col. Patterson has not yet returned—expect him soon.

The Weather is a little more pleasant than usual but still very warm. . . . yours as ever, Charles O. Musser

List of the losses in Co A, 29th Iowa Inft, since first Organized, August 22nd, 1862, up to July 9th, 1863. . . .

Died of Disease: 1. Corporal Henry P. McElroy, 2. pr'vt Joseph Shadden, 3. pr'vt Hiram Boyle, 4. pr'vt Sylvester Orsler, 5. pr'vt Eli Deal, 6. pr'vt Jonathan Custer, 7. pr'vt Samuel Coffelt, 8. pr'vt Jordan R. Wittum, 9. pr'vt Albert Rauschenberg, 10. pr'vt George Reed, 11. pr'vt John Fierstine, 12. pr'vt Erastus Clark, 13. pr'vt William Peterson, 14. pr'vt Lester Slocum, 15. pr'vt George Holeman, 16. Sergt Anson Hedge, 17. Sergt Curtis Burroughs

Killed in Battle: 18. Sergt. Isaac T. Lucas, 19. pr'vt Edward Harl

Discharged on account of disability and wounds in Battle: 20. pr'vt Welcome R. McElroy, 21. pr'vt William T. Hunter, 22. pr'vt Henry Custer, 23. pr'vt Albert Mansfield, 24. pr'vt George W. McConn, 25. pr'vt Samuel J. Robinson, 26. pr'vt Joseph Holeman, 27. pr'vt Moses Nixon

Deserted from the reg't: 28. pr'vt William Reed,[4] 29. pr'vt Wm H. Deardurff, 30. pr'vt Benjamin Williams

Absent on sick leave: 31. John Martin, 32. Gerhard Seltz, 33. Daniel D. Johnson, 34. C. Se. Cole[?], 35. Hiram Lewis, 36. Aleck Smith, 37. E. T. Hardin. . . .

Camp Helena, Arkansas   Aug. 5th, 1863

Dear Father: . . . We are now busy making preparation for a long march across the country to Little Rock. it is Said a very large provision train is being fited out.

A boat came down the river last night, loaded with Wagons and Mules, also a regiment of troops from Alton, Ills. it is the 77th Ohio. The expedition will consist of a very large force of Infantry, Cavalry, and artillery. two brigades of our division will go and Steeles old comand—in all, about twelve thousand men.

We may start Sooner than we expect—our set time is five days. . . . There will be a great many sick and convalescents left behind in camp. none but the most hardy of the boys will go on the march.

. . . When we leave here, our mail will be very irregular, and you must not think hard if you do not get letters often. . . . i cannot carry much writing material along with me [in] this hot weather. . . . your affectionate Son, Charles

Helena, Arkansas   August 7th, 1863

My Dear Mother: Your kind letter . . . was received this morning with great pleasure. . . .

probibly before this reaches you, we will be on the march toward Little Rock. we now have marching orders and are to Start as soon as we can posibly get ready.

. . . News is very good from all points, and the prospect for peace is geting brighter and more encourageing. but months will roll round and may be years before peace will Smile all over one land. If foreign powers keep hands off, eight months will wind up this rebellion, but if otherwise, it will be some time, and oceans of blood will yet be spilled. America will never bow the knee to a crowned head. let us end this present war, and the North and South unite, and the combined powers of the old world can never conquer us. I heard yesterday that North Carolina wishes to comeback into the Union again and furnish men to whip the rest of her rebellious sister states. The people of Arkansas are also wishing for peace, and this state will soon have a new government and will be represented in congress.

The supposed object of our march upon Little Rock is to take posesion of the capital, and repair the Memphis and Little Rock Rail

Road, and open comunication with the civilized world up north. We will find no enemy on our march worthy of notice, only the Myriads of Nats and Musquitoes.

... I should like to go home and go to School next winter, but my country wants my humble services a while yet befor i can look for pleasure. What is home to one without a government? If this war lasts five years, and i live and have good health, i will help end it. No one out side of the family circle cares for me, and i do not know that i care for any one and have no one depending on me. So what is there to hinder me from making this, a soldiers life, my ocupation for life? The reenlistment of the old soldiers into a Veteran Volunteer army for three years will Soon comence, and a great many of the boys are in for reenlisting. ... if some of the boys from our company enlist, i will go with them. i have duly considered the case and think it is the duty of all the young, unmaried men to Still serve their country, even if peace is made soon. we Still want an army and will need the best men in the country. We will have to be separated at some future time, and now we are far apart. you are doing well, and i am doing as well as a soldier in active service can do and will soon have a chance to better my position in the army.[5] ...

The weather still very warm.

Troops and army stores [are] constantly ariveing from above. all is bustle and activity. it will be ten days before the army will move from here.

... i would like to have the pictures of the whole family but cant expect them [until] next pay day. i will Send money enough to the girls to have their pictures taken and sent to me in groops of two or three.

... Kiss the little ones for me. ... your unworthy Son, C. O. Musser ...

Camp Helena, Ark.   August 10th, 1863

Dear Father: ... We have just returned from a grand Review. the troops composing the Arkansas Expedition was reviewed by Major General Steele between the hours of 9 and 12 this morning, preparatory to our march.

We start tomorrow, and today is all activity and bustle throughout all of the camps at the post. we are all in good spirits and are ready for the tramp. We leave all of our extra clothing behind: Overcoat Coat, dress coat, 1 pair pants, one shirt, 2 pair drawers, one blanket. We Box them up and leave them in care of the post Quarter Master and receipt for them.

. . . you must excuse this short letter and bad writing, for i am in a busy time. . . . your affc Son, Charles

---

The campaign for Little Rock proved to be a relatively bloodless affair of march and maneuver. On August 11, at Grant's order, Steele assumed command of all Arkansas north of the Arkansas River and led his Arkansas Expedition Army—12,000 men and 42 guns—out of Helena.

With Davidson's cavalry providing a screen, the main column, accompanied by Steele, undertook the first leg of its march in oppressively hot weather. The heat troubled Steele's men more than the Confederate horsemen who were trying to delay them—sunstroke felled several members of the 29th Iowa the first day out. By the time the column arrived at Clarendon, a thousand men were too ill to march. The Federals began crossing the White River August 17, then took six days to reach Devall's Bluff, where they dug fortifications, established a supply depot, and built a hospital to care for the sick.

As Steele's juggernaut lurched forward, the Rebel cavalry under Walker and Marmaduke, heavily outnumbered, judiciously fell back. They dug in on the west side of Bayou Meto, a sluggish stream with steep banks. Recognizing that this position was vulnerable, however, Price funneled all but one brigade of his infantry into the unfinished works at Ink Bayou. On an ominous note, he also initiated preparations for the evacuation of the capital.

As Price had anticipated, the thin Bayou Meto line survived all of forty-eight hours. On August 27, Walker decreed a retreat after concluding that the line was about to be flanked. He did take the precaution of having a critical bridge destroyed, leaving pursuing Yankee cavalry wallowing in the muck of the bayou. A frustrated Davidson withdrew to Brownsville, where he awaited Steele's arrival.

Steele quit Devall's Bluff on September 1. The infantry now faced an unforgettable ordeal: a twenty-three-mile forced march across the parched Grand Prairie. The heat continued to exact a heavy toll as the column snaked its way toward Brownsville, the only available water being the small

amount in each soldier's canteen. So many of Steele's men suffered sunstroke that there were not enough ambulances to accommodate all who could not march. It became necessary, according to a historian of the 29th Iowa, "to fill the ambulances to their capacity, send them ahead of the marching column as far as it was deemed safe to go, leave them by the road-side and return to others. Thus, for the greater part of two days prior to reaching Brownsville, the sick were subjected to most intense suffering." [6]

The entire Arkansas Expedition Army was assembled at Brownsville by September 2. Here Steele considered the final leg of the advance on Little Rock. Davidson's cavalry scouted the left flank of the last-ditch Confederate line at Ink Bayou but found this approach unacceptably roundabout. Meanwhile, Brigadier General Samuel A. Rice's Third Division made a grueling forced march from Brownsville, staging a diversion to cover Davidson's reconnaissance and probing for the enemy's main body. As a result of Rice's efforts, Steele concluded that a frontal assault on Little Rock would be too risky. In the end, he made the obvious choice, deciding on an end run around the Southern right. While Steele's infantry held the attention of the Rebels, Davidson's cavalry was to lay a pontoon bridge eight miles below Little Rock, cross the Arkansas River, and take the roads leading to the capital.

The numbers were against Price—he had fewer than 8,000 men to oppose Steele's advance—and his options were few. Marmaduke had command of 6,500 troops dug in north of the Arkansas River, shielding the railroad and the northern approaches to the capital. Walker was south of the river with only 1,250 men to watch the vulnerable crossings downstream as well as two roads leading to Little Rock. To make matters worse, on September 6, morale was dealt a blow when Marmaduke mortally wounded Walker in a duel. [7]

Steele's column maneuvered into position, crossing Bayou Meto on September 6, and on the morning of September 10, Davidson bridged the Arkansas. Colonel A. S. Dobbin, succeeding to command in this sector upon Walker's death, had arrayed his whole force in opposition. But Davidson expertly massed the Union artillery for a two-hour barrage, saturating the south side of the river so that any effective resistance was impossible. Dobbin pulled back to Fourche Bayou. Price, informed that Yankees were now south of the river in force, ordered the Ink Bayou line abandoned. He also reinforced Dobbin, hoping to delay the Federals until the army could slip away.

While Davidson's advance was temporarily stymied at Fourche Bayou, the Rebel withdrawal got under way. The state government fled to Wash-

ington, Arkansas, and at 5:00 P.M. the last Butternut exited Little Rock— just as Davidson's cavalry entered. The weary Federals pursued only half- heartedly, and the lead elements of Price's army reached Arkadelphia on September 14. On balance, the capture of Little Rock, which cost Steele only 137 men, was a serious blow to the Southern cause in Arkansas. Price fum- bled his best chance to save the city by not making a stronger stand at Bayou Meto. The evacuation did mean that Price's army would live to fight an- other day, but the loss of Little Rock denied the Confederacy the use of northern Arkansas as a base of operations against Missouri and the Middle Mississippi valley. Furthermore, both Missouri and the Indian Territory were lost as recruiting grounds.

For his part, Steele, with an eye on the attrition his army had suffered due to sickness, elected to rest and refit at Little Rock rather than invade the southwestern part of the state. The campaign's aftermath had convinced him that the war in Arkansas was all but over. Numerous deserters and seces- sionist civilians were coming into the Union lines, prepared to renounce their allegiance to the Confederacy. Now deep in enemy territory, Steele was content to establish a reliable supply line to support an army of occupa- tion. Contrary to his instincts, however, there was much more fighting to be done in Arkansas.

Camp at Clarendon, Ark.   August 16th, 1863

Dear Father: We are now camped on the bank of White River near Clarendon. we arived here late yesterday evening, prety well used up.

We left Helena 2 oclock in the afternoon of the 11th, marched four miles and stoped for the night, started early next morning. went to Lick creek, took dinner, and then [marched] off again by sundown. got to Big Creek 12 miles from Helena. here we found the bridge burned and had to build a new one. that day, we was the rear guard and did not get across the bridge untill nearly sundown. the Guerrillas shot one of the ambulance drivers while crossing the river or creek. it was eight at night when we got into camp and had to be up and going before light again.

So that is the way we have had it since we started. a great many men give out and had to be hauled. we all got our Knapsacks hauled for us, or we would have been the worst used up army that ever marched through an enemys country. . . .

the boys are all well except John Boulden. he has a speell of the chills. . . . yours as ever, Charles O. Musser

Camp Near Clarendon, Ark.   August the 18th, 1863

Dear Father: Tomorrow morning, we will take up our line of march again for the capital. . . .

Troops have been crossing the [White] river for two days past and are not over half over yet. our vanguard is seven miles out on the other side of the river. they had a little Skirmish with the rebs the other day. It is the opinion of most of the men that we will have a fight soon. the rebs are gathering head and intend to Stop us if they can, but our force is sufficient to go through them unless they are fortifyed. we have a very large park of artillery, . . . and a great many of them are rifled Parrotts.

Our pickets extend up and down the river for fifteen miles. we captured two Steamers from the rebs a few days ago, up the river Some distance. they are small boats but will be very serviceable to us as ferryboats. . . . they had been up the White River for over twelve months and dared not to Show themselves. they were on the river last winter when we were here. The river is in Splendid order for boating. the largest Mississippi boats can run up to Clarendon with ease. it is a narow river but very deep and free from Sand bars.

We have to leave a great many men here sick and a force to guard them. thirty of our regiment took sick since we left Helena. the complaint is Swamp fever and the ague. We Camp on a low, flat botom near a Swamp and use the river, which is very bad. . . .

Two boats just now arived from Helena. they probibly bring the mail for us. . . . one of the boats is playing on the caliopi or steam organ. it sounds fine playing National aires. it can be heard for miles.

. . . Harvey Meginniss is siting by me writing to his wife, and Sam Underwood is lying on the ground faning himself with his cap, and James Robinson is puffing the weed. the men are siting in groops and squads all round. . . . Some [are] writing, some cooking, and Some playing cards, but there is very little of that done. it is not alowed. gambling is Strictly forbiden by the comander in chief.[8]

The comisary department is now isueing rations to the different companies ready for the march tomorrow. We are now Seventy miles from Little Rock, and it will be a Six days march unless we make a forced march. . . .

I have been very well since i Started and live in hopes that i will still keep well. this campaign is a hard one on us, and many a poor fellow will leave his bones to bleach on the accursed Soil of god and man forsaken Arkansas. several have died of Sunstroke and a great many will in traveling over the hot, dusty roads without water fit for hog to wallow in. there is a space of country between here and Little Rock called the plains that is fourty miles across and very little water on the route. . . . where an army of twenty thousand men marches over it, there is but little . . . [chance] for the rearguard to get any. . . . your Affectionate Son, Charles O. Musser . . .

> **Camp of the 2nd Brigade of the 3rd Division**
> **of the Arkansas Expedition**
> **Devall's Bluff on the Little Rock Rail Road**
> **August 24th, 1863**

Dear Father: . . . we left Clarendon the evening of the 21st and marched six miles in the night. reached our outposts about midnight, Stoped there all next day, and yesterday morning early, we started for this point, fifteen miles from where we camped the 22nd. We are now on the direct route to Little Rock. we was up here last winter while on the famous White River Expedition. . . . We will probibly Stay here a few days. I have heard it rumored that there is going to be a military post established here, it being the most important point on White River, and this will be the base of our operations against the enemy.

the rebels are Said to be intrenched within Strikeing distance of here on the west Side of a larg Bayou. . . . it is a body of water extending north and south many miles, and ther is only one crossing in our route. . . . we will have to dislodge him before we can effect a crossing. . . .

This is a Splendid country here, to all appearances. yesterday, we crossed Some very nice Prairie, the first we had Seen since we left home. it looks very homelike. the first Scope of prairie was, in extent, several Square miles, and as level as a floor, and entirely surrounded by heavy timber. it looked more like a lake of Still water than land. it was four miles wide, and our column of troops reached clear across, and we could not see more than half of them. then we crossed two Such lakes of grass in our route. but one great disadvantage to this country keeps it unsettled, and that is there is no water worth Speaking of along our line of march but Wells, and they are not sufficient to water only one plantation. we have to make long marches on acount of the water. this part of the State is well wooded, but the prairie will not produce. it dries out like an ash heap.

I heard this morning that there has been a train of cars captured by Davidsons cavalry out some twenty miles from here, but [I] cant put much confidence in the rumor.

the boys are generaly very well but Sore from marching. i feel "Bully" this morning. . . . your Aff. Son, Charles Musser

Devall's Bluff, Ark   August 24th, 1863

Dear Sister [Hester]: . . . we are now Encamped on the west Side of White River on a hill under the Shades of the large White Oaks. we have no tents with us, and we have to Sleep in the open air.

we are all geting as Swarthy as gipsies and tough as men can get from liveing as we do. i have not Slept with my clothing off Since we left Helena. we are all dirty and care for nothing. [We would] just as Soon mete the enemy as not, especialy when we have been marching all day without "grub." we would fight them like demons, and when we Stop at a plantation, the poultry, pigs, and beef has to Suffer. Some of our boys just now passed here, driveing a fat Steer. they are taking him out of Sight of the officers to kill him. We play some Sharp games on our officers. What an old soldier can't think of is not worth thinking of in the way of forageing or any thing connected with the life of a Soldier. when there is orders not to Shoot, we bayonette the hogs and beef. the bayonette is more used for such purpose than any other, and our regiment cant be beat at anything we go at, even fighting. we have the best marksmen of any regiment in the brigade.

. . . i will write every opportunity i have, but i will have to write Short ones while on the march. you must write often. . . . your brother, Charles . . .

Camp Near Brownsville, Arkansas
September 2nd, 1863

Dear Sister: . . . we are now about one and a half days march from Little Rock. our boys have had Some very severe skirmishing all the way from here to within six miles of the capital. our loss in the Several days fighting is variously estimated from thirtyfive to sixty killed and wounded. the vanguard of our cavalry had quite an engagement in Brownsville. the rebs were there in large force and had the fenses all let down, ready for a charge, when our boys came through the lane. but our scouts smelled a . . . [trap], and the order was artillery to the front, and the first thing the rebs knew, Some Shell and grape [shot] was on their track. they did not stand long, but took [illegible] Tactics and went as fast as their confederate leggs would cary them. the rebs loss is not known, but our loss was four killed and sixteen Wounded. there is a large number of rebel prisoners in town now, taken in the fights.

We made a long march yesterday in order to get to good water. we marched about twentyfour miles. the day before, we only marched eight miles. about ten miles from here is our next camping ground. . . . the march yesterday was most too much for me, and it made me very nervous.

I will Write only one letter home each week hereafter, for my writing material is runing short, and [I am] so far from any place that it could be got at. I have written a great many letters since we left Helena. allready it is not yet a month, and half of my stationery is gone. . . .

(Camp Near Brownsville Sept 5th) . . . late yesterday evening, we arived in camp from a two days march.

we, the 3rd Division, was ordered early on the morning of the 3rd to be ready to march by six oclock with two days rations in our haversacks and our India rubber blankets. . . . (Brigadier General Rice commands the 3rd Division, which is composed of two Brigades under the comand of Acting Brigadiers Benton and [Charles W.] Kittredge.)[9] the first Brigade of Cavalry also was ordered to march. we started in good time. the intention was to reach Bayou Meto by eleven oclock. it is eighteen miles from here. we did not get to the Bayou untill nearly two in the afternoon, and then over five hundred men gave out and had to be hauled. the cavalry went down the Bayou five or Six miles, and crossed, and went on toward Little Rock while we marched up to the bridge. Saw the rebel pickets in retreat and threw some shell at them. they disappeared beyond the bluff that is fortified. we were not sent to bring on an engagement, and we fell back to an old rebel camp and stacked arms for the night. our march was only a feigned movement to draw the attention of the enemy So that the cavalry could get in the rear. it is said that they have a strong position . . . some Six or

84

seven miles farther on [at] what is called Ink Bayou, five miles from the city.

well, the next morning at nine, we started back for camp. arived just at dark [and] found that the cavalry fource had beat us back. Our reconoisance prooved Satisfactory to General Steele, and that was all we wanted. but Such forced marches are hard on us, especially in Such hot weather.

When we were ordered to march back to Brownsville from Bayou Meto, the boys all began to curse and swear, Saying that they would rather fight than march. . . . after marching eighteen miles, and [having] found the enemy, and then have to march away from them was too much to stand without Saying Something. I never Saw a Set of men So mad in my life. it would make the blood run cold to hear some of them curse the Officer in comand. when we arived at the picket lines, the men that were here would ask "how far have you been out?" The first answer would be "go to h———ll" or Some other like answer. i guess they thought our comand was a crabbed set of men. I tell you, when a soldier is tired, footsore, and hungry, he will not take a word from his best friend. . . .

I received a letter from Jane not long since, and she told me that she had heard from William but gave but few particulars. I am Sorry that i have to fight against a brother, but fate So ordered it and [I] cannot help it. . . . William may have fallen at Helena, but i think not, for i seen about all of the dead Officers that was left on the field, and he may not now be in the service at all. i hope not for his sake and the sake of our family.[10]

. . . I have a very poor pen to write with, and my hand is very unsteady from marching, and you must excuse the bad writing. . . . your Affectionate Brother, Charles

Camp Near Little Rock, Arkansas   Sept 22th/63

Dear Father: . . . we have moved camp from the East Side of the river to a camp once used by . . . Shelbys Misourians of Prices army.[11] there is now only one Brigade of Prices force that he can trust, and they are geting So reduced in numbers that ere long, the great rebel army of the Southwest will be among the things of the past.

A few days ago, i had a long conversation with a parolled rebel Officer from Missouri by the name of Yates. . . . I made Some enquiries about William. he Said he knew a young man by the name of Musser in the Comisary department. . . . Said he was not personaly acquainted with him but Knew he was a northerner by birth. . . . he Said he thought William was dead if he was not among the prisoners taken by Grant at Vicksburg. "Cap[tain] Yates" Said William, for i am prety certain it was him ranked as first Lieutenant or Captain in the Comisary Department. If he is gone, i say peace to his soul. I hope i will die a more honoreble death when my time comes.

Business is begining to get quite brisk in the city. Hotells, Shops, stores, and other public houses are being opened again after being closed for many months. Farmers bring in their produce to Sell and get good prices for it. young men that have escaped the Conscription and Deserters are coming in and enrolling themselves as a State Militia and geting arms. they are allready doing good Service as Scouts. they are acquainted with the country and Know who are loyal and who are not. they have brought in a good many Guerrillas and bushwhackers. the Penitentiary is nearly full of rascals of that character, and they will . . . leave there only for the *grave.* The Citizens generaly Seemed glad to see us and treat us with great Kindness. there is Some very *fine people* in the city.

One lamentable accident occurred the day we took the city. Some rebs crouded into the Street and fired at us, and we unlimbered a gun and threw some shell among the rebs. . . . one shell was thrown too far into another street, and a little child happened to be in the street when it exploded, and the child was cut in two by the fragments of the shell. . . . its mother near by [was] going to get it—poor thing did not know the danger it was in. it was only two and a half years old. The rebs have it reported now that we killed innocent women and children when the confederate army was gone. that is one way the Southern people are *So* bitterly against us.

We have allready got a printing press into operation in the city. the paper is isued weekly. it is called the *National Union.* it is Edited by a Loyal Arkansasian. it calls loudly on the people of Arkansas to rally for the old union, Since the dark cloud of rebellion and anarchy has passed over, and the bright sun of our union now Shines gloriously over a once oppressed people.

If the people at home were only more united, our Soldiers in the field would do their duty with a better will. but [there is] So much partyism and quarreling among the men at home that ought to be looking to the welfare of the families of Soldiers and to the good of our country. Some of our boys get letters from their friends at home, and they Say we are represented at home as being clamorous for peace on any terms. now i tell you, it would not be good for the health of the men that represent us to the people in that way if we would get them into our hands. the sneaking, cowardly, villianous Copperheads are the ones that keep up Such a "fire in the rear." I do not care how much they talk, So long as they do not touch us Soldiers. there is Some men in the Bluffs that if they were here with us they would *ride* on the Bayonette very quick. Some of the Soldiers that have Shared our hardships, fought on bloody fields with us, have now turned and are runing on a Copperhead ticket for offices of trust and profit. Yes, in our own state of Iowa it would have been better for them if they had went and hung themselves [to] a man. . . . their manhood and principles ought to have been killed on the field of battle. then their names would have been recorded in the book of fame. [Benedict] Arnold at one time was a great man, but one act spoiled all. there is yet Some Arnolds left.

. . . i hope by next Spring to hear of the declaration of peace and the rebels all back to their allegiance. Oh what a day that will be to us, but our hopes may be all vain. our castles in air may vanish, and we still Stay in the Service and have to fight Louis Napoleons Grenadiers and Veterans. let them come. We can whip americans, and We Know we can Whip *Frenchmen* if it comes to the test.[12]

We get but little news here, and it is generaly Stale when it comes. i am not very well posted in the movements of our armies, but from what i can learn, all is favorable. I expect by this time Charleston is ours. Chattanooga is ours also.[13] all will Soon be Ours. . . .

The weather is Still warm through the day and cool at night. our tents and clothing that we left at Helena have been sent for and will be here Soon. Act[ing] Adjutant . . . Lyman has gone after the men that were left at the Convalescent Camp [in] Helena. from that i judge we will Stay here all winter. . . . your Affectionate Son, Charles O. Musser . . .

Camp Near Little Rock, Arkansas   Oct 3rd/63

Dear Father: . . . glad to hear from home again. it has been Some time

Since i got a letter from home, and i had almost began to think you had quit writing to me but better late than not at all.

We are going to build Barracks next week, So i have heard, but there is no certainty of it. there is Some talk of our Brigade doing Provost duty in the city. if we do, we will not build Barracks.

The weather is geting some cooler than it has been. fall winds are Stiring—nights geting very cool. . . .

. . . we have lost but few men since we came here, and they were old, chronic Cases. one of our boys died last night. he has been Sick for over Six months. his name is Thomas Loynd. he is the boy i tended on when we were at Sioux City last fall. i Saved his life then only [for him] to die a lingering death down here in Dixie.[14] I expect you have heard of the death of John W. Peck of our company. he died the 14th of September of a hurt he received last Spring at Helena. he was ruptured Some very inwardly. he was appearantly well when we left Helena and done duty with the rest of us most of the time untill he was taken down sick. inflamation took place, and he died very sudenly. we made a box for him and buryed him with the honors of war. fired a last farewell volley over the grave of one that served his country faithfuly and died with a prayr for the welfare of our country.[15] one of our boys that was left at Helena died since we left. he was from Harrison County. his name was Alexander Smith.[16] another one that was Sent to Memphis died lately. he was a good boy and a faithfull soldier. his name was Wm Cox, also from Harrison county.[17]

Our company is now very Small. but it is tough and rough enough to make up for numbers. we have only about thirty men [fit] for duty. . . .

Captain Gardner is going to Memphis and [is] perhaps home . . . now. he is in comand of an escort that is taking rebel prisoners from here up north to exchange or be sent to Alton [Illinois]. he will try and get a furlough. if he can, he will give our county a visit before he returns. he Starts in the morning. If he gets up there, he will give you a Statement of affairs in our regiment. . . . your Son, Charles M. . . .

Camp Near Little Rock, Ark   October the 6th, 1863

Dear Father: . . . I just returned last night from Devall's Bluff by the nine oclock train. I was Sent in comand of a detail of thirty men from the 2nd Brigade to escort Some rebel prisoners to the Bluff and then load the train with the goods and . . . camp equipage of our Brigade. we started the morning of the 4th from camp, marched to the Depot, and waited for the prisoners, 330 of them. (the escort that was to take them to Memphis is comanded by Capt Gardner. he is going clear home before he joins the regiment again. . . .) as soon as the rebs were on board of the boat, we went to loading the cars with our goods. we did not get them all loaded untill next evening. we then got on board of the arkansas rail cars and Started for . . . Little Rock. it [Memphis & Little Rock Railroad] is the roughest road i ever saw. it is twice as bad as the . . . North Misouri Road, and that is a very bad road. this road is the straitest one i ever saw. the country is so level that there is not more than one [illegible] on the road that is over eight feet deep. there are but few bridges [and] only two of any importance: one on Bayou Meto and one on Ink Bayou. there is a regiment of cavalry encamped at each of the bridges to prevent the Guerrillas from burning them. all along the road, it is a very wild looking country. the hand of civiliza- tion has done but little there. game is plenty, Such as deer, turky, bear, opossum, coon, etc.

as we were coming along yesterday at a very good rate upon the Prairie near Brownsville station, a large, fat buck jumped up out of the grass and started to run when a man of the 28th Wis hauled up his enfield and cracked away at Mr deer. he made a couple of leaps, and down he come. he was fourty rods off when he was shot, and the cars [were] going very fast. the old Iron Horse would not stop for us to get our venison. we hated to go off and leave him lying there on the Prairie to be devowered by hogs and woolvs. I tell you, we have some of the best marksmen i ever saw in our brigade. we tried our guns yes- terday as we were coming from the Bluff. we would shoot at trees from two to five hundred yards off, and we hardly ever missed our mark. I have with my enfield hit a targot the Seiz of a man at the distance of eight hundred yards. they will Kill a man a thousand yards if the sights are elevated properly. we have drilled considerable in targot shooting and in computing distances over ground that is deceiving to look over.[18]

Charleston, that nest of treason, is gone. i hope it will Sink and the salt water cover it fathoms deep. The southern Confederacy is melting away very rapidly, and ere long it will be among the things of the past. The Grand Army of the West now ocupies nearly every stronghold of the enemy on the Old Father of Waters. General Grant now has an army that will drive the Frenchman from our Sister Republic of Mexico. (let foreign Powers Come on. Americans can whip all of them.) Old Rosey [Major General William S. Rosecrans] and [Major General Ambrose E.] Burnside has formed a junction and are driving the rebels from their camps, forts, and cities.[19] Lee and [General Braxton] Bragg will, before long, be caught in a trap.

One Week from today is Election day, and i want to See Our union ticket go strait through. I will be entitled to a vote this time. I will give it to the man that ought to have it. a few of the boys will go the democratic ticket.

I would lik to have Some of your Molasses. now it has been sometime Since i had any. I am glad your cane was not spoiled by the frost. Corn is very cheap down here. we go and get it for nothing—only the trouble of gathering it. Sweet potatoes very plenty here.

from what you say, I am sorry to hear that Moses Nixon has took to drinking again. If i was a cripple as he is, had lost an arm in the service of my country, and was at home discharged honerably, a copperhead that would insult me or abuse me in any way had better Keep from my Sight if he did not want his cowardly, traitorous blood Spilled. for as sure as i am now existing, i would Kill him if i was hung for it the next minit. nothing raises my blood So quick as the ranting of the Blackhearted villians in the north called Copperheads. I only wish our company was in Council Bluffs on election day. if a copperhead would then dare to Say a word, he would Soon go to Davy Joneses . . . House.

When we were at Camp Dodge, our Co. was Said to be a rough set of men. but now what are we? we [would] just as soon fight as to eat. but one thing is certain. there is not so much liquors drunk as then, [and there is a] good reason for it. . . . it can't be had, and it is a good thing too, for there would be more men killed in sprees than any other way. a few nights ago, a squad of cavalry went to town . . . to have a spree. they got their canteens full of comisary Whiskey, and it was not long before the men were full. . . . then the old boy began to rise in them. they concluded to go to a certain *House* and "clean it out." they went there [and] found a party about equal in number to their own and about as full of the *Principal.* . . . the cavalry Ordered them to clear out, but they would not go. so they got to quarrelling, and next to fisticuffs, and finaly revolvers were drawn, and bang, bang they went, and a general engagement ensued. over fifty shots were fired by both parties, when a company of guards came and stoped the fuss. three men were Killed and eight or ten wounded—quite a skirmish among our own men. they are not frequent. . . .

Deserters still Keep coming into our lines. there is now quite a force of Militia organized here, Some where near fifteen hundred, So i have heard. they are doing good service.

business is geting quite lively. everything in the provision line is geting plenty.

there is being an expedition fited up here. it is all cavalry. they are going to follow the remnant of Prices army, going to either capture it or break it up entirely. if they are let alone this winter, they will all desert but a few hot heads. none but misourians will follow Price, and but few of them will follow the broken fortunes of the Hory headed old Traitor. there will Soon be none but a few Scattering bands of Guerrillas in the State of Arkansas.

If the French invade Texas, we will drive them clear from the American continent. Mexico Shall not be rulled by a crowned head. i will Serve ten years in the army rather than see the petty tyrants of the old world rull an independant American Nation. "no Sir." I will never bend my Knee to a crown.

The weather is cool to day. it rained a little this morning.

The health of the boys is excellent—better than it has been since we have been south. I never was Sleeker in my life than now: weigh nearly one hundred and fifty pounds [and] have grown in highth half Inch in the past year. . . . your Affectionate Son, Charles . . .

Camp Near Little Rock, Ark.
Wednesday morning, October the 14th, 1863

Dear Sister [Hester]: . . . I am well and harty—Stouter than i ever was before. the health of all the Soldiers here is eccellent.

I like this country so well that [I] dont know yet but what I will make this my future home [and] Marry Some loyal Arkansasians fair daughter. there are plenty that wants to marry. I was to church last Sunday and almost lost my heart among the beautyfull Daughters of the "Sunny South." they are not quite so Buxom and rosy cheeked as our Northern lasses and generaly not So intelligent and So well edjucated. but they are clever and amiable—good company to pass time with.[20] Here i must Stop my Soliloquy, for if a *certain person* at Home Should read this, i could then Say "Alas, Vain hopes, i have trusted too much to thy fickleness." Why, i am geting poetical. . . . It is a pity to waste this paper with Such nonsense as i am writing, to be the laughing Stock of all who read it. . . .

Refugees are coming in daily to take the oath of Alegiance. 30 came in last night, direct from Prices army, and i saw two come in this morning. they were in a Complete Confed rig. Price has but three thousand men left of his great army of the South West, and they are as good as So many prisoners, for they have to be watched to Keep them from deserting. even the guards Stick their bayonets in the ground and leave their Posts to come to our army. we are almost overrun with prisoners and men out of employ.

I can't help but pity the poor women and children here. a great many are in a Suffering condition. all is being done for them that can be done. families that were once in affluent circumstances are now reduced to want and are glad to even get washing and Sewing to do to clothe and feed the little ones. Its enough to make anyone Sick of the war to See the Sufferings and misery it causes. I have seen Some of the women Spining coton to make clothing for the winter. I tell you, it is rough material to make clothing of. it puts me in mind of our gunni Sacking, rough as can be. I wish you could take a peep in to some country dwelling here. you would think of the "Squatters Hut" on the frontier. The furniture, if i may call it that, is of the roughest Kind: Stove, Bedstead, Stools, a few shelfs, Spining Wheel, and last of all, but the most important, is the "cradle" or "crib" for the "Wee" ones, of which there is allways a goodly number. I have hardly Seen a woman Since i left Helena but what had a . . . [baby] in her arms (*or was going to have*).

. . . my compliments to your school Mistress!! She directed a letter for you once, did she not? I allways had a kind of regard for School Mistresses (fear of the whip). . . . I would like to peruse a letter from your teacher, though [she is] an entire stranger to me. it would be kind of romantic, and i like romance. "What!" have i again run into the ridiculous? . . . your Brother, Charles . . .

Remember: I am not writing this for publication, nor do i call it a political letter. it is merely a boys letter to his *"little Sister."* I Beg your

Pardon. I mean younger Sister, for i expect you are as large as i am by this time if you Still Keep growing as you did when i left home.

Election day is past, and our voters have all cast their [ballots]. . . . I have not heard the returns yet, but i Know the "Union War Tickets" Swept the field like an Avalanch from the mountains Side. You can talk about Election days at home, but ours was *one of them*. If you had heard the noise, you would have thought that all the *"North American Savages"* had congregated together to try how much noise they could make. Some of the boys and even Officers got pretty well to *"Windward"* with the effects of too much of the "Principal." I do not want you to infer from what i Say that they were *"drunk."* Oh, no, by no meanes. it was only an *overflow* of their *Patriotic feelings*, and *love of country*, and their *zealous support* of the great *"Principals"* of our government. I was not an eye witness to those *Scenes.* i was on Picket all day, but i have good authority for it. "Election" only comes once a year, and Such *times* are not of frequent occurence—*glad of it, too.* I long now to hear from our old Iowa. i wait patiently for the news.

. . . we receive our pay this evening—two months wages. I will try and Send a little home this time by some means or other.

. . . it is my opinion that Rebellion is in its last agonies, and Soon our "Brave Volunteers" (this dont include me) Will return Home.

(Thursday morning, October the 15th, 1863) . . . I have just heard the Election returns from the Iowa regiments. the 29th gave [William M.] Stone 360 and [J. M.] Tuttle 77 votes. the 1st Iowa cavalry gave Stone over 600 votes and Tuttle but few. the 40th gave Tuttle a Small majority. the 33rd and 36th gave Stone a large majority. the 27th and 32nd Infantry, and the 3rd Battery, and the 3rd Cavalry all gave Stone a large majority. four fifths of the votes cast was for Stone. now if the voters at home do as well as the Soldiers, Stone is our governor.[21] "Bully for Iowa." Copperheadism is about "played out" in our State. . . .

(Fryday Evening, October the 16th) It is quite cool this evening, and i closed my tent to Keep out the cool air that comes from the Washita Hills. . . .

I am going down the country toward Pine Bluff in the morning with a lumber train. there are several steam sawmills there, and we get lumber to build winter quarters with.

I can not any more tell what we are going to do than if i was at home. One day we have Orders to do a thing, and the next day orders come countermanding the first order. I will not attempt any more to tell you what we are going to do untill it is all over with. . . . A Soldiers life is as changable as the wind, and he soon gets so that he is not surprised at any thing that happens in the way of "duty." *"its all in the three years any way."* no use to grumble, but considerable is done once in a great while. "grumble we may, but *Soldier* we must," as an old captain Sais.

It is geting late, and the Bugle has Sounded Tatoo, and our lights must go out.

(Saturday evening, Oct. 17th) I have just returned from the Rocky Hill Mills. i tell you, the road is well named, for i never had Such a jolting in my life as i had rideing in our old government wagons over the rocks. hardly anything but Rocks and Pine trees are to be seen. a mule would Starve in Such a country as that. Of all country i have ever Seen, give me Iowa—that is, if a person has to make a liveing by hard labor, Such as the tilling of the Soil.

(Oct. 19th) There has been no mail yet, and i have had no chance to Send my letter. The Guerrillas have torn up the Rail Road track and thereby the delay of the mail. We have had no news of any kind for near ten days, and I am almost geting the blues.

I was to the Catholic Church yesterday during hours of Service. Went home with an old gentleman and his daughter, dined with them, had a very polite invitation to call again. think i Shall. . . . I am very fond of company, especialy of that kind. . . . Ever your Aff Brother, C. O. Musser

Camp, 29th Iowa Infantry
Little Rock, Arkansas   Oct. 23rd/63

Dear Father: . . . I never Saw as little Sickness among so many men beffore as there is here. . . . most of the cases are ague.

The weather is not So pleasant as it has been. we have had one Slight frost and Some cold rains. it is quite comfortable with our great-coats on early in the morning, but we can go without any coat in the middle of the day.

duty is not very heavy on us now, but drill is plenty. we have company drill every morning and Brigade [drill] every other day, So we have but little time to play. for my part, I am busy all the time at Somthing or other. I take regular lessons in "Caseys Infty. Tactics." [22]

You Say that Baker and Eugene Griffin has been converted to unionism. they may prove good men—at least i hope So. but *I have no confidence whatever in galvanized unionists,* especialy such as Baker and Griffin, woolves in sheeps array.

I am very anctious to hear the results of the election in our state. we have done our part, and if the citizens do as well, Stone is our governor by a very large Majority.

Refugees from the neighborhood of the rebel army Still continue to flock in, from ten to fifty a day. Prices men are deserting him by hundreds. he is now at Washington near the borders of Texas, and if any demonstration is made in that way by us, he will march on. no telling where he will Stop—perhaps not untill he gets to China, and then if a Chinaman would Say, "the yankees are coming," he would Still go on round the world.

. . . I wish we were into active Service again. i do not like this inactivity. I almost get the Blues. Sometimes this is the dullest Camp i ever was in—nothing to revive the Spirits. only one thing over and over: the Same old routine of camp duty.

I expect before [this] reaches you, Cap Gardner will have given you a visit and have told you the Statement of affairs around Little Rock.

I See by the papers of the 13th, our latest, that Roseys army is still in its old beat, but the news is delayed so coming here that it is Stale when it comes. next mail i expect to hear Some good news from the east. Charleston is Still where it was and Richmond Still in Virginia. it will yet take Some western men to clean out them eastern Confeds. It is the opinion of the Soldiers generaly that the war is near its termination, but i think it will take another Summer Campaign to end it. War on as gigantic a scale as this is not ended in a day, nor month, nor year. it takes *years* to end Such a conflict, where there is almost millions in the field and such an extent of Territory to work in.

The Emperor Napoleon had better Keep his "frogeaters" at home if he does not want some badly whipped Frenchmen. for if he ever meetes any of our western men on our own Soil, we will drive him back quick. we are not half civilized Mexicans as those he is now fighting. I would ten times rather meet the french than my own countrymen. it Seems So much like fighting my own relatives and friends, but Still they are as great an enemy, if not greater, for they are trying Just . . . [what] a foreign enemy would try to do and that is to tear down our national flag and the institutions of our country. [They are] Jealous of a republican government. . . . your affectionate Son, Charles O. Musser . . .

Camp of the 29th Iowa Vol. Infty   Near Little Rock, Ark.
November 5th/63

Dear parents: . . . I do not See the reason why i get no more letters from home or from anywhere. I dont get one tenth as many letters as i used to. If my friends are all deserting me now, what are they to a person when at home? the last letter from home was written over a month ago. letter writing will Soon "play out" with me if i do not get more from home. I do not mean you right at home but out side friends. I will not hire any one to be my friends. bought friendship is but little deeper than the purse. . . .

Weather begining to get winterish. Cool rains coming on.

[We are] expecting to comence a winter Campaign Soon—talk of going to reenforce Old Rosey [illegible] Chattanooga. I hope we will. I am geting tired of lieing still. again, active Service Suits me best. we may follow old Price to the Gulf and not get a fight out of him. he is good on the run, can beat us at that, and when that is said, all is Said.

we have not heard the returns of our election in Iowa yet. in fact, we get no news at all from any where. we are clear out of the world— at any rate, out of america. . . . your affectionate Son, Charles . . .

Little Rock, Arkansas   Nov. 15th/63

Dear Father: . . . I am glad to hear that the union war ticket has come out Victorious in our old Pottawattamie [County]. it will let them know that they will not rule the north any more, and all Such Traitors as [Clement L.] Vallandigham Shall find no favor, even among his own neighbors and friends.[23] I have not yet seen the returnes of the Election in Iowa but think Stone will have ten thousand majority over Tuttle. . . . Democracy [the Democratic party] is truly nearly played out.

The Soldiers are nearly all of the Same opinion as yourself concerning the War. they think this winter will about wind it up. I hope So, for no one ever wanted to get home worse than i do. not that i fear the dangers, but i want to get home to help you along. I Know it is hard for you to See to every thing there. I done wrong in enlisting, but i thought it was my duty to Serve my country above all things. what would my home be to me without a government? nothing, nothing. I care not for my life at all, but for your Sakes it [is] that i want to get Home.

If you can do better in town, why, sell out and go to town. but i can never make my Home in a town. do as you please, and it will suit me anyway. School privliges will be a great deal better in town, and that is one great advantage over the country.

If i live and Keep my health, i expect to have money enough to give me a start in the world by the time i am mustered out of the service. I have as yet sent but little home, but i have the money and intend to save all i can. the first year in the service, a Soldier Saves but little. some of the boys borrow and send it home, but when next pay day comes, he has none to send, so i can see no sense in borrowing. this year our clothing bill greatly overrun our allowance, and it comes out of the wages. So you See, there is not much saved the first year. the first year we draw overcoat, Blankets, ponchos, dresscoat, and they will last a Soldier three years. I will give you a list of the prices of our clothing, and you can then form an idea how much it will cost a person a year. we are allowed three dollars and a half a month for clothing, and if we draw more, we pay out of our wages. . . . your Aff. Son, Charles

List of Prices, government Clothing, for the year of 1863/62: Uniform Hat $2.03 (1), [Uniform] Cap $.56 (1), [Uniform] Coat $7.21 (1), [Uniform] Pants $3.55 (5), Unlined Blouse $2.40 (1), lined [blouse] $3.14 (1), Over Shirts $1.46 (3), Under [Shirts] $1.30 (4), [Under] Drawers $.95 (6), Pair Stockings $.32 (8), Pegged Shoes $1.48 (3), Sewed [Shoes] $2.05 (3), Over Coat $9.50 (1), Pair Blankets $7.20 (1), Poncho/Tent/Blankets $2.90 (1).

The number of pieces of each article i put opposite the prices. on marches i have lost clothing Several times, and that is my loss. Several times i had an extra pair of shoes and lost them. some of the boys lost all their clothing several times.

I now draw seventeen dollars a month, where the first year, i only got thirteen. i receive a Sergeants pay and allowances. . . .

Little Rock, Arkansas   November 27th/63

Dear Father: . . . after reading your letter over, i find by the tenor of it, there is one letter that i have not yet received that was written before this. you Speak of receiveing a letter from William, and in this letter, you speak of haveing received another. So from that, there must be Some rascality practiced Somewhere on the mail line. . . .

When you write again, give me all the news respecting William and his address So that I can write to him if it is allowed. I want to Know what position he holds in the reb army and his view of the matter at the present time. you Say you do not Know whether to help him or not. I say, if it is in your power to help him, do so. for we do not Know how soon i may be in Some Southern prison, and then would it not Seem good for some kind hand to help me in my time of need. consider that, and then I Know you will do all for him you can. he has been fighting for the destruction of our government, but now i hope he has seen the error of his ways and will try and redeem that blotted name by sincere repentance. and he is Still my Brother if he is a rebel. that even can never efface those feelings that are due a brother. [It makes] no difference what a man may Say at times when his angry passions rise. it is all talk. let me Know his address, and i will write to him.

As i write, the rain is pouring down in torrents, but the thin Canvass sheds rain like a roof. not a drop gets through. We have built good winter quarters. . . . your Affectionate Son, Charles . . .

Little Rock, Ark   Dec. 11th/63

Dear Father: . . . the Same old Song: no news to write, plenty of duty.

[I] almost got the blues to day. Jim Wilding says [he] dont think you are geting along very well. I am indeed truly sorry for it. I do wish i was at home to help you, as you are all alone. it is very hard geting along. I hope, ere long, the day will come that i can do you Some act that will in Some way pay you for the neglect and wrong i done you in enlisting. yes, i ought to have known better, but i did not. I will not say any more on that subject this time. . . . your affectionate Son, Chas. O. Musser

Little Rock, Pulaski Co., Ark.
Thursday, December 17th/63

Dear Father: . . . This time we can complain of the cold weather as well as you can. last night was the coldest time we have had this winter—ground froze about half an inch deep. no snow as yet, though. I am now writing in my tent without fire. . . . we wear more clothing than when at home. we are well fixed for the winter. no danger of much suffering unless we are called away from here.

We are just now enjoying ourselves. long evenings pass away very pleasantly talking of times past and to come, building castles in the air, which will vanish away.

I have become acquanted with Several of the citizens in the city and spend some evenings very pleasantly with them. they, of course, are Unionists. among those friends is one whose name is McDonald, a gunsmith [who] has been a resident here about fourteen years. he has been a Staunch Unionist all the time of the rebel rule in the city [and] was imprisoned several times. . . . the day before we came here, he was taken prisoner by some of Marmadukes ruffians, but he escaped from them, and after hideing in the mountains awhile, he got to our lines and is now doing a good business.

We have had no very late news, but all is going on to our Satisfaction all round, and I think this winter will wind up the *Southern Confederacy*. the rebs in this Section of the Confederacy are nearly played out. thirty of them was brought in prisoners only yesterday.

. . . but a few days ago, a Scout of forty men from the 1st Missouri Cavalry started out on a Scout from Benton and went about twenty five miles when the advance guard saw some rebel cavalry. [They were] about two hundred strong, all out in line of battle on each side of a lane, on each Side of which was a deep dich that no horse could leap. at first the boys was badly scared, but they soon found out that they would be captured if they did not do their best. the rebs told them to surrender, or they would give them no quarter. . . . now the Missouri boys all have eighteen Shots: a pair of revolvers and a revolving carbine. So they drew their pistols and told the rebs to come on, and then fired a volly, wheeled about, and off they went [with the] rebs after them. but when they got out of the lane again, our boys wheeled and fired. they now found the rebs trying to surround them. they were hemed in on all sides by five times their number and no quarter asked nor given. it was a desperate act, but the boys resolved to die rather than be taken by the ruffians. they drew their Sabres and in one hand they held a revolver, and with a yell they charged on, cut their way out, leaveing only one man dead and two wounded. but many a rebel charger was without a rider. when the boys got out, they formed and charged again, Sabre in hand. this time it was too much for the rebs. they haveing no sabres, they got panic stricken and broke pell mell, and away they went, our boys after them, and many a one was cut down with our Sabres. Some raised the white rag, but no such thing was in the thoughts of our boys. So no prisoners was taken. our boys chased the rebs ten miles and give up, beat in the race, but one of the boys that was in the fight said he saw twelve dead rebs in a Short piece of the road. . . . they nearly all had their *heads Split to their Shoulders* by sabre Strokes. our loss: one Killed, two wounded. could not find out the rebel loss [but] can yet if [we] take the pains to go and see, for they *all lie on top of ground yet* if not buryed by their own friends.[24]

A few days ago, a Spy was arested and sent to prison. . . . nothing being proved against him, he was released and went and stoped at the houses of some of his friends [near] where his wife was sick. . . . one day, one of our detectives watched him, and in a short time, [the spy] met one of his friends, and the friend called the gentleman by name. [Recognizing the name], the detective went to the Provost Marshall and asked for a Sergt. and squad of men to arest a spy. . . . in a short time, Mr. Spy was before the Provost Marshall. . . . [He] came in to learn our strength and to see his wife. he is now in a cell of the Penitentiary awaiting trial. . . .

Great excitement here now in camp about the reenlistment of men for the *Veteran [Volunteer] Corps.* some regiments have gone heavy. over half of the 77th Ohio are now in again. over two hundred of the 29th would go . . . if they had a chance and all the other regiments in proportion. So *Uncle Sam* need not be afraid of runing out of soldiers. With your consent, i would again enlist on condition of geting a *position* above *Private* or *noncommissioned Warrant officer.* I guess i will wait awhile yet and see how the Mashine works.

I have wrote to William but no answer yet. . . . Your Son, C. O. Musser

The weather made New Year's Day, 1864, a memorable one for the 29th Iowa. At dawn, the thermometer read sixteen degrees below zero. Sleet had fallen, and ice covered the ground.[1]

Little Rock, Arkansas   January 1st/64

Dear Father: . . . I cannot Say this time "we have fine weather." on the contrary, it is very cold, and the hills are now clad in their white winter robes. it comenced Snowing yesterday morning and Snowed all day. this morning, the sun came out and made Some dark Spots on the hillsides, and in a Short time, all of that frigid representative of the Polar regions will be gone forever.

It is almost needless to repeat the old song of "All well and harty," but a soldiers letter is not complete if nothing is said in regard to the health of comrades.

. . . it is rumored that Price is coming this way with twenty thousand men within fifty miles of here: commanders [Kirby] Smith, Price, [Dick] Taylor, [William] Steele, Fagan, all joined together for the purpose of retaking this city. *let them come* is the cry of all here. We will Soon have Some *"Linkum Gunboats"* here, and the rebs of Arkansas have a mortal dread of them kind of engines of war Since the 4th of July/63.

The message and proclamation of the President has not only been read with interest but will be the means of redeeming this State from

102

the hands of traitors and once more bring peace and prosperity to the country. once the poor, deluded rebel soldiers hear of their free pardon, they will lay down their arms and return to their allegiance.[2]

The "Homeguards" or, as they call themselves, the "Mountain Feds," have done good service and are Still increasing in numbers. besides the Mountain feds, there is a regiment of [Union] troops almost full, all Arkansians, called the 4th Ark. Mounted Infantry. The policy of Genl Steele has won thousands [of Rebels] back and has recruited the Federal army with thousands of good men. . . . if he had addopted a policy Such as some rabid retaliators wished, men that now wear the blue would then have been driven to desperation, and cursed the federal rule, and lay in ambush to revenge themselves.[3]

It would just suit the rebel leaders [for us] to use the citizens with cruel, relentless severity so as to drive them from home and join their army, which is daily growing less by desertion and death. but as it is, it has caused their soldiers to desert the citizens, to withdraw their aid and sympathy from the traitorous cause, and has rendered them almost helpless and discouraged.

Why is the Army of [the] Potomac So slow? have the leaders no energy, or are they [so] afraid of traitors that they do nothing? they have now gone into winter quarters, and it will be june again before they move on to Richmond. how often have we heard the words, "All quiet on the Potomac"? what is that *Grand Army* good for, lying there when an enemy is within a days march of them? they want our U. S. Grant there awhile to conduct affairs. I hope there will be a change of Comanders Soon there.[4] . . .

I will now close, wishing you all a happy New year. . . . your Affectionate Son, Chas. O. Musser

(January 2nd, 1864) . . . it was very cold last night and has the appearance of another Snow storm. . . .

Late news is that rebel Scouts came within twenty five miles of this place. Prices Headquarters [is] at Camden. a great many firmly believe that we will have to fight a battle here with the Same old rebs that have been whipped so often. . . .

Little Rock, Arkansas   Jan 17th/64

Dear Father: . . . the weather is So very disagreeable that a person can hardly move out of his tent. rains all the time—mud every where.

Still, we drill every day—no rest for the wicked. if we had not the constitution of Locomotive Engines, it would Kill all of us. we came South to Soldier, and we will Soldier. Our Company is no longer doing Infantry duty. we have been detailed to man a Section of the 3rd Iowa Battery, they haveing run short of men. our position may be permanent till the war ends, and [then] again, [maybe] only this winter— hard to tell. I hope it will be a permanent detail. we get rid of considerable hard duty. we drill two hours every day Artillery practice. . . . most of our boys will make Splendid Cannoniers and Artillery drivers. My gun—that is, the one I have charge of—is a six pounder bronze [that] was at the Battle of Pea Ridge. [It] was struck by a rebel shell on the muzzle and a small piece knocked . . . out—done no harm.

I am glad that William has some notion of makeing reparation for past acts by leaveing Jeff Davis army of Traitors and once more come under the protection of that dear old flag, the Stripes and Stars. we must forget, as near as we can, the past [and] bury it in oblivion. I will be glad to hear of his safe return home, and if I never Should get home, you will have one to Comfort you in your downward path of life perhape better than I could. one son that has been lost and is now found ought to be used like the Prodigal Son of old. I wrote a letter to Wm Some time ago—not long enough to receive an answer yet. . . .

You do not Speak very well of your old town. it does look as if its loyalty was to be some what doubted, but [they] cant make Soldiers out of every man. Some have a natural military talent and like it while others would not make soldiers if [they would] Serve till gray haired. a man must [not] be very Patriotic that will buy himself out of the Service—unless in certain instances where a father and mother who are old and feeble or something of that character. then he has Sufficient cause. if I could be freed from the army tommorrow by giveing fifty dollars, I would not take the chance. on the contrary, no mans five hundred would buy me from the army. I am no creature of Sale. I came into the army for my country's good and not for money. there is too much of this *"Green Back" Patriotism* in the army.[5] this war has been prolonged by the influence of them *miserable, low flung Villians wearing the Uniforms of American Army officers*. if they were out of the way, this war would Soon end. . . .

. . . we hear nothing from the east at all. have not had any "Northern Papers" for about a month—only the *Nonpareil* and that is only a drop in the Ocean. Will have to be content this winter with reading old News Papers and letters. Your Son, Charles O. Musser

P.S. cant write often on account of the Scarcity of Postage stamps. government sends no stamps to this place, and consequently, [I] have to depend upon individuals going up river. . . .

Little Rock, Arkansas   February 8th, 1864

Dear Father: . . . I am always anctious to hear from home, but this time more especialy, for in your last [letter] you said that Some of the family was Sick, and of course, [I] wanted to hear from them.

We are all well—or nearly so—this time, with the ecceptions of Severe colds. Measils have done more toward thining the ranks of our regiment than all other diseases together.

We have very pleasant weather. it is so nice that I would like to be tilling the Soil of Iowa at this time if it was as pleasant there as here.

Soldiers Still reenlisting rapidly—will Soon have an Army of veterans here. I guess I will wait untill next fall, and if *Uncle Sam* still wants men, i will Serve him through the war. I think Cap. [Marquis L.] Andrews is rather fast in his conjectures concerning the close of the war. he need not fret himself about not geting back to this place befor we are ordered home. *he will yet march many a day with the 29th Iowa before being ordered home.* Father: *Cap Andrews is a recruiting Officer and trying to get recruits. it is to his interest to look on the Sunnyside of Soldiering.* you understand. . . .

I am Sorry to hear of David Breese being in Such a bad fix, poor fellow. he Shortened his life in the Service of his country.

All those that wish to marry these times, let them do So. but here is one that will never bind a woman by the ties of matrimony So long as the war lasts. . . . there is but little love of country or respect for the graves of their forefathers that fell in defense of it in the men that would marry instead of helping to end this war.

You say Dave Nixon wants to enlist badly and will run away if they dont let him. the best thing they can do is to let him go. he will Soon get cured of his fervor. . . . your affectionate Son, Charles O. Musser . . .

Little Rock, Arkansas   Feb 15th/64

Dear Sister Hester: . . . I have been Sick for about six days, most of the
time confined to my tent, but now I feel considerable better—Still
very weak and nervous. . . .

The weather is warm and pleasant. I only hope it will continue so
untill summer.

the boys are pretty generaly all well and in fine Spirits. . . . they
are laughing and yelling over their ball playing and Such like amusements.

it will not be long before the farmers here will begin to think of
Sowing their grain. the ground has not been frozen any worth men-
tioning this winter here, but I expect soon to See it almost deluged
with rain, march being generaly the wetest month in the year.

I am glad you are all geting along so well with the measles. you
have been more fortunate than many families much smaller. we have
allways been very fortunate in all cases as far as sickness is concerned,
and [I] hope our good fortune wil not desert us.

Jane ought to go to school all the time, for she needs Schooling
badly. . . . when an opportunity offers it must be improved, or She will
come out lacking in the end. If I was out of the service now, I would go
to school untill I got a good education. but if this war lasts ten years
and I am able, I will never quit the Army untill the last rebel lays
down his arms. . . . a young man at home has no patriotism about him
if he does not help to Subdue the rebel and Support the President in
all his acts and policies.

I hope Jane will have more respect for us all than to marry that
cowardly Copperhead Lewis. I mean what I say. it will be a disgrace to
her, to us, and to her country for anyway encourageing Copperhds. I
have seen men down here that have served nearly three years in the
rebel army and finaly came out and acknolledged they were wrong,
like men. one of them is more honerable than the mean, . . . cowardly
copperheads. yes, ten times more and I would rather a sister of mine
would marry one of them reclaimed rebels than a renegade Tory,
comonly called copperhead.

John Tucker had better stay at home awhile longer before he goes
soldiering. he is too young to stand the hardships. because he is now
stout and robust, it is no sign that he will stand the service. I noticed
the death of David Burroughs published in some paper. . . . "verily it is
hard," but such is fate.

Never fear but what your letters are entertaining enough for me. so long as I dont complain, you may know they are "all right" in that respect. only Send a few more and more frequent is all I ask. If my own letters dont bore you, I will think that we all do well enough for *country people*. . . . So long as letters come from home, it matters not how much or how little they contain. they are allways welcome to a Soldier. with Some, the first thing [said] is "got a letter from home," then [the boys ask] "how is the folks?", "how is the weather?", "how is times?" next question then is, "did you get a letter from your *'duck'*" [sweetheart], which has to be answered in Some way to the Satisfaction of the boys, of course.

I guess Eliza hears often enough from me—or at least would if the mail was regular—to know that I am all right side up with care. you think I had better write often, or she will get one of them *home pets*, do you? She is her own mistress and will do as she pleases as far as that is concerned. . . .

. . . Write Soon and [give] all the news—not war news but home news, home gossip. . . . your Affectionate Brother, Chas. O. Musser . . .

Little Rock, Arkansas   Feb 19th, 1864

Dear Father: . . . I am well again and fast recovering the flesh and Strength that I lost during the few days of Severe . . . Sickness. I never lost pounds So fast before. . . .

The weather has been quite cold for a few days past, but this morning is a little pleasant, and in a few days, . . . [we] probibily will have some rain.

Business is quite brisk in the city. the Streets are continualy crouded with country wagons and government teams, coming and going constantly. . . . you cant look any way but what your gaze will encounter Soldiers in groups, Standing here and there all over the city. . . . you occasionaly meete a Squad of the "City Patrolls" [military police] and [are] asked for a pass. . . . if [you have] not got one, you march along to the lockup untill next morning, and then [you are] brought before the "Provost Marshal" to give an account of yourself: why [you are] in town without a pass. if it is the first offense, you go free, but if you have been in [the] presence of his honor before for the same offense, you go back to the "Stone Jug" again for perhape ten days. I have always been fortunate enough to get a pass.

... By deserters from Prices army, we learn that he is on his way to Texas. [He] left his Camp near Camden when deserters left him and was crossing Red River a few days after. his fource, the deserters Said, did not exceed Six thousand, and a great many of them was threatening to desert if Price undertook to force them into Texas. every few days, one or more deserters come into our lines. If old Pap Price still haunts this country in the Spring, we will again take his trail and run him out of his hole or tree him befor we stop. we have learned from very reliable sources that an Expedition is in contemplation by the Commander of this department, to be fited out by the middle of May, ready for a trip into Texas. the fact is, a large number of men has been detailed from the different regiments to repair Wagons, Harness, gunn cariages, ambulances, Saddles, guns, Sabres, . . . tents, and every thing nessesary for a long march and a Campaign.

General Steele is now in comand of this "department," the "Department of Arkansas," and the troops Composeing the "Seventh Army Corps." our Division commander is Still Brig. Genl [Frederick S.] Salomon, our dutchman, and our Brigade is commanded by Brig. Genl S. A. Rice, formerly Col. of the 33rd Iowa. The 29th is commanded by Lt. Col. R. F. Patterson and will continue to as long as he is well. Col. Benton is the fifth wheel to our wagon. he is now President of the "Court Martial" for the "3rd Division" of "7th Army Corps." Lieut R. R. Kirkpatrick is in command of our company. Cap Gardner is a member of the "Court Martial."

Our Company is geting pretty well Scattered, So many men . . . [are on] "detached Service." Some have been away from the company for a year. A. E. Larue is Hospital Steward, Hindman Hospital, Helena. Wm. H. Sherratt is in the Ordnance dept, Helena. Lieut. Jacob Fulton and three of the boys are at the Depot on the other side of the river. Lieut Fulton is in command of the R. Road Guard that go out to Devall's Bluff and return each day, and another one of the boys is at the Bluffs on Detached duty. and Wall McFadden is in the employ of Capt [Charles A.] Henry, Chief Q.M. [quartermaster] of this Post, and Frank Brown is on duty also in town, and Ben Palmer is also detailed in the Saddler Shop. two more are detailed as teamsters, and one for an ambulance driver, also two in the Regimental Hospital. So you See, in all, quite a force is detailed from our company and other companies about the same. we need recruits badly. I would like to see about three hundred recruits come to the 29th before the Spring Campaign opens, but recruits seem to dread going into old regiments. but it is the best place for a recruit. he has the Judgements of *older Soldiers* to guide him, which is a great advantage to him.[6]

. . . you will find quite a job reading my letter this time. I am yet so nervous that it is quite an undertakeing for me to write. . . . . your Affectionate Son, Chas O. Musser . . .

(Feb 24th, 1864) . . . I have just returned from the depot. I was sent in charge of a detail to work on a new engine house. the old one was burned by the rebs. . . .

it is very warm to day. Some of the citizens are makeing [a] garden. . . . They are trying to hurry the season, I think. Still, it [is] warm enough to plant corn. . . .

P.S. Our Orderly, James Trenor, has been Promoted to a Captaincy in the Sixth Arkansas Infantry (Niggers), just organizeing in this City.[7] "'Tis well," "verily.". . .

Little Rock, Arkansas   March 7th, 1864

Dear Father: . . . We are all well as usual and have very fine weather. Some days are almost too warm to be right comfortable.

A Squad of recruits came last evening for our Company, and among them was Joseph and Benjamin Meginniss and Edwin Eggleston. they all looked as natural as ever. fourteen months has changed them but little.[8] it has changed us more than it has them. they say the boys look more manly. the time has changed me in looks less than any of them. I can now pass most any where for eighteen years old and would not be doubted.

. . . it is reported that the Rebbels are massing a large force at Shreveport on the Red River and are going to dispute our posesion of the Red River country. their force is said to number twenty thousand under the Command of Smith and Price. I tell you, they will have a fine time Stoping us if we Should go on an expedition down there. a few Gunboats on the river and our army to work in cooperation will make it a little too warm for Mr. Price and Mr Smith. I do not hardly think there is ten thousand rebels in all that country, and they will run from us like scared Sheep whenever we advance upon them. there are so many rumors Set afloat that we cant tell what to believe lately. So I give you the above news for what it is worth.

Business is very brisk in the city [with] Streets crouded all the time. if it was not for the warlike appearance of bodies of Soldiers moveing about, you could hardly realize that there was a war going on but a Short distance from us.

It is geting late, and I must close for to night. Tatoo has just sounded, and [I] must put up my Portfolio. Good Night.

(March 8th) . . . it is very pleasant this morning. a Steamer came up the river this morning and reported the rebbel Scouts very troublesome at Pine Bluff. our boys frequently have a brush with them and whip them, but they wont stay whipped long. . . . but the 5th Kansas and 1st Indiana boys make them retreat in rather a disorderly way every time they get after them.

Now I will have to quit writing again—got to "relieve" the "Arsenal Guard." just the way—nearly every time I sit down to write. but duty first all the time.

(March 9th) Have Just been "releived" at the Arsenal, and it is raining hard. last evening was clear and cloudless, but [I] was surprised this morning to find it raining.

I am glad that I do not have to "walk a beat" or "stand Sentry" in this rain. dont believe I would Stand it. any way, [I] would not like to. it is now nearly eleven month Since I "stood Post." my "Guard Duty" is quite easy. all I have to do is to "march the Guard to the Post," "form the Releifs," give the Instructions to the Corporals and see that they are given properly to the Sentinels, and then make out a "Guard Report" [and] Send it to the "Head Quarters" of the "Post Guards.". . . I am then done with my work for the day unless the General or "Officer of the Day" Should come around. then I have to "Turn out the Guards," "form," and "Present Arms" untill they pass, and then we disperse.

There is a heap of forms and ceremonies to be performed in the army that looke likes foolishness, and our regiment is one that has to come up to the "Army Regulations" to the very letter. [There is] no Slighting the work with us, for if we do, a "Court Martial" Stares us in the face, and two months wages or our "Chevrons" is lost. but [it] is just as easy to do our duty as to refuse and I think a little easier. I find it is no use to complain, and I am one that never—or at least do not often—complains. I can do my duty and will. no one can say that I ever have yet Shirked my duty since Uncle Sam had control of me.

It is just nineteen months today since I enlisted. It does not seem to me as if half that time had passed Since *that Saturday afternoon, the 9th of August,* 1862, at Crescent City, Iowa, *When I pledged myself to my countrys use.*

. . . I write to pass time, and read to pass time, and when not on duty, most of [my] time is spent in my tent alone, Studying and writing. . . .

(March 10th / 1864) . . . The weather is warm this morning, but it is misting rain and is not very agreeable to be out. . . .

Father, I am Sorry I have not got the money to Send you this time. my money is about all in the Shape of Notes, and I cannot collect any untill next pay day, which is not far off. we will be payed between the midle and last of this month. then I can Send you fifty dollars, if you wish it, and not discomode myself in the least. but now it is not comeatable.

Now I will Say a word or two about that other little affair of Tatling and Storytelling. I do not want to Say any thing against my comrades without just cause. but I have now "grounds" and will Say my mind about James Wilding. first, about knuckling to officers, I will Say I do my duty and do not *curse* my oficers for what I can't *help*. and I dont *Shirk* my duty off onto my *comrades* Shoulders. . . . as to a little petty office in a company, I dont go to the officers and *fawn* like a dog for favors. . . . as to his being offered the *stripes*, it is a base lie, and [he] could not get them if he wanted to. the Captain dislikes him for a careless and duty *Shirking* man. and besides that, his own "Bunky" wont trust him with anything he wants kept a Secret. I have never associated with him, had but little to say to him, and will have less hereafter. I can get twenty men to Sign their names to what I have written above. we will see in the end who is the most thought of: the Soldier who does his duty and asks no questions or the one who *plays off sick*, and *shirks* duty, and *knuckles* and fawns before officers for small favors, and then accuses . . . others who are far from asking a favor of *any* officer, especialy the one in question. . . . your Affectionate Son, C. O. Musser

P.S. I will send you that money as soon as we are payed off and ask no Pay back when I return. I owe you a debt that will take me some time to pay and probibly never will get it payed (that is, all the care in child hood). money cant compensate the trouble. . . .

As 1864 opened, Lincoln was intent on showing the Union flag in Texas to discourage Louis Napoleon's empire building. Major General Nathaniel P. Banks was to lead a column up the Red River toward Shreveport, Louisiana, while another column under General Steele came down from Arkansas. The two armies would then join forces and advance into Texas.[9] *Steele balked, however, preferring to stage only a feint in support of Banks's Red River campaign. He had not budged after occupying Little Rock, concluding that his men were too sick and supplies too low to chase the retreating Confederates.*[10] *But Grant, the newly appointed general-in-chief, wanted an all-out effort and overruled his subordinate. The matter of supplies would loom large in the forthcoming campaign—likewise transport, for the expedition would be entirely dependent upon wagons to carry food for the men and forage for the animals.*

On the Rebel side there was a command shakeup. General Holmes returned from sick leave and resumed command of the District of Arkansas. Charged with the responsibility of defending what remained of Confederate Arkansas, Holmes concentrated his forces at Camden. But the memory of Helena lingered, and in March 1864 he was replaced by erstwhile subordinate "Pap" Price.

Little Rock, Arkansas   March 13th, 1864

Dear Father: . . . we now have "Marching Orders" and are all packed up, ready to Start at short notice. There will be a Review of the troops in the morning, and we will probibly start soon after. Our destination is not known farther than Hd. Qrts. but there are a great many conjectures and opinions as to where we are going, and the most probible one I have heard is that we are going down on Red River towards Shreveport to work or Cooperate with Banks. the force at Fort Smith and Pine Bluff are ordered to move forward at the same time we do. Every man able to walk has to march. we take no tents, one change of underclothes, and will go for Mr. Price in a hurry. a Captain came through from Bankses Army with despaches to Steele, and before twentyfour hours, we had Orders to be ready to march. So we will now open the Spring campaign in the west, and the rebs will have to run or surrender before many weeks. . . . No telling but what the marching Orders may be countermanded yet before morning.

The boys are all well and in good Spirits, eager to again take the "war path."

The weather is fine—just cool enough to make good time on a march. Recruits will have a kind of a rough innitiateing spell of it, but all are willing to give it a trial. Nothing has suited me better for a month than the receiveing of marching orders to day. Sunday as it was, we had to pitch in and work like fine fellows boxing up our surplus clothing.

Lt Col. Patterson has been very sick and will not be able to go with us. he was not at one time expected to live from one minit to another. he has the Quinsey. Col. Benton is now in Command of the regiment and does as well as any other old granny could do.

. . . I will take a small amount of writing material along with me. cant take much. it is too cumbersom to cary. may be gone long and again may not. . . . your Son, C. O. Musser . . .

Little Rock, Arkansas   March 20th/64

Dear Father: . . . we yet remain, but it is now thought we will march in a couple of days. great preparations are being made, and this time we will go Sure. The Supply trains are being loaded and Coraled on the Parade ground in front of St Johns Hospital. it is completely covered with them, and the Parade Ground is in extent about forty acres. no sham about this movement. it is too true to joke about—or will be before we march many days.

I am glad that our county has filled her quota of recruits. I wish the recruits for our regiments was all here. I have been Drilling Jo and Ben Meginniss and the rest of our Co's recruits Some. they will get drill enough on the march no doubt. . . .

. . . I am not very well at present but not on the sicklist—only a Slight touch of the ague, which is, however, not very agreeable. John Nixon had a touch of it, too, but is knocking round as lively as ever. he is geting as gray as a rat. when he came into the army, he was begining to get gray, but now he has ten gray hairs to where he had one then. if he has to serve his time out in the Army, he will be white headed.

The day before yesterday, two Guerrillas were hung in front of the Penitentiary. one was a Captain by the name of Earnest. the other was a member of his company. it was proved positively that Earnest was accessory to the hanging of twenty three Union men in and around this city. Some since we came here was hung by him but a few miles from town. Several more will be hung soon if justice is done them, and it is probable that justice will be done. There are hundreds of men in this that deserve hanging as much as Ernest did, and if a man ever did need hanging, he certainly did. . . .

I would like to attend some of them Spelling schools you speak so often of. it was always my delight to be at Such places and partake of the exercises. I don't know but what I will go to school a year or two when I get out of the army and then turn Schoolteacher . . . , a Wielder of the ferule and pen instead of the musket. but [I] dont know but what the hoe and plowhanders are more appropriate to my use than most any thing else that can be named. But hold on. I am looking too far ahead, building air castles, which will vanish . . . , for all my bright visions of future prosperity, like bubbles on the sea—"Vain Hopes."

Now I have written what Shakespeare calls "an infinite deal of nothing." So I will quit and call it a bad job. . . . Your Affectionate Son, C. O. Musser

---

The Camden expedition got under way March 23. Steele's column set out from Little Rock on what would become a 250-mile odyssey. When joined by Brigadier General John M. Thayer's provisional Frontier Division, which left Fort Smith the same day, the Federals would have 13,000 men and 30 guns in the field. Brigaded with the 33rd Iowa, 50th Indiana, and 9th Wisconsin, the 29th Iowa marched under Brigadier General Samuel A. Rice's command.

Mounted Rebels led by Brigadier General John S. Marmaduke, too weak to stop the Union column, resorted to harassing attacks. On April 2 Rice's brigade and Captain Martin Voegele's battery were escorting the supply and pontoon trains—450 wagons that stretched out 3 miles. The 29th Iowa and a section of Voegele's battery constituted the rear guard. Suddenly, hundreds of gray-clad cavalrymen descended on the wagon train as it neared Terre Noir Creek. The Iowans opened fire, momentarily checking the onslaught. Meanwhile, Voegele's artillery unlimbered and "after a brief and spirited contest," Colonel Benton reported, the Rebels withdrew. The rear guard took advantage of the lull, crossing the creek and retreating to the crest of a ridge. The Confederates regrouped and "made a desperate charge," Benton recalled, but were driven off after an hour of "hotly contested action." [11]

Relieved by the 50th Indiana, the 29th fell back quickly, hoping to catch up to the wagons, which had moved on. The Rebels attacked again and were again beaten back. The rear guard then withdrew, and after stumbling along bad wilderness roads in the dead of night reached the Federal encampment at Okolona. Roll call revealed that the Battle of Terre Noir Creek had cost the 29th Iowa four killed, nineteen wounded, and four captured or missing, but none of the all-important wagons had been lost.[12]

On April 3 Rice's brigade followed that of Colonel William E. McLean to Elkins' Ferry and camped along the Little Missouri River. Early the next morning, McLean's command repulsed a Southern attack. While the 29th Iowa played a marginal role, suffering just one man wounded, Brigadier General Frederick S. Salomon, commanding the Third Division, commended the regiment for "rendering efficient service at the close of the action."[13]

Steele's column pressed on. By April 7 it was 100 miles from Little Rock, just north of Prairie De Ann—some 25 square miles of open, undulating country. "One of the prettiest little spots in wild Arkansas," a historian of the 29th Iowa called it.[14] *There, on April 9, Thayer completed his rendezvous with Steele.*

As Steele's ranks were swelling, "Pap" Price was organizing his defenses. Unfortunately, he could count on little more than half as many men as the enemy commander. Expecting Steele to march on the new capital of Confederate Arkansas at Washington, Price had earthworks built along the prairie's southern and western edges and positioned his main body along a ridge commanding its northern entrance.

The Federals broke camp April 10. After a short march to the edge of the prairie, Salomon's division formed battle lines and advanced. (Thayer's division did not come up until the following day.) The thin Rebel line on the ridge was turned, the defenders falling back to their prepared works. Next day, after a late start, Steele advanced cautiously on a two-mile-wide front, and darkness brought operations to a halt. In view of this impressive show of force, Price thought better of making a stand on the prairie, choosing instead to withdraw toward Washington and defend the capital on more favorable ground.[15]

Steele now made a decision that changed the course of the entire campaign. Rather than march on Washington, he would divert the army to Camden. "Our supplies were nearly exhausted," Steele later explained, "and so was the country. We were obliged to forage from 5 to 15 miles on either side of the road to keep our stock [12,000 horses and mules] alive."[16]

Once at Camden, he could rely on the Washita River as a new, shorter line of communications, even resuming the offensive after stockpiling supplies. For now, the initiative went over to Price, who elected to countermarch to Prairie De Ann and strike the rear of the Union column. He did so April 13 at Moscow but disengaged after meeting stiff opposition. Despite more Rebel harassing attacks, three days of marching brought the Federals to Camden on April 15.

Little Rock, Ark   May 4th

Dear Father: We are once more quartered in our old camp at Little Rock after one of the hardest campaigns on record, considering the time we were out: forty two days hard marching, and twenty of them we had to cut our way through the enemy. on the 30th day of Apr., the Hardest Battle ever fought in Ark was fought between Steeles Army of ten Infantry regts. and Prices Army of Six or Seven thousand well clothed and disciplined troops. . . .

March 23rd: we left Little Rock, marched 8 miles, and bivouacked on Fourche Creek.

24th: marched 16 miles, camped on the Saline near Benton.

25th: march 9 miles, camp on a tributary of the Saline River.

26th: march 18 miles, camp near Rockport on the Washita River, advance guard skirmish with a squad of rebs (none of our boys hurt).

27th: cross the river two miles below town on a Pontoon [bridge], march 6 miles, and again camp on the river.

28th: march 12 miles, camp on a tributary of the Washita. . . . we again skirmish with the enemy and kill a Lieut and one of his men. we have no loss.

29th: march 9 miles and camp near Arkadelphia on the Washita. Pickets fight with the rebs. none hurt.

30th: we lie in camp all day.

31st: Still in camp. one of our boys is shot accidentally while on Picket duty.

April 1st: our advance roll out early. we march 12 miles and camp near a little town called Spoonville. our advance skirmish and capture a few of Shelbys cavalry. none hurt.

2nd: we start late this morning. it is about noon when we start out, our regt being the rearguard. we have two pieces of the 9th Wis. Battery with us. we have an immens train of wagons along, which is a great encumbrance to an army.

we march scarcely 3 miles from the Vilage when our extreme rearguard, consisting of a Sergt and ten men, is fired into by a party of rebs in Federal uniform.[17] our boys returned the fire and unhorsed some of them and went forward as fast as they could to join the command, they being about two hundred paces in the rear of the Regt. the rebs came upon us in large force and opened with two guns. we fell back and fought until our two guns were brought into action. we repulsed them and kept up with the train all the time, it being our duty to guard it.

a steady fire was kept up with both small arms and cannon on both sides until we came to a hill commanding the road and Valley of Terre Noir. here we made a stand and formed line of Battle with our force, about five hundred strong. the rebs crossed Terre Noir creek and also formed a line across some fields in front, it being open ground in front and heavy timber on our flanks. the rebs numbered about two thousand men, all well mounted cavalry and dressed in our uniform. our guns kept up the fire, and the rebs also used their cannon while we reserved our fire until they came onn. at the Sound of the Bugle they came slow at first, and as they neared they came faster, and finaly with a Yell they came like a Hurricane upon us. we reserved our fire until they came close, then we let loose upon them Such a Volley that they were thrown into confusion and had to fall back. they Soon formed and came again, wilder and fiercer than ever. we poured volley after volley into them, and right in the heat of the Battle, the 50th Indiana came back on the double quick and just in time to pour a deadly volley of rifle balls among them. we did not See them until they fired the first time, So engaged were we with our work. . . . when we saw them, we cheered, . . . gave the rebs a double dose and drove them off about 1/4 of a mile, . . . took up our line of march and still skirmished with them.

we came to a cross road and was told that a squad of our cavalry went out on the road and was driven back by a large force of rebs. when we passed [the crossroads], both forces formed [a line of battle], and [the rebs] prepared to attack us again. we had also got reenforced by two more canon and the left wing of the 9th Wis. Infy, and that with the 50th and our regt, made us more than a match for them. so when they came on to us, we mowed them down like grass and routed them. they left 20 dead on the field. in the last charge, we gave them a parting volley and again took up our line of march [and] reached Okolona about 9 at night.

our loss in the days Battle: 67 men; rebbel loss: over two hundred. the loss in our regt: 27. in our company, only one wounded: Lieut. Kirkpatrick by a piece of Shell. the 9th Wis. lost 14. the 50th lost 26. rebbels had over 70 horses killed on the field and a great many crippled. they did not make much at the Battle of Terre Noir.

Apr. 3rd: marched 6 miles and camped on the Little Missouri. a force was sent back this morning to bury the dead and take care of the wounded. they had quite a fight with the same force and whipped them.

4th: the rebbels attacked our Pickets in force this morning and drove them in. we were ordered out in line and went across the river. the engagement became general, and we, after a pretty hard contest, drove them from the field with the [Rebel] loss 40 men Killed. our loss: 24 Killed & Wounded. we captured a rebbel Major here, a member of Genl Marmadukes Staff. . . . [This is] Called [the] Battle of Elkins Ford. in this engagement, General Rice was wounded by a ball in the head slightly.

5th: Still in camp on the river and Battlefield. all quiet today around our lines.

6th: we advance upon the enemy and skirmish with him all day. they retire slowly. we march only 6 miles and camp.

7th: remain in camp today.

8th: still in camp. the Fort Smith forces under Thayer camped on the Battlefield of Elkins ford last night. Some Picket skirmishing to-day. not many lost.

9th: Thayers Command, 6 thousand strong, join us today. Still fighting on the picket lines. a few of our men shot.

10th: we again advance upon the rebs and drive them Several miles. they finaly make a stand on the edge of Prairie De Ann. after a sharp engagement, we dislodge them and follow until night. they do not drive very well. we lie in speaking distance of them. they keep up a sharp musketry fire for some time. about midnight, they charge upon one of our Batteries and are repulsed with heavy loss. they fall back a short distance and shell our camp—or rather lines. we slept on our arms until day light. the rebbel line of Battle is but a short distance off. we skirmish all forenoon. . . .

. . . the evening of the 11th, we again advanced and drove them into the wood beyond . . . , then fell back to our former lines and slept on our arms all night. next morning, we were up early and in line of Battle.

the 12th: we advanced upon them and drove them clear across the Prairie . . . from a long line of earth works with but small loss on our side. we then took up our line of march and stoped for the night a short distance from the town of Moscow. our loss in the three days fight is small. the exact number I do not know—about 10 in our regt. one of our company, Harmon Shoemaker, was wounded badly.[18]

13th: we march 10 miles today. the rebs attack us in the rear. we turn upon them, drive them across the prairie, and Kill about 60 of them, and go on to camp. This is called the Battle of Moscow, and the three days fight is called the Battle of Prairie De Ann.

14th: march 8 miles and again skirmish with the rebs. our loss light. Rebs [loss] not known. one of our scouts wounded.

15th: again we advance upon the enemy who are posted at a place called the Crossroads. we skirmish at first and finaly have to plant a Battery. the fight is very Spirited for nearly two hours. we finaly dislodge them and drive them several miles. . . . they leave the main road with their Artillery. we continue on our route and enter Camden about dark. with but Slight resistance, we take posesion of the fortifycations and camp for the night. our loss at the Crossroads is about 20 in all.

16th: our army [is] in camp in and near the town. our whole force is but small to come so far through the enemys country with. . . .

Reports filtered into Steele's headquarters that Banks's campaign had come a cropper, his army in retreat after suffering a reverse at Mansfield. With Banks neutralized, there was the danger that the Rebels would turn on Steele. In fact, on April 9 General Edmund Kirby Smith, commanding the Trans-Mississippi Department, started three infantry divisions north from Louisiana. When all units were assembled, 14,000 men would be available for an offensive against Camden, personally led by Smith, who replaced Price as commander of the Army of Arkansas.

In the meantime, Yankee foragers set out to gather supplies. Rebel cavalry patrols harassed them and burned or carried away the food and forage they were trying to collect. Guerrillas dumped animal carcasses in local wells to spoil the water. On April 16 Steele sent a detail to secure a large store of corn eighteen miles west of Camden. Two days later, a Confederate task force routed this foraging party near Poison Spring, seizing 170 wagons heavily laden with the corn.

History repeated itself all too soon. On April 19 Steele sent a column, which included the 29th Iowa, under Benton's command to escort a supply train en route from Pine Bluff. Next day, 150 wagons brought hardtack, bacon, coffee, and salt, temporarily relieving the supply problem. Just as important for morale, the train delivered mail—the first received since the expedition had begun. The Pine Bluff train was then ordered to return for another load, and on April 23 211 wagons set out under escort. Southern cavalry ambushed the column at Marks' Mills, capturing most of the escort and, worse, all of the wagons.

A crisis was at hand: men and animals on reduced rations, meager prospects for foraging, and a significant loss of wagon transport. All this and the presence of a reinforced, aggressive enemy persuaded Steele to quit

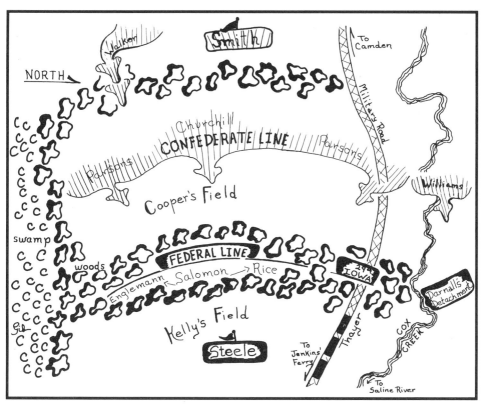

Battle of Jenkins' Ferry, April 30, 1864. Map by Gaile Beatty.

Camden and fall back on Little Rock. The evacuation commenced under cover of darkness April 26, with Salomon's division bringing up the rear. Kirby Smith was taken by surprise, his men reoccupying a ghost town on the morning of April 27. The pursuit got off to a bad start, as a miscommunication ordered the pontoon train back to Louisiana. Consequently, a raft bridge had to be built from scratch to span the Washita River, and it was not finished until the following morning.

April 28 was an excessively hot day. The 29th Iowa's march commenced at 8:00 A.M., and by noon men were falling out of the ranks. The regiment halted at Princeton, sixteen miles from Jenkins' Ferry, at 3:00 P.M. and went into camp with the rest of the army. More than half the Iowans were missing at first, but these stragglers eventually came in.

As the retreat continued next day, rain began to fall at noon—it would not stop raining for the next eighteen hours. (Charles and his comrades would spend the night of April 29 in a soggy cornfield.) Late in the afternoon, from the rear of the Union column, came the rumble of artillery fire between the claps of thunder. Lead elements of the hard-marching Confederate army had overtaken the rear guard.

At the other end of the column, the advance guard had reached Jenkins' Ferry, the crossing point on the Saline River. Steele was eager to cross the river—wagons and guns first—before the enemy could attack in force, which they would surely do at first light the following day. But the rain-swollen river was too deep to ford; a pontoon bridge had to be laid. Moreover, the storm was turning the military road where it crossed the river bottom (the bottomland extended for two miles and more on each side of the Saline) into a sea of mud that mired wagons and artillery. Fatigue parties were organized to help the teamsters and pioneers corduroy the road.[19] Despite a prodigious effort, at daybreak wagons and guns still waiting to cross the Saline stretched back two miles from Jenkins' Ferry. A crisis loomed as Steele's men, worn down from forced marching, lack of sleep, and reduced rations, now had a confident enemy snapping at their heels.

Kirby Smith's divisions had closed rapidly on the Federals, covering a remarkable twenty-eight miles on April 29. (His pontoon train had been turned around but still lagged far behind the main body.) The head of Smith's column was now within striking distance of the Yankees, who were foundering in a sea of mud.

Fighting was now imminent. A Union officer described the soon-to-be battlefield, the bottomland west of Jenkins' Ferry, in his report: "The ground ... *with the exception of two open fields near the road [Cooper's and Kelly's], was a majestic forest, growing out of the swamp, which it was very difficult to pass through on horseback, the infantry being most of the time in the water up to their knees."* [20]

General Salomon had a life-or-death assignment: hold the bridgehead so that the remainder of the army's wagons and artillery could get across the river. Shortly after 6:00 A.M. he had Rice form a defensive line in a belt of timber separating Cooper's and Kelly's fields: the 29th Iowa on the right and the 9th Wisconsin on the left. The 29th's right flank was firmly anchored on Cox Creek, which was close to overflowing its banks.

Rebel cavalry opened the battle by attempting to develop the Federal position. The going was easy at first, but resistance mounted. At 8:00 A.M. Brigadier General Thomas J. Churchill appeared with his infantry division, and Kirby Smith ordered him to reinforce the horsemen. Two Arkansas regiments, the 19th–24th (Consolidated) and 27th–38th (Consolidated) were deployed in line of battle. Upon discovering Yankee skirmishers partially under cover in a swale, these regiments charged at the double quick across Cooper's field. The Union skirmishers withdrew to their main line, joining a flock of sheep fleeing before the Southerners. Both the 29th Iowa and the 9th Wisconsin then poured several well-directed volleys into the ranks of the 19th–24th Arkansas, halting its onslaught. The Confederates, caught in the open field, found some cover in the water-filled swale and began to return fire. Meanwhile, farther to the right, the 27th–38th Arkansas gained little ground. The 33rd Arkansas charged next but was also stopped at the swale by volleys from the Iowans and Wisconsinites.

The Rebel leadership fell into a pattern of feeding troops piecemeal into the battle, mostly in futile frontal assaults. More regiments were sent forward. These men charged across Cooper's field and were pinned down in the swale like their predecessors.

On the other side of the field, Rice took advantage of a thirty-minute lull to shore up his flanks. He sent a detachment, which included elements of the 29th Iowa, under Captain Marmaduke Darnall across Cox Creek on the right. Lieutenant Colonel H. G. P. Williams' Confederate pickup force soon tried to turn this flank, but Darnall's detachment and sharpshooters from the 29th Iowa stopped them. The Rebels renewed their effort and, after half an hour of hard fighting, managed to dislodge Darnall's men. Salomon sent reinforcements, however, and the Southerners were pushed back. They made no more moves against these pesky Yankees, who were able to lay down enfilade fire on anyone attempting to traverse Cooper's field.

At this point, the 2nd Kansas (Colored) of Thayer's division relieved the 29th Iowa and 9th Wisconsin. Both regiments, low on ammunition, retired to the ordnance wagons parked in Kelly's field, refilled their cartridge boxes, and returned to the front, taking a position behind the Kansans.

Kirby Smith now committed another division of infantry under Major General Mosby M. Parsons. At 10:30 A.M., Parsons advanced but made no more headway than Churchill.

Both sides employed artillery sparingly, as horses and guns mired in the soft ground. One Confederate artillerist, Lieutenant John O. Lockhart, would have reason to regret going into action. Ordered to Cooper's field, Lockhart took along a pair of six-pounders that commenced firing double canister at 250 yards. This disconcerted the colonel of the 2nd Kansas (Colored), who requested and received permission from Rice to charge, reinforced by the 29th Iowa. Assistant Surgeon William L. Nicholson recalled, "Colonel Benton waved his sword and on went the boys with a yell." All through the fight, Nicholson wrote, "the wildest enthusiasm animated the men. They forgot cold, hunger, and wet." "I detected only one case of skulking."[21] The Federals captured the six-pounders with caissons and seized one other abandoned enemy fieldpiece. They removed the ordnance from the field, then returned to their breastworks.

The Iowans' work was not finished, though, as they found themselves assisting in the repulse of the enemy's final assault. Major General John G. Walker commanded the last of the three Louisiana divisions to reach the battlefield. Walker's subsequent offensive failed, in part because two brigade commanders were mortally wounded. (Yankee officers were going down as well. Rice was shot in the ankle and had to relinquish command.)

With the Rebel army growing stronger and probably regrouping for another attack, Salomon concluded it was time to disengage. It was noon, and most of the army had safely crossed the river. Within two hours, the last of his division was on the east bank, too, and the pontoons were removed. To everyone's relief, the rain stopped, and Kirby Smith did not pursue. The Southern commander had no pontoons, and his men had no fight left in them anyway.

Smith tallied 1,000 killed and wounded of 6,000 engaged to Steele's 700 killed, wounded, and missing of 4,000 engaged. Federal casualties for the

campaign totaled 2,750 men, 635 wagons, and 8 guns; Confederate losses in-
cluded 2,300 men, 35 wagons, and 3 guns. The 29th Iowa sustained 108 ca-
sualties at Jenkins' Ferry (15 killed , 79 wounded, 14 captured or missing),
the most for any battle in the regiment's history.[22]

The trek from the Saline to Little Rock, which commenced May 1, was
a miserable one. The road consisted of "mud that no mules leg would
fathom," wrote one member of the 29th Iowa.[23] *Steele's solution was to order*
all regimental wagons burned, along with nonessential property, although
this action still left the wagon train more than two miles long. The column
entered Little Rock on May 3, with the 29th Iowa proudly escorting the cap-
tured guns. Along with these trophies, the 29th could point with justifiable
pride to the role it had played in saving the Union army.

17th: a large forage train of 192 wagons under the escort of the 1st
Kansas Colored, . . . the 18th Iowa, and two guns of the 2nd Ind Battery, [all] under the command of Col. [James M.] Williams of the 2nd
Darkies [1st Kansas (Colored) Infantry], went out today about 14 miles
after forage for the [wagon] teams and cavalry Horses.

18th: the train has been attacked by an overwhelming number of
rebbels and is finaly taken. the boys fought desperately against great
ods and had to retreat. the rebs murdered the wounded negroes and
the prisoners, but the rebbels payed dearly for the train. they lost 800
men in the Battle. it was fought on the Same ground we fought on the
day we came here. this is the 2nd Battle at the Crossroads. the loss in
men is only 200.[24] . . .

19th: we are ordered to go out on the Pine Bluff road and escort a
train in with supplies for us. three regts go. we march 14 miles and
camp near the train. all is quiet to night.

20th: We return Safe to Camden with our supplies. Still fighting
on the Picket [line] on the Shreveport road.

21st: Sharp Skirmishing continualy all round us.

22nd: the train that we brought in started back for the Bluffs today, escorted by the 2nd Brgd. they have two Sections of the 2nd Mo
Battery along. we have quite a fight on the Picket line today. rebs
charged upon a post and . . . was repulsed with the loss of 7 killed, 2
wounded, and 15 taken prisoners.

23rd: a large force of the enemy came in on the Shreveport road,

... planted a Battery, and attacked our outpost of about 100 men. we had a very sharp fight before we drove them off. our regiment was ordered out as soon as the fireing began. we did not lose a man. we were guarding a . . . Bridge and had the advantage of the rebs. rebbel loss not known.[25]

24th: all quiet today around our lines.

25th: our train on the way to Pine Bluff has been captured, . . . the whole force Killed and taken prisoners, and the four guns also captured. our boys fought as long as any hopes remained and had finaly to give up to overwhelming numbers. the rebbel force was three Brigades. we had a large mail on the train. it was destroyed.[26]

26th: Our whole army is on the move from Camden. we cross the river, and march 8 miles, and camp for the night on the Little Rock Road. we cut down and burn 86 of our wagons.

27th: march 13 miles and camp for the night.

28th: march 18 miles and camp near Princeton.

29th: march 19 miles and camp 2 1/2 miles from the Saline River. rebbels attack us in the rear just this side of Princeton and followed up all day—some right sharp fighting.

April 30th: Between four and five o clock this morning, the rebbel army under General Price attacked us and drove in our Skirmishers. we marched out and met them with our whole force of Infantry except 3 regts: the 18th Iowa, the 2nd Ark, and the 1st Kansas Colored. our line of Battle was formed with Rices Brigade on the right, Engelmanns the centre, and a part of Thayers command on the left.[27] rebbels had two guns in position in front of our right in a field. Scarcely had the line of Skirmishers been driven in when the engagement become general. our whole line was attacked at the Same time, and the roar of Battle was awful. Charge after charge was made on both sides in gallant stile, and the ground was soon Strewn with dead, wounded, and dieing. So heavy was the musketry that we could not hear one another speak at four feet distance at the highth of the fireing.[28] our regt and the 2nd Kansas Colored Charged upon the two rebbel cannon and took it and all the men at the guns that were not killed or wounded. every horse at the guns but one was killed—and he was wounded. the 50th Ind Charged upon a regt of rebels that was coming up with colors flying and in good order. the charge was awful, the contest hot but soon over with the colors captured, and 7 of the 8 colorguard was shot down in defense of their traitorous duty. . . . we gained ground upon the rebbels and poured upon them such heavy volleys of musketry that they gave way after about 8 hours of the hardest fighting ever done in Arkansas. after we took the Battery, not one shot was fired from a cannon, and the Battle was mainly fought in very heavy timber and the ground almost entirely covered with water from rain of yesterday, and all night, and all this day. . . . the carnage was dreadfull—the Battlefield in every direction covered with dead and wounded of both sides. I do candidly believe that at one time two thousand dead and wounded was on the field.

. . . we drove the enemy about half mile off the field and held our ground untill we had orders to cross the river, for it was riseing very fast and would soon cover the [pontoon] Bridge. when we got to it, it was covered two feet on one side with water and riseing rapidly. we camped a short distance from the river.

our loss is somewhere near 800 killed, wounded, and prisoners. rebbel loss is not less than 1500, and some say two thousand. our regt is among the heavyest losers. we lost 117 killed, wounded, and missing. Genl. Rice was wounded seriously in the foot. he is one of the Bravest men i ever saw. he does not fear anything, and he has a Brigade that will fight for him lots. Rice ought to be in command of this army instead of that rebbel encourager, and rebbel guarder, and Army Selling General. this Springs campaign has been a disastrous affair for us. we have lost over 2000 men, 8 pieces of Artillery, and 600 wagons, and 2400 mules besides an immense ammount of camp and Garrison Equipage. Steele is hated by all. even the Secesh here call him a fool. blunder after blunder was commited. our trains being taken was a blunder of his or it was intentional. I would rather believe the latter. he is an old villain and a whiskey bloat and not fit to command a flatboat.

May 1st: march 13 miles. midnight before we stop.

May 2nd: march 18 miles. camp on Fush Creek 9 miles from this city.

May 3rd: Once more in our old camp at Little Rock and hartily glad we are here and not in the field where we can be sold by our own General. I hope he will be superseded Soon by a *man*. we accomplished nothing, although we whipped the enemy in nearly every encounter. only at the capture of our trains where the escort was overpowered [were we beaten]. the rebbels are far the greatest losers in men, but we are in army stores of different Kinds. [It was] all mismanagement, blundering, or all intentional. Rice is our only General. pity but what the Bullet that struck Rice had not struck Steele.[29] it would be well for us. . . . your Son, Charles O. Musser

126

Southerners did not take kindly to fighting ex-slaves, and reports of atrocities escalated as more of them entered the Union army. At this stage of the war, it was the Confederacy's official policy to treat African Americans in uniform not as soldiers but as slaves in rebellion. If captured, they were to be turned over to civil authorities for disposition, which could mean enslavement or execution. But it was not unknown for Rebel officers or enlisted men to decide their fate on the spot.

Victorious Confederates roamed the field of Poison Spring after the fight was over, shooting or bayoneting wounded black soldiers. The 1st Kansas (Colored) suffered 182 casualties, of whom 117 were killed—an extraordinarily high percentage. Two weeks later at Jenkins' Ferry, members of the 2nd Kansas (Colored) bayoneted three captured Rebel artillerymen, probably in retaliation for Poison Spring. Also at Jenkins' Ferry, the 29th Iowa's surgeon, Nicholson, reported that an enemy officer rode up to a group of wounded lying in the muddy yard of a field hospital and unceremoniously shot three who were black.

The Battle of Fort Pillow, Tennessee, was the most publicized of such incidents. On April 12, 1864, Major General Nathan Bedford Forrest's Confederate cavalry attacked and overran Fort Pillow, garrisoned by a mixed force of black and white troops. The fact that only 58 of 262 blacks survived the fight inspired Northern accusations of a massacre, charges Forrest denied. But the preponderance of the evidence suggests that some wounded blacks and others who had surrendered were shot.[30]

Little Rock, Ark.   May 11th, 1864

Dear Father: . . . The letters from home always come like a ray of Sunshine after many days of cloudy weather. . . .

You Speak of the anxiety that will be felt at home untill the particulars of our fighting is known. Yes, many an anctious Father, mother, Sister, and Wife will wait long in vain for a letter from the absent ones. many, *many* that left here on the 23rd of March in good Spirits now fill a Soldiers grave on many bloodstained Battlefields. Oh, how anctiously do we look forward to the time when we can Say the foe has been conquered, and the rattle of musketry and the roar of cannons have ceased, and millions of hearts [are] Shouting the glorious paean: America is free from War.

I received a letter from Grand Father [John] Souls a Short time ago, Stateing that Uncle Charley had entered the Army and that Uncle John was still a prisoner of war in the hands of the enemy at Danville, Virginia. Such is the fortunes of war.

So far this Spring our Army has gained nothing. Banks' Army met with a very severe reverse, and at Plymouth, N.C., the enemy gained the day, and at Fort Pillow [Tennessee], and Union City, Ky, and Paducah [Kentucky], and our Spring campaign has accomplished nothing.[31]

we lost an immense ammount of Government property. the enemy Captured about 400 wagons from us and the mules also, Six to each wagon. and we destroyed about 200 wagons, and a large number of tents, and Camp equipage, and Some Ordnance Stores wer burned. . . .

they have got near 2000 of our men prisoners. we took but few prisoners, and I wish the *number was less.* I want *no prisoners.* if they raise the Black flag, we can fight under it. they have raised it at Fort Pillow, and at Camden, and in North Carolina, and I say give rebbels no quarter, and the feeling is the same throughout the army in the west. *we will retaliate.* no prisoner will ever be taken by me, and I ask not to be shown any quarter by a prisoner murdering traitor. General Rice told his Brigade that he did not want one of his men to take a rebbel prisoner that was found in our uniform, as a great many of them are. Shelbys whole command wear our clothing, and Strange to tell, none of Shelbys men are to be found among the prisoners. we have a right to Shoot our [enemy] over clothing if we want to, *and we do it.* that is what we call a *private Parole.*

The murderer [William Clarke] Quantrill was all the time near us, and if he or any of his men are taken, they never will have the chance of Spiritual Advice or time to write their wills. Old Quantrills Band surprised a small Squad of cavalry of the 2nd Kansas at Roseville on the Ark. River above here a short time ago and murdered nearly all. he did Kill all that fell into his hands.[32] when this war becomes a war of extermination, it will be quick and decisive. When an enemy looses all honor and violates the laws of warfare and laws of Nations, they cannot Stand. the world will be against them, and *God will be against* *them too.*

I will be very glad if you can gain the release of William. I am Sorry that I have to Say that a Brother of mine ever was in the Army of traitors that are lost to all honor and everything else that is good. as long as they fight like men, we will respect a rebbel Soldier, but when they become Barbarians, we will mete them as such. . . . your Affectionate Son, Charles Musser

(May 13th) . . . We have just heard of heavy fighting on the Potomac and of the Advance of the whole Army. I hope they will be more Successful than we have been in the west.[33]

Banks' defeat caused us the loss of our trains and a retreat of 120 miles. the enemy, after the defeat of Banks, was able to throw a heavy force Against us, which cut off our entire communication and Source of Supplies and threw us in a very critical Situation. . . . our only way was to get back to Little Rock as quick as possible. wherever we met the enemy in force, we punished him severely.

we have heard more particulars from the Battle of Jenkins' Ferry of the 30th of April. a [Confederate bearing a] flag of truce came in and reported the rebbel Army in a bad State. their loss in killed and wounded was tribble our own, and a great many deserted in time of Battle—not to our line but ran like Scared Sheep in every direction. . . .

there was one Brigade in the Battle that called themselves the "Mississippi Tigers," and are Said to have never backed [up] before our boys untill that time. but Some of the Prisoners Say when they hear our yell when we charged, they "knew they were gone up," for they never heard Such a yell from our troops before and Such deadly volleys of musketry.

this flag of truce I speak of said that they could not have followed us if they had been so minded, for the whole Army was disorganized and in confusion. he speaks of one regt that went into Battle 500 Strong and came out with only 17 men unharmed, and another regt in the same Brigade went in 400 strong and had 72 men left not hurt. he reports the reb force at 17.000 men and says 7000 will not more than cover the loss in Killed, wounded, and missing. the missing are mostly Straglers and Deserters, but he estimates their actual loss at 3.000 and says it is the hottest Battle that ever has been fought where Price and Smiths Army has been engaged. he Says the Battle of Mansfield, Banks Defeat, is no comparison. he said that he never Seen So many

Officers Shot in one Battle. This is the Story of a rebbel Major. I think it is greatly exagerated. our whole force engaged did not amount to as much as his reported loss on their Side. but as to the Officers being Shot by his story, I dont think he misses it far, for I seen a great many dead and wounded Officers on the field. I know that I took very good aim at three or four Officers at but short range with my Enfield. dont know as I hit any of them, but if I did not, it is not my fault, for my will was good enough. there was probably a hundred rifles levveled upon the same Officers and fired when I did. it is hard to tell who shoots the man in time of Battle. for my part, I dont want to Know.

Genl. Rice is geting along finely. Lieut Kirkpatrick has started for home. have not yet heard from John Nixon or Jo Meginniss yet.[34] to any certainty [possible], the rest of the wounded are geting along as well as could be expected. Henry Meginniss is here now and feels bad about Jo. he says he would give all to have been with me. he regrets it greatly.

I never Saw men So much exasperated about anything as the troops here are about the Fort Pillow Masacre. they Swear vengeance against all rebbels. if a person ever speaks of it, the first thing heard is some fearful curses upon the rebbels. even the Colored troops are wild about it. if the rebbels would now attack us, blood would run in torrents.

Charley Hunter was Slightly wounded in the arm but is doing duty right along. Charley is a good Soldier.[35] . . .

Our regt is now prety well filled up with recruits, and had we not lost any in the Spring Campaign, we would have a large regt. Our Co. is the Smallest one in the regt. we have but few recruits. Cap Andrews . . . misrepresented our Co to many of the recruits and persuaded them [to go] into his own Company. Cap Andrews represented our Co. as being a set of ruffians and anything but Gentlemen. . . . of course, a stranger would not know any better. he will hear from us often, you better believe. What can a man gain by such work? our Company is bad enough even if the truth is told. the worst thing our Company is generaly guilty of is geting on a *Bust* once in a great while, but there are men in our Co that does not even drink liquor. one thing I know to be a fact, and that is Co. "B" has the *most men of the least Sense* of any company in the regt. there has always been a coldness between our Co. and "B" Co, and Andrews does all he Can against us in the sneakingest way *he can.* . . . Your Son, Chas Musser

130 Dear Father: . . . The weather is very warm.

The boys are generaly in good health and Spirits. a great many of the wounded are able to get around on crutches. Our duty is not very heavy, and we have plenty to eat, Such as it is. Considering all things, we have pretty easy times. Still, I dont want it to last long. I would rather be on a march, but if all our Campaigns terminate as our Springs Campaign did, it would be more of an advantage to government for us to be inactive.

If our Expedition was realy as bad as some northern papers represent it, it was a great defeat. Our losses are greatly exagerated by the Newspaper Correspondents. I noticed an article in the *Missouri Democrat* written by the Special Correspondent of that paper, and only once in a great while he happens upon the truth. he wrote from hearsay and was at Pine Bluff when he wrote. . . . That correspondent Says Steele lost about twenty guns on the Expedition. now if I did not Know better, I would say nothing, but I knew to a gun the number we started with and also the number we returned with. we came back with *6 guns less than we started with*. we rolled one rebbel gun that we captured from them [at] "Jenkins' Ferry" into the river, and the other two we brought along with us. the Special Correspondent also says we are beleaguerd, and every point around here is menaced by Price, and almost as much as Says the 7th Army Corps is Demoralized. Such ones as that Special Correspondent ought to be drumed out of our lines. he is fit only for the company of *prisoner murdering rebbels. All Newspaper Liars* ought to be driven from our lines. then the papers would not be filled with exagerated stories and misrepresented accounts of Expeditions and Battles. . . .

You Spoke of the backward Spring at home and frosts the 1st of May. what will you think when I tell you we had frost after the middle of April down here? the Citizens here say this has been an unusualy backward Spring. I guess it is about the Same every where this Season.

Vegetables are very scarce here. Potatos are so high that none but Brigadier and Major Generals can afford to buy them. Butter—that is, some less than 20 years old—Sells for 60 cts per pound. Stock is very high. an ordinary Horse sells for from 180 to 200 dollars. . . . Some Hard money [is] in circulation—more than has been for some time.

I think John Dingman deserved *Several* [illegible] for taking up again with that woman. I think a Bachelors life would be preferable to liveing with a woman that would never give one any peace. [I] would rather enlist and war with men than women.

David Nixon Soon got tired of Soldiering. it is best for such boys to stay at home and help their parents. they are of no account in the army. too many are now in the Army. the enlistment of children ought to be stoped. if they are large enough, they should have the age also. I have been in the Army long enough to learn that boys has no business in the army, that is, in the field. they will do well enough at Garrisen or post duty.

I think you have come to a wise Conclusion in finding out Williams feelings and opinions before taking any steps for his release. If he does not relent, let him suffer the penalty of his misdeeds, though he is my Brother. I would use him as I would any other man in his place. . . .

(Sunday morning, May 22nd, 1864) . . . It is now rumored here that Grant has posession of Richmond and routed Lees army completely, capturing most of them. I am afraid the news is too good to be true. cant put much confidence in the rumor.

rebbel cavalry scouring the country all round us on the west side of the White River. there was fighting near Brownsville yesterday. have not learned the result and there was a fight up the Ark. River a few days ago—rebbels routed.

Shelby crossed the Arkansas River near Lewisburg, 50 miles from here, a few days ago. his force [of] 2.000 men [and] four pieces of Artillery are all Misourians and the best rebbel Cavalry in the West. they are all mounted on the best kind of Horses. the men wear our Uniforms. they will fight, for we have felt of them and can vouch for that fact. they killed, wounded, and took prisoners 27 of our regt, but they paid dear for them: at least four for one and a great many Horses on the 2nd of April.

Price's Army is said to be now on its way to Shreveport. Fagans Division of Cavalry and Mounted Infantry is not far from here with three or four thousand men, and it is said that he (Fagan) and Shelby are the only forces now near us.[36] and both forces will number not over 6.000 men and 12 guns.

We are geting large reinforcements and a large amount of transportation. I hear that the 12th Army Corps is ordered here.[37] the 9th

Iowa and 16th Michigan Cavalry came here a few days ago, both full

regts. Several Veteran Regts have also returned from the North. The 3rd Iowa Battery returned a few days ago with a Splendid Battery of Six ten pounder Parrott guns. the 1st Missouri also came with the same Kind of guns. So you see, we are geting a large force here again. In a short time, we will have 20.000 effective Infantry, and [I] cant tell how much cavalry and Artillery. 800 Wagons are on their way here.

From the way things are working, it looks very much like another Campaign Opening Soon. I hope my predictions will prove true, for I have enough of being in camp already. want to see this war end soon So [we] can go home.

Just heard from the fight near Brownsville. the rebbles were routed and Some prisoners taken. our loss was very light.

The Paymaster has just arrived and will Pay off the troops soon. I want to send most of mine home this time, if I can collect it all this pay day. Some I will never get. it lies on the Battlefield of Jenkins' Ferry. I will never dun the widdow of a fallen soldier for the debts he contracts. . . . your Son, Charles

5 ↤ HOME FRONT   June–November 1864

In the wake of the Red River and Camden failures, Grant scaled back opera-
tions in the Trans-Mississippi. In May 1864 the Federal army in Arkansas
was incorporated into the Military Division of West Mississippi, com-
manded by Major General Edward R. Canby. Canby was simply to hold
the line from Fort Smith, down the Arkansas River to Little Rock, east along
the railroad to Devall's Bluff, down the White River to Clarendon, then east
to Helena. Steele, already on the defensive after Jenkins' Ferry, was only too
happy to follow the new orders Canby passed down—to the letter. Restless
subordinates accused Steele of deciding to sit out the war in the comfort of
his Little Rock headquarters.[1]

Little Rock, Arkansas   June 6th, 1864

Dear Father: . . . we got a letter from Lieut Kirkpatrick Several days
ago, and he Said he had seen . . . most of our boys, friends and relatives,
around [home]. So W. W. Wilson has got back to the Bluffs. well, after
all is said and done, he is not as bad a man as Some imagine. true, he
made considerable [money] while in the Q.M. [Quartermaster] Dept.
personaly, I have nothing against him. he was always very good to me,
whether in Camp or on a march. . . . Lt Kirkpatrick will give you about
as true an account of our Campaign as any one and more correct than
any newspaper account that I have Seen.

We have had no news from the east for Several days—last was
very favorable—verry little from the South. Canby is geting Banks old
Command in fighting trim again.

Pap Price is now at Shreveport. got there with four thousand men—less than he started with. Jenkins' Ferry was not a very healthy location for him. Marmaduke is Somewhere about Camden, and Shelby is not far from here. seventeen of his men came in yesterday, escorted by some of our mounted Infty. they were taken in a little fight down on the Ark. River.

Our Army is going to be Reviewed today by Major General Daniel E. Sickles, the one legged General. he lost his other one at "Gettysburg." [2]

Our Brigade was reviewed yesterday evening by Col. [Charles E.] Salomon, Commanding the Brgd. Since Rice was wounded, our Brigade has *no leader*, and it is one of the best Brigades in the 7th Army Corps. it is composed of the following regts since reorganization: 9th Wis., 29th Iowa, 33rd Iowa, 50th Ind, 28th Wis. the whole Brigade will number about three thousand Strong. One Co. of the 9th mans two Sections . . . of Field Artillery: four guns. they are attached to our Brigade. Col. Salomon of the 9th, a Brother of the Generals, is now in command of the 1st Brigade of [Frederick S.] Salomons Division. I am afraid Genl Rice will never get to his command again. we have full confidence in him as a Commander and would be very Sorry to lose him. Salomon is a perfect old Swill tub and Whisky blout and cant talk but little English. [3]

we have heard from our wounded boys and prisoners. they are at Princeton, all Parolled, and as soon as they are able to be caryed, we will go after them. Surgeon Nicholson of our regt is in charge of the Hospitals, and the prisoners are acting as nurses. John Nixon and Jo Meginniss are ther, and Jo is geting along fine. John is tending on them. Tell Jo and Johns folks that they are doing well and not to feel bad about them because the fortunes of war threw them into the hands of the enemy. they are treated kindly and speak well of the Jonny rebbs. . . .

. . . it is cool to day and has the appearance of rain.

we have plenty of work to do now. our lines are a complete chain of redouts, Forts, breastworks, and riflepits. . . . it would take more men than Price, Dick Taylor, and Kirby Smith could get together to drive us out of here.

I think, before long, we will try a little of the driveing game ourselves. I think Canby will not take So many *Paper collars* and more amunition than Banks did when he *went to take* Shreveport. *Puting on Stile* and Generals rideing in *fine Cariages a la Steele* wont whip the rebs in this country, let me tell you.

Our Regiment is one of those Stileish regts, but if the bone and Sinews were not there, . . . [we] would not fight much. we have Orders at parade, Orders at supper, orders to sleep on, orders to get up, and orders for breakfast, and orders for dinner. . . . Our thoughts are about Orders, whether sleeping or awake. We would not live if it was not for the fear of not haveing orders *hereafter*. Orders are as great a mania among us. . . . Your Affectionate Son, C. O. Musser . . .

Little Rock, Ark.   June 12th, 1864

Dear Father: . . . you are about the only one that writes at all to me, and I do not want that to Stop. most of the boys get letters often, but I am one of the unluckey ones. at one time, I had *eighteen different correspondents*, but now most of the names are rubbed out. . . .

The weather very warm and Sultry most of the time.

we are Still working on the Forts. we will Soon have works enough finished to mount Sixty cannon. we have two regular Forts. the rest are Redoubts and Ravelins [small defensive earthworks], though very strongly made.

a very large force of Cavalry arived here not long Since. . . . there is also Several regts of Infty and Some Batteries. . . . they are from Batesville and Memphis. [Brigadier] General [Joseph R.] West, I think, is in command of the Division.

General Sickles left here on the 9th for the armies down South. he Seemed to be well pleased with the condition of our army. Said that he never Saw a better regulated army and congratulated General Steele highly for the fine appearance of his men.

We have no very late news from the east. all Seems to go well there. [Major General William Tecumseh] Sherman is Still driveing [General Joseph E.] Johnston before him.[4]

you have no idea how quick the daily papers are Snatched up when the News Boys come round. many a dollar is spent in that way in our camp. I buy one nearly every day, and occassionaly Northern papers Come round. then we get the true reports of the movements of our Armies.

I wish we could be transfered to the "Army of the Potomac." I would rather go there and run the chances of being Shot than Stay here all Summer. most of the boys would like a change of Department, and if this campaign is to be the decisive one of the war, we would like to partissipate in it. we cannot possibly get where bullets flies thicker than at Jenkins' Ferry but can easily get into it on a larger Scale.

. . . our total loss [at Jenkins' Ferry] in killed was 300, and wounded 680, prisoners 63. . . . your Affectionate Son, Chas O. Musser . . .

Little Rock, Ark   June 18th/64

Dear Father: . . . I am realy Sorry for Lucinda Nixon, but it is useless to . . . [carry] on So. the boys will do well enough. John has been taken to Camden and [so have] most of the boys. but I think it will not be long befor they are exchanged and be with us. Mary Meginniss Shows the right kind of pluck. She will do for a Soldiers wife.

The weather is very warm [and] reminds us of last Summer.

The boys are all well and in good Spirits but waiting patiently for the Paymaster. it . . . [has been] Six months since [we were] last Payed, and we are about all *"Strapped, dead Broke."*

Mr Halls going to Idaho turned out just about as I expected. . . . It must be very lonesome in our Neighborhood, So many persons haveing left there in the past two years. I know I would not be contented if at home now. . . . The army is not a very desirable place to be, but I would reenlist if discharged at this time. home is no place for me while the war lasts.

I am Surprised to hear of Aaron Graybill and the Motts enlisting. they, I expected, would be the last *run* of *Shad.* Poor Simeon. aint it hard to lose your boy? I hope a few more of that clan will have to Serve Uncle Sam—be taken in . . . the Draft. I wish that three hundred dollar law was repealed.[5]

The news from the East Seems good. our U.S. has began to *dig.* Sherman is doing very well. [Major] General [David] Hunter gained quite a victory over the rebs in west Virginia near Staunton. but to offset it, old Forrest . . . out[foxed] [Brigadier General Samuel D.] Sturgis and [Brigadier General Benjamin H.] Grierson in Miss, South of Corinth.[6]

we Still have Some Skirmishing with the rebs around here, but they wont Stand up to much of a force.

Old Marmaduke has got down about Gaines' Landing on the Miss but does no damage of any note. Shelby is now Somewhere about Batesville and Jacksonport on White River. there is a cavalry force after him from this place and two other forces from this point. Shelby is trying to form a junction with [Brigadier General Dandridge] McRae in the edge of Missouri. they will find warm times this Summer in that Section of the country.

. . . [Colonel Randolph B.] Marcy, the Inspector Genl of the U.S. Army, is here, Stoping with Genl Steele. I expect we will have another "Grand Review" Soon. we are Still working hard in the ditches and on the Forts.

Old Abe is bound to be our next President. no other Candidate will stand any Show in the Army. Uncle Abe is the Soldiers Choice. If you do your part at home, we will reelect Lincoln for the Presidency. . . . your Aff. Son, Charles O. Musser

Little Rock, Ark.   June 27th/64

Dear Sister [Hester]: . . . The weather is very warm.

Lieut Kirkpatrick was very kind in going to See the friends and relatives of our boys before he again left for the Seat of war. I hope he will get safe through so we can talk of home and friends.

I hope Jane and her husband will get along hapily together and set an example for some others of our *kinfolks.* I am very Sorry indeed to hear of Eliza being unwell. I have had no letters from her for a long time. . . . The fact of the business is I have had Scarcely any letters from any one since the beginning of the Spring Campaign.

So Mr Tripletts folks are geting very Aristocratic, are they? I like to hear of the prosperity of our Neighbors if they come by their gains in the right way. and dont blame them for their Aristocratic feelings if it has a good foundation and Intelligence to rest upon. *May they continue to prosper.*

I am sorry you have no school this Summer. the time [you spend] ought to be improved. you must have a chance to go to school, if it is to be found, and become a teacher So that you can help yourself. I will help Father as soon as we are paid off. I will Send him enough to get along with for a while. we will get Six months Pay, and I have a considerable amount of money loaned out that [I] will collect in as soon as [I] can.

you ask me if I will vote for Abe Lincoln for the Presidency. I answer: *I will* if I have a chance to vote at all. *We will not change Pilots in the most difficult part of the voyage. Lincoln will remain* at the *Helm.*

So Mr. & Madam Peterson has Joined the Saints [Mormons], have they? Good luck to them. *I suppose they will inherit this land when the Gentiles are all killed off.* . . . your Affectionate Brother, Charles . . .

The failure of the Camden expedition gave Confederate forces in Arkansas renewed life. The Federals holed up in fortified enclaves at Little Rock, Devall's Bluff, Helena, and elsewhere, allowing Rebel marauders the freedom of the countryside. Chief among these was Brigadier General Joseph O. Shelby, who posed a serious threat to Steele's lines of communication. Shelby's cavalry division crossed the Arkansas River in May and commenced several months of raiding.

While Shelby failed to wrest control of central Arkansas, his activity diverted Union attention from an impending invasion of Missouri. "Pap" Price was slipping across the Arkansas with the main body of the Southern army, intent on seizing that key border state. (Shelby's force soon joined Price's.) But Price returned to Arkansas in December after losing more than half his 9,000-man army and failing to liberate Missouri. Active, organized Confederate resistance in the Trans-Mississippi was at an end. Many Federal units were subsequently withdrawn from Arkansas—the 29th Iowa was one—and assigned to operations against Mobile and other points east of the Mississippi.

Rebel efforts in Arkansas continued, though conducted by bushwhackers. Neither Steele nor his successor, Major General Joseph J. Reynolds, could find a way to counter their vicious brand of warfare. Reynolds stepped up the imprisonment and execution of guerrillas, to no avail. The war in Arkansas wound down in stalemate.[7]

Little Rock   June 28th/64

Dear Father: . . . There has been Some pretty hard fighting done within a few days [past] near here on White River. Our Cavalry Brigade, 3000 strong under the command of Brig. Genl. [Eugene A.] Carr, Started out from here in pursuit of Shelby, who was at Clarendon, fireing on our Steamers as they passed up and down the river and almost cutting off our communication with the outer world. a few days since, one of our wooden Gunboats was destroyed by Shelby. his forces, about 3500 Strong and [having] eight pieces of Artillery, Joined McRae's of about 600 men and were just going to play hob with our transports on the river. Carr went down the river to Clarendon and found the rebs, had a very Sharp fight, routed the rebs, captured half their cannon, left 100 rebs dead on the field, and pursued the rebs, picking up straglers. the country is so that the rebs will have to destroy the rest of their guns, or Carr will capture them. the rebs are scattering in every direction. Carr's loss was 12 killed 40 wounded.[8]

A Scouting party of three Cos of the 3rd Regular Cavalry went out toward Benton and came across an equal force of rebbel Cavalry. a Skirmish ensued. the rebs were routed and chased a couple of miles. our boys returned to town without the loss of a man. Several of the rebs were killed and wounded.

The Guerrilla Colonel, [Douglas H.] Cooper from the Indian Nation, is now on the Ark River with Seven or eight hundred men and two guns, fireing into our boats between here and Fort Smith.[9] they will get out of there pretty soon if nothing hinders our boys that are now after them.

We now have a force of about 9000 Cavalry at this place, Devall's Bluff, and along the Rail Road, and at Pine Bluff Clayton has about 2500 Cavalry and two regts of Mounted Infty. So in all, we have quite a large force of Mounted troops.

Our works around town are becoming quite formidable. we have done an immense ammount of work in the past Six weeks. We have four strong Forts Named after some of our Generals: first, Fort Steele, Fort Salomon, Fort Rice, Fort Carr, and several Redoubts for two or more guns. if it was nesessary, we could mount on our works about 130 cannon.

It is rumored around here that Price is going to try the Strength of this place. he is Said to be at Rockport, his advanceguard at Benton. the rebs that the 3rd Cavalry had a Skirmish with was Supposed to be Prices outpostguard. Price is Said to have a very large force, about 35000. Fagan is Said to be at Bayou Bartholomew, 15 miles from Pine Bluff, with 8000 men. I give you this as rumor has it. . . . one thing is certain. every thing is being put into the best state of defense possible, and the Pickets have very Strict Orders. every regiment and detachment of troops at this place has its particular post to defend in case of an attack. every thing is in complete order and works like good machinery. I do not like fighting any better than most people, but I wish Price would give us a call. we would put him in mind of the 4th of July 1863.

I do not like to hear persons boast of their own prowess, but it is a good thing for Soldiers to have confidence in themselves and with it determination. these times we want no cowards with us, and another thing almost as bad is rashness. . . . I come pretty near loseing my life at Jenkins Ferry by rashness. a young man of our Co. by the name of [James W.] Fletcher Saved my life by Shooting down the reb that was in the act of Shooting me. we were not over thirty Steps apart. I did not see the reb, but he saw me and had his rifle to his shoulder when Fletcher fired. I was several paces in front of our line and needlessly exposed. just as the man fell that Fletcher shot, another reb fired at me, and the Ball whizzed not three inches from my head. I turned and saw the reb just in the act of geting behind a tree. his back was toward me and about thirty steps from me. I raised my Enfield to my Shoulder, looked along the sight, pulled trigger, and when the Smoke cleared away, the reb was lying on his side in a pool of water. about that time, the command *forward* was given, and we moved ahead a few paces. I stood by the reb that fell when I fired. he was dead—never moved after he fell. there was a bullet hole between his Shoulders. I emptied his Cartridge box, put them in my own, being about out of Cartridges. I broke the gun against a tree, and left the horrible sight. when we left the Battlefield after driveing the rebs off, we passed the Spot again where I came so near being Shot. there lay the dead rebbel just as he fell, his face as white as a sheet, the life Blood all drained out. poor fellow—he showed bravery worthy of a better cause. [letter incomplete]

Lewisburg, Arkansas   Aug 1st, 1864

Dear Father: . . . we was four days marching to this place, a distance of about sixty miles. this is a miserable out of the way place and very unhealthy. we will be stationed here perhape all fall, and it will be a very difficult matter to send mail off from here, as the river is So low that none but the lightest draught boats can come up.[10]

The boys are generaly in good health. my Eyes are yet very sore.

The object of sending us here is not yet known by us. news is very scarce. we are all in the dark as to what is going on around us.

. . . most of the boys have no writeing material with them and cannot write. they wished me to let their folks know the circumstances in which we are placed, so they need not expect letters from them soon. Gus Breese wants you to let his wife know that he is all right.

we have not been paid off for so long that the boys have been greatly disappointed in sending money to their families. no telling when we will get our pay. . . . your Affectionate Son, Charles

Lewisburg, Arkansas   Aug 5th/64

Dear Sister Hester: . . . The 4th of July passed with us as all other days usualy do, that is, with the Same routine of daily duty of a Soldier.

I am glad to hear that everything is geting along well at home. it cheers me and enlivens the Spirits, makes time pass more cheerily. I would like very well to help you gather Some of these Raspeberys you speak of. I have seen none for a long time now. once in a while, we would get Some Blackeberys while at Little Rock.

I do myself wish for this war to end as hartily as any one, but wishes do not amount to much now a days.

We have had no news from our Armies in the East for a long time. we do not know what is going on hardly in our own immediate vicinity.

In about twelve months more, I will begin to think about Seeing home and friends again, and if the war is *not over and cant content myself at home, will enlist again*—for the period of my life time, *"I Spect."*

I am glad to hear you have again a good School. Oh, how I would like to go to school. I am so ignorant that I am almost ashamed of myself sometimes when in company with well Educated men. on such occasions, I generaly hold my peace and try to learn from observation. I now, more than ever, See the need of a good education. it is better than a fortune. I would think more of a relative that would give me as a legacy an education than one that would leave me a large fortune to Squander away in ignorance. . . .

I will give you a short description of our camp and vicinity. Lewisburg is on the North bank of the Arkansas River in the mouth of a deep valley. we are encamped about one mile from town in a northeasterly direction and upon a very high hill or rather mountain, as the

Surrounding hills are Spurs of the Ozark Mount[ain]s. . . . we can look down on the river and town from our camp, and it presents a fine scene. our Camp is in the heavy timber under the best kind of Shades. we have built bowers and live a regular Nomadic life. we have to cary water almost a mile from a large Spring that affords water for our regt and a Battery. these hills are all covered with rock and are very rough in Some places. in Some of the valleys close [to] here are farms with orchards and gardens upon them, and we live upon the fruits of the rebellious Soil partialy—not exactly rebellious soil but rebellious owners.

we just about have our own way among the "Razorbacks." they give way to the Iowa Boys quick. I am Speaking of the Arkansas Soldiers that are stationed here and citizens, too. . . . Your Aff. Brother, Charles

P.S. The Paymaster has finaly arrived, and we will get our pay tommorrow. I will send most of mine home as soon as [I] possibly can. Tell Father that he can look for a few double Xs [twenty dollar bills] soon.

Lewisburg, Arkansas   Aug 6th, 1864

Dear Father: . . . we got a mail much Sooner than we expected, and upon the Same Steamer with the mail Came the Paymaster. . . . [He] Paid us our long owed Greenbacks, Six months wages, all in a heap— quite a heap for boys that have been Strapped for five months. . . .

. . . I am not very well at present—caught a very Severe cold and it Settled upon my lungs. I was very sick for a while and had a touch of the lung fevere but got it checked I am now Stirring about but Still not sound. I wount give up to Sickness untill it gets me down, and I find it is the best plan to never give way as long as [I] can get about.

I expect the Mormons will Soon rule in our neighborhood Since John Thomas, David Evans, and Co. has got to holding forth. Whiskey and Mormonism are near akin and Should go together. no doubt Thomas needs some of the ardent to raise the Spirits of prophecy. And Dave Evans is a pretty Speciment of humanity to try to preach the Gospell. I have done with the mormons long since.

I am glad you have the School in operation again. I wish I was at home to go a few terms and partialy make up for lost time. I think if I had a small chance, I could teach as well as Wesley McCoid. I do not know him, but I know his Brother George in our Company.[11] he says Wesley is rather quick in the business. he may do very well. . . .

It is rumored now here that Petersburg and Atlanta was taken and a large number of Prisoners taken. If Such is the case, Richmond will Soon fall, and the rebs will Soon have to dig farther South. [Major] General A. J. Smith gave Forrest a good Cleaning out at Tupelo, Tenn.[12] and we hear of the Maryland raiders being whipped and a large number of Wagons taken loaded with Plunder . . . from Maryland. It is too bad to let them get away so easily, but I guess, in the longrun, they did not gain much by their raid.[13]

. . . my Eyes are still Sore, and it bothers me to write. . . . Your Son, Charles

Camp Near Lewisburg, Ark   Aug 17th, 1864

Dear Father: . . . our healths are improving fast. this is not So unhealthy a place as we, at first, Supposed it to be. we get an abundance of vegetables and have but little duty to do. I am as hearty as ever I was, with the exception of the Sore Eyes. they are not any better. it is a very difficult matter for me to See to write. . . .

if we should Stay here two or three months, we would all run wild. The officers can now hardly controll the boys. if any Orders are isued that the boys do not like, the officers are hooted and booed every time they come into the quarters of the men. as Soon as we came here, the Colonel (Patterson) Ordered drill. the boys concluded it would not do, so that night, the Officers was run out of their tents, and stones flew thick as hail around them. Soon all was quiet. next day, the line officers got up a petition to get the Col. to countermand the Orders concerning drill. we now have but little drill, and the Officers are as good to us as can be. their Stile and petty Tyrany is about played out.[14]

The 29th Iowa has easy times now and will have as long as we stay here, detached from our Brigade. . . .

. . . I will enclose a little money with this and wish you would send me some Postage Stamps Occasionaly. we can not get any here.

. . . I expect it will be a long time before you get the money I sent you. $100 in Green backs is not much but too much for a Poor Soldier to lose. that is five months wages since the soldiers wages has been raised. . . . Your Affectionate Son, C. O. Musser

Camp Near Lewisburg, Ark   Aug 24th/64

144   Dear Father: . . . I got three letters from home. . . . they were all welcome favors. . . . Writing material is So scarce here that [I] will have to make one stamp cary all the answers. I brought a large supply of writing material from Little Rock . . . , but I shared with the boys untill about all is gone, and there is not a bit of paper or envelopes in this town.

. . . we get very little news from the East or South.

It is Still very warm through the day, but the nights are cool.

the boys are all harty. I never felt better in my life, with the ecception of the sore Eyes. they are improving Slowly.

I wish that I was at home to help you get hay this fall, but this and another fall will pass away before I can help you.

We have heard nothing from our boys that are prisoner for a long while. I expect they are in Texas at a town Called Tyler near the borders of Louisiana.

We get plenty of vegetables here now and at a moderate price. we set our own price upon everything that comes in.

I think I can manage to weather through this year and then will try home. by the time this reaches you, [I] will have served the first month of my third year.

[Harmon] Shoemaker or Billy Sherratt has not written to the Co. Since they left, that I know of.[15] you can tell the boys that we have been payed off now and have some money, but most of the boys sent theirs home.

That young man that Saved my life at Jenkins' Ferry has left for parts unknown. he deserted about two weeks ago. another man left with him. probibly you know him: Edwin Eggleston of Crescent City, Son of Esq. Eggleston of Great Salt Lake City U.T., a follower of Brigham [Young] the Prophet. James Fletcher was a Misourian and lived in Shelby Co.[16] . . .

. . . Gregg is still farming his old way, is he? he will never do better untill he runs through with all he has got. If I get home again, [I] will Show him how to farm on a small Scale. if Gregg was down here, he would Starve to death in Six months if he depended upon his farming for a liveing.

. . . That Colt you spoke of I will accept . . . as a present from you and give you many thanks. the Colt may be of some use to me if [I] get safe home again, which I hope will be the case in about eleven months. . . . your Affectionate Son, C. O. Musser

Lewisburg, Ark.   Aug. 24th/64

Dear Sister Hester: . . . We are away out here in the woods and get no news and See but little that would interest you to write about. just wait untill I get home, and I can tell you more in a day than [I] can write in a month and will interest you more. I can spin some long yarns [that] will almost rival Dave Breeses old Stories. [I] can tell of greater wonders than Old Billy Smith could. . . .

I cant see why Bouldens dont get letters from John. he writes about as often as I do, but he dont get letters as often as I do by a long way. I think his folks neglect him. they ought not to complain. . . . your Affectionate Brother, Charles

---

The lengthening casualty lists of the spring and summer campaigns, which apparently failed to bring the war any closer to an end, solidified opposition to Lincoln's war policies. No one saw this more clearly than the president himself, for on August 23 he composed the now famous memorandum predicting his own defeat in the November election. Meanwhile, Democrats rallied around former Union Major General George B. McClellan, who held out the hope of peace. McClellan's running mate, Congressman George Pendleton of Ohio, was an ally of the Copperheads and an unabashed Southern sympathizer.

Many Southerners saw Lincoln's ouster as their last, best chance for independence, and as the presidential campaign opened, they recognized that continued stalemate on the battlefield would go far toward realizing it. But Lincoln's political stock rose considerably when Major General William T. Sherman marched into a burning Atlanta on September 2. Moreover, Major General Phillip H. Sheridan followed with a string of victories (Third Winchester, Fisher's Hill, and Cedar Creek) that wrested control of Virginia's strategic Shenandoah Valley. Acknowledging the success of Union arms, McClellan backed away from his party's "Chicago Platform," which called for an immediate cease-fire and peace negotiations. This decision cost the candidate the support of some Peace Democrats.

Little Rock, Arkansas August 29th,1864

Dear Father: . . . we arrived from Lewisburg yesterday after three days marching. we left Lewisburg a little Sooner than we anticipated. but we are here now in our old camp, and it seems kind of homelike to us. our duty will be very hard now, but I guess we can stand it. we are a tough set of boys. Nothing but a bullet can kill us now. we are case hardened [and] used to the rubs.

My Eyes were almost well when we started from the Burg, but the march has made them almost as bad as they were at the worst. I have to keep [to] my tent all the time.

while at Lewisburg, we got the intelligence of the death of Mrs. Kirkpatrick and that the Lieut. had again started home. he did not leave the City when we did, so he has been but a short time with us since he came [back] to the regt. The loss of his wife will be a heavy blow to him. his children are fortunate in being left in as good circumstances as they are. I do not think Kirk will resign. he always seemed to like the service. . . .

what is Mr Triplett doing now days? I have not heard anything of him for a long time—geting rich, though, I suppose.

If you had a load of your garden Truck here at this place, you could get quite a pile for it. vegetables are not as cheap here as at Lewisburg. . . . melons that sells for 10 cts at home are worth 75 & 80 cts here, and Cucumbers are about fifty per cent higher. in town you cant get anything of the kind. they dont get nearer than the Camps around town.

I am sorry that Asa Downs was so unfortunate as to lose his horses, but he can better stand the loss than a great many other men. Gregg is very unfortunate with his Children. it seems it is hard to lose the children as fast as they get large enough to begin to help their parents. . . .

I have been busy helping the Capt. make out our Muster Rolls and quarterly and monthly returns. we have about one weeks work to do to get all made out. we have to make Clothing, Ordnance, and quarterly returns to the War Dept., the Adjt Genl. of Iowa, and to the Hd. Qts. of the Dept., and District, and Division, and Brigade. so you see, a great many documents are used. and last month, we could not make the returns at the proper time, so we have two months work on hand.

To day, the Chicago Convention meets to nominate a man for the Presidency. Old Abe will get my vote this time if [I] get a chance to poll it for any one. I dont like these windy candidates. . . . your Affectionate Son, C. O. Musser

Little Rock, Arkansas   September 5th, 1864

Dear Father: . . . your letters always come at regular intervals of about ten days. I always know when to expect them, and they are read with great pleasure. I wish I could write letters as good as yours, then it would be Some pleasure for me to sit down to write home. but as it is, there is nothing to write about here. . . . the Same thing over and over again is a bore to me, and it certainly is to the folks at home. . . .

I noticed in a northern paper not long since an account of Some Indian depredations being commited about Fort [Phil] Kearny. they can do a great deal of damage to the frontier at this time. they are no doubt led on by rebbels and Secession sympathizers. nothing but a war of extermination will do any good there now. wipe them all out of existence: [every] man, woman, and child, Harney style.[17] if I was at home now, I would shoulder the rifle and try Indian fighting awhile, but I am fast for nearly one year yet without Indian fighting to wind up with.

we are expecting an attack every day from the rebs. we are in line of Battle at 3 oclock every morning and remain under arms untill Sunrise. the rebs are said to number 15000 strong and only a short distance from here. our Outposts skirmish frequently with the rebbel advance. a large detail from every regt gos to the Rifle Pits every night. We have a long line of works to defend and but few troops to defend them. our Brigade, with the ecception of a few detachments, is all the troops that are [here] now, though I heard that the 3rd Brgd got in last night. they have been gone a long time after Shelby. there is still three Brigades out yet: one of Infty and two of Cavalry. what success they have had on the Campaign I have not learned, but some Prisoners were brought in. . . .

The way things are caryed on in this Dept is enough to discourage any army. you cannot hear a soldier say one word in favor of the *Commanding General. he is branded as a Traitor, a rebbel feeder, and a friend of the secessionists in this City. it is true. he has a Brotherinlaw, not many miles from here, commanding a division of Prices army. his name is Fagan. our Major Gen'l Com'ng has scattered our little army in every direction for two hundred miles up and down the Ark River and the same on White River. 10.000 rebbels could take this city and all within it. there is one thing strange here. you will hear the Secesh praise the Gen'l, and all loyal men condemn him. There was not long since a man put in chains and Confined [to] the Military Prison for calling the Gen'l a "Traitor." the soldier belonged to the 2nd Kansas Cavalry. the whole Brigade that the soldier belonged to Swore that if he was not released, they would burn the town and have the hearts blood of the Gen'l. . . . the soldier was released secretly by Gen'l Order.* the men curse Genl "———". the officers curse him. you can hear nothing but curseing. I never saw such dissatisfaction.

the men and Officers deplore the death of Gen'l Rice. he was a *man* among many. his loss is deeply felt by all. ten Gen'l "———" could not replace him. his old clothes are more thought of than Genl "———" whole body. I firmly believe that this place *will be evacuated* in less than *six months* unless the *head* of the *7th Army Corps* is *cliped off.* Corruption is no name for it—*Treason, high Treason.* The only leader we could depend upon is *gone. [He] fell gloriously.* his name will ever be remembered by the soldiers under him. his blood is upon the hands of *another*, [as it was] caused by his (Genl "———") missmanagement. The truth must and shall be told.

you people at home know not what is going on in the Army. you read the Official reports [and] the Newspaper reporters tale. you hear of a defeat. it is smoothed over and looks very well. you hear of a failure of some expedition caused by some unforeseen obstacle. it is all smoothed over and finaly make it a great feat, a display of Generalship in extricateing an Army from such perilous positions. and you hear of an army being overpowered by numbers when in reality it was only superior display of Gen'lship [by the enemy]. the rebbels are as good fighting men as we are, and the leaders are as good. There are good Gen'ls enough to have one here and why not have one? *Stars* do not make the Gen'l. neither do puffs in Newspapers. . . .

. . . I can tell you [that] the Politics is awfuly mixed in this army— cant tell how the machine is going to run. Yet the Republican Party is split, the Democratic Party is Split, the Abolition Party is split. all is split. it is a regular conglomeration of all sorts of political opinions, but I believe the Democratic Party will win this time. Abraham is geting very unpopular among the soldiers. he is loseing supporters every day. I hope it is not so at home, for if it is, Father Abe can prepare for an evacuation of the White House the 4th Day of March next. I hope, if we are beaten, we will get some good man in the Presidential chair. I am willing to let the Majority . . . rule in all cases.

I hope we will get a President that will end the war quick and honerably. I do not want to see this war last twelve months longer. lives enough have been lost, and treasure enough has been expended for a century to come. none but those in the midst of it can tell what a terrible thing war is. it makes demons of men. it corrupts the *pure and innocent*. it is Sickening to see what a degraded state the *once pure and innocent ones* come to from the evil influences of Armies. one could hardly believe it untill it is seen. families that were, before the war began, honest and upright in their ways are now as low as mankind can sink. want and poverty brought them down, down, on a level with beasts. homes destroyed by the desolateing hand of war and old grey haired parents, young innocent girls, and helpless children cast upon the cold and unfeeling world to shift for themselves. and [with] temtations of the strongest kind beseting them on every hand, . . . they fall, poor frail creatures. We ought to be very thankfull that war is not caryed on in our own Section of the country. But it is no telling how long it will be before such may be the case. God grant that it may never be. . . . [letter incomplete]

Little Rock, Arkansas   Sept. 12th, 1864

Dear Father: . . . The weather is Still very warm.

our boys are in the best of health and spirits.

The expected attack from the rebbels on this place has been, I guess, postponed to some time more suitable to them. we are now ready for any force that the rebbels might bring against us, large reenforcements having arrived. The enemy is undoubtedly in this vicinity in force. rumor has [Major General John Bankhead] Magruder at Princeton with 17000 men, and Price is Crossing the Arkansas at Dardanelle. his forces are estimated at 15000 Strong and 18 pieces of Artillery. he is trying to make his way towards Missouri. we are willing for him to go there and Magruder, too, if he wishes.[18]

General Davidson is here now in Command of our Cavalry, which will number about 12.000 effective men, and with Davidson as commander, they will do more good than the whole 7th A.C. with Steele at its head. Steele and Davidson are not good friends at all. the latter is too *bitter against the rebbels and the rebbel Simpathyzers* to Suit our over lenient commander.

There will be a force started from here soon, and the 29th will undoubtedly be with them. we are ordered to hold ourselves in readiness to march at a moments warning, So we may consider ourselves under marching Orders. I only hope we will march again soon. I am geting so tired of this digging and fortifying all the time. I want some of the active Soldiering again. I always feel much better on a march than in camp.

Harmon Shoemaker got back to the company two days ago and is well and harty. he was twenty five days on the way here. he gives rather a gloomey report of the State of affairs at Council Bluffs. he says there are nearly as many rebbels there as here, only they are protected there. before he went home, he was a McClellan man. now he says he wont vote for any man that will accept a nomination from the renegade Democracy. he says there is only two sides now, Union &. Disunion, and Lincoln is leader of the Union Party. we have pretty warm times here somtimes argueing Politics. The Democracy is prety strong, though now I think the other Side is a little the Strongest. The Democrats here are not like the Democrats at home. they are for the Union strong. the motto is *"Peace when the Union is restored, war untill it is"* and war to the bitter end. we will make a Killkeany Cat fight of it before we will acknolledge the Southern indep[endence].

The Nigger question is quickly settled among us now. we have nothing to do with him. we dont like the nigger. we wish they were in Guinea. we have seen too much of them. now let those that love them have them. for my part, I avoid them, dont have anything to do with them at all. we dont want the negroes among us. but as it is, they are here, and we cant help ourselves and have to make the best of it by saying nothing about them. . . .

I heard of Isaac Cooper being among the missing at the late Battles at Atlanta. I am Sorry for Isaac. he is a good fellow and a good soldier. he was in command of his Co for a long time. he is an Orderly Sergeant and a good officer and will be missed greatly in his Company. but so goes the fortunes of war. I also heard that Benton Marshall was missing. it seems as if misfortune come pretty heavy upon the people of our vicinity. the list of killed, wounded, and missing Soldiers from our county in the past year is great. and many a family has to mourn the loss of a member.

I hope the Indian trouble will prove to be not very serious after all, but it is hard to tell. they are urged on by a set of renegades from Missouri and other states and will not stop untill a large force is called into the field. and then I Say exterminate them, wipe them out of existence, and be troubled no more with them hereafter.

I am glad you got done with your Hay so quick. you got through . . . about as Soon as [you] usualy [do]. . . .

So Moses was ready for the fray, was he? moses is no coward in a fight. he will stand fire like a true Soldier, as he was. I wish he was with us yet and his arm all right.

we hear from John and Jo often. they are Still at Camden. our boys are runing away from the rebs all the time. four or five men came all the way from Tyler in Texas. they were seventeen days on the way. they run away from a Corral of Prisoners where most all of our boys are sent that are taken in the west. there is about Six or seven thousand there, so the rebs say, but [I] cant see it in that light. dont know where they were all taken at. it is reported that there will be a general exchange of Prisoners in this Department Soon, and then our boys will be released from the Corral. John Nixon and Jo. Meginniss get along well with their rebbel Captors. they are allowed many favors. they go about town once in a while without guards, and that is very fine in "the *Johny rebs*."

I expect to See Some recruits coming down here soon for our regt. we need them badly. Drafted men will be as good as any, and we will welcome them as hartily as any that comes volunteerily. Our Adjutant is now up in Iowa to See about haveing our regt filled by drafted men. Lieut Kirkpatrick will, I expect, get Some recruits and but a little Some, in my opinion. we want 280 men to fill our regt to the minimum number. our company has run down to 57 men all told, and a great many of them has been away for over a year on detached service. we have not men enough to allow us a full complement of Commissioned Officers.

I will give you a list of [Commissioned and Noncommissioned] Officers in our Co.: Capt. C. V. Gardner, Lieut R. R. Kirkpatrick, Orderlie Sergt Wm H. Meginniss, 1st Sergt C. O. Musser, 2nd Sergt H. Lewis, 3rd Sergt Thos. H. Hutton, 4th Sergt E. T. Wilson, Corporal I. E. Huffman, Corpl. John Nixon, Corpl. Elias Owens, Corpl. Dominic Heagney.

I could have been Orderlie Sergt my self but did not want it. so I done all I could to get Harve Meginniss appointed, and I succeeded. he is a good Orderlie, and if the Co is filled up, he will be a Comish [Commissioned] Officer before six months. I will tell you the thing. . . . I wanted Harve to have the Position after I refused [it]. . . . it next fell upon another Sergt, one Jacob Case, and the whole Co was opposed to him. So I got up a Petition to the Capt recommending Harve to fill the vacancy caused by the Promotion of our old Orderlie, James Trenor. I got very near every man in the Co. to Sign it, and I signed it myself and handed it to the Capt. . . . he took it to the Col., and Harves recommendation was accepted, and his appointment soon followed. . . . this Sergt Case I spoke of above got wrathy and threw up his posish [position]. we have now a good set of Non Com Officers. and in case Harve is Promoted, he will make a good Lieut, and I will be urged to take his place as Orderlie. I dont like it. it is very hard work to do. . . . more is done by the Orderlie than by the Capt., and it is hard to please a company of men and do ones duty as I allways have done and shall continue to as long as I am able.

I have the good will of the whole Co. I dont think I have got an enemy in the regt. or any where else. I use every man alike and use all as a gentleman should. The Army is the place to find out the weak and strong points in a mans Character. every trait will Show itself in Spite of all deceit and cloaking. if a man is a friend to you here, he is a friend that you can depend upon anywhere. There is a something in soldiering in the associations connected therewith that binds one soldier to another like the ties of a Secret Brotherhood. I have noticed it often. . . . I have been just long enough in the army to find out just how to get along well with all persons. I have been a great observer, have studied human nature considerable Since [I have] been here, and there is not a better place in the world for Such Study.

and here is a good place to try the Strength of a mans mind [and] his will to resist evil influences. I tell you, a man has a Strong mind and an iron will that can resist all the evil influences connected with the life of a Soldier. you are surrounded in Camp by Temptations of every kind except to do good. There is So much profanity, Such awful swearing all the time in Camp. I can never get into such a habit, for the more I hear of it the worse it Sounds to me, and still more I cannot forget those first lessons I was taught in my childhood. they remain indelibly fixed upon my memory. . . . what was taught me by the one who first gave me life is held sacred, though none is free from guilt, and I, too, am bad enough. and the use of intoxicating liquors is abused awfuly. it is used to excess. Some get in trouble about things at home. his mind is troubled and to forget it gets to drinking, and his influence will get others to drink, and so it goes. good men are led into it to drown trouble. there is not in our company a half dozen men but what drinks liquors. yes, I might Say there is not *four*. I saw So much of it and its bad effects that I thought total abstainance was the best plan. . . . I swore to not drink another drop while in the army, and so far, since the resolution was formed, I have not tasted one drop of any intoxicating drinks.[19]

We had a Chaplain once in our regt, but he did not stay long with us. Our Officers were too hard a Set of men to Suit him. I will tell you confidentialy what kind of a set of Officers we have got in the first place. *There is not one Officer in our regiment but what I have Seen under the influence of Strong drink*. I will commence at Lieut Col.—no higher, for old Thomy [Benton] is a good man. I hardly ever consider him in the regt, for Patterson is in command most of the time. In what I said above, *I do not except one* Caps, Lieut, Adjutant, Major, nor anyone. . . . (Total number of [line] officers [captains and lieutenants in the regiment's ten companies]: 21. number required to fill vaccincies: 9. so you See, 9 commissions are at stake, and if we get the required number of recruits, the number of officers must be had.) Several of the officers now in the regt ought to be out. they are nuisanceses. they do no duty, are *sick* all the time, and their *sickness* was brought on by their own irregular habits. it is a disgrace to their families and friends at home. Such *Sickness* has got no less than *four* [of] their resignations accepted. and [these were] men that had good wives and a family of Children at home. only a few days [ago], one of our Lieuts was mustered out of the service on the account of *disability*, and another one, a Capt, will go out the same way in a short time.

I want to get home but not bad enough to go in Such a way as some of them officers, with disgrace attached to my name. the outward world may not know anything about such matters, but we of the regt do, and we will at some future period form a portion of the civil world. (I do not often write anything personal, and then I am carefull who I write to. it is a bad plan for any one to be so personal as I have been in this, but it is only to you that I address my remarks. So I am not afraid of offending any one by my plain talk. a great many Soldiers write all they hear and see and add Some to it in their letters home, but I never made a practice of Tatling and do despise it.) So

with what I have written you can judge the moral Character of our leaders, and just imajine the men under them to follow partialy their example. . . . your Affectionate Son, Charles

Little Rock, Arkansas   September 18th, 1864

Dear Father: . . . as it is Sunday and [there is] nothing to do, I thought it better to Scribble a few lines and Start them for Home than to Spend the time in indolence. . . .

It is very warm to day and but few people [are] Stiring about. . . .

Our duties are about the same as usual: *very hard.* we have but few idle moments to spare.

the troops are mostly all gone again from here after Price. he is now on his way to Mo. with about 8.000 men. Those reenforcements that I spoke of in a former letter are all after the rebs. . . . it is a detachment of the 16th [Corps], one Division Commanded by Major Genl [Joseph A.] Mower. it is composed of both Eastern and western men. . . . 17 regts in all of the Infantry and two Divisions of Cavalry. there is about 12000 cavalry and 5000 Infantry after Price, and he will have to work some headwork if he gets South of the Arkansas River again. General Mower is an energetic Commander, a fighting Genl, and will not Stop for small obstacles. he is none of your *rebbel lovers* as Some one of Our Genls not far from here. he was (Genl Mower) in Com[mand] of the Divis under Banks on Red River. Genl A. J. Smith and Mower Saved the *Whole Army* there from destruction. Mowers Divis took Fort De Russy, and at Pleasant Hill, the 16th Corps done most of the fighting.[20]

Old Banks and Steele Ought both to be where Benedict Arnold ought to have been. The War Department dont Know who they have in Command here, or they would remove him at once—Though I can stand . . . [it] if Government can afford to throw away money on a piece of pride and corrupt ambition, a Government thief. All may turn out right yet in the end like a novel Story, but I cant see it in that light yet. But I am not here to Judge the actions of the *Brave commanders of our Armys.* . . .

I would like to know how the "Draft" is coming on at home—or the volunteering. I will bet a hundred there has been no "Draft" this time. and I am Sorry for it too. . . . all the *true* and *Loyal* men will Soon be gone from home and none will be left but the rebbel *Sympathizers* and "Copp[erheads]." I want to See them "Drafted." it would take off some of the Copper, and we would have *some* good Soldiers.[21] . . .

"Old Abe" is gaining Strength lately here. if *Pendleton* was off the Democratic ticket, McClellan would get a great many more votes, but *Pendleton* is too barefaced a rebbel, even for most of the McClellan men. "Old Abe" will Sit another four years in the Presidential Chair. . . . Your Affectionate Son, C. O. Musser

P.S. Dont forget the Political News when you write. . . .

Hunterville Station, Ark   Oct. 1st, 1864

Dear Father: . . . The weather is begining to look like a Southern winter. it has been raining for several days and is Still raining.

I came to this Station about a week ago with a detachment from our regt. we are doing Guard Duty. we have very easy times—no exposeure to the weather at all. we are trying to get a permanent detail for all winter, and I think we will succeed. this Station is on the Memphis and Little Rock R.R. but a few miles from the city.

we have . . . the late news from [Major General Phillip H.] Sheridan: his great Victory over [Major General Jubal A.] Early in the Shenandoah Valley.[22] we are expecting a mail in this evening, but the morning train from Devall's Bluff is now four hours behind times. yesterday, one train run off the track this side of the Bluffs and was delayed several hours.

Hunterville is entirely a new town. it has been built within a year. it is composed principaly of Government buildings and the houses of Government employees.

I was over to the City yesterday to see the Little Rock Militia drill. all of the business houses in town was closed, and every man on the rolls were out drilling. it put me in mind of our drilling while we were at Council Bluffs before we went into Camp. Some of the young Southern Bloods dont like it very well. The Jews take a great interest in it and do their duty like old Soldiers, as near as they Know. . . . your Affectionate Son, Charles

Little Rock, Arkansas   Oct 3rd, 1864

Dear Sister Hester: . . . I am well and hearty as ever, with the ecception of weak Eyes. I cant See to read or write by candlelight, which deprives me of much pleasure. before my Eyes got sore, I was—most of my time when not on duty—in my tent reading or writeing, studying anykind of works I could get. [I] even [turned] to *Caseys Tactics for Infantry, Cavalry, & Artillery*—which is very interresting to me—*when [I] cant get any thing better.* . . .

Father Says that Sarah Hall is off to School again. Young folks must be very Scarce in our neighborhood now, [with] most of the young men gone away and the girls leaveing or geting married. . . . I believe in people Marrying young, Say the ages of the parties 16 and 20. that is the right ages for young people to start on lifes voyage. but I cant start that Soon. my time is now about 25 . . . or there abouts. you say I had better hurry home, and get a *better half*, and settle down. It is a very easy matter for me to get a better half. . . . goodness knows, any one is better than I am. But candidly, I would not Marry while this war lasts if that was *ten years*. for I dont expect to stay at home while the war goes on if it does not end within my present term of service. and I dont want any one depending upon me for a Support while my life is in danger all the time and liable to be laid low and leave them to Suffer. No, I think it is wrong, very wrong for any Soldier to do Such an act of injustice by any woman.

I am realy sorry for Lieut Kirkpatrick. If I was in his place, I would either resign or find a good place for the Children and return to the command. I guess he gets but few recruits for our Regt. at least I have heard of none from there. there are too many Copperheads at Council Bluffs to get many volunteers now days. The draft is what we want. there ought to be no more volunteering allowed, but an Order for the Draft [should] be enforced immediately. . . . Your Affectionate Brother, Charles

Little Rock, Arkansas   October 8th, 1864

Dear Father: . . . The mail is becoming more regular of late. . . . almost every mail brings us good news from Our armies in different Departments. not long since, we heard of Sheridans Success over Early & [Major General John C.] Breckinridge. and to day, the news came that

Grant had gained a glorious victory over Lee in front of Petersburg & Richmond.[23] you know not how it cheers us up to hear Such news. Genl. Steele had 100 guns fired in honor of Sheridans victorys, and the Booming of them cannon Enlivened us up and made us feel like *waideing into the Rebs again.*

I learned to day that Magruder was trying to cross the Miss. River below Napoleon and that his men refused to go across and was deserting him by hundreds. his force is said to number about 15000. Price, Fagan, Shelby, Marmaduke, Cooper, [Colonel J. T.] Coffee, & [Lieutenant Colonel Benjamin] Elliott with their respective forces are now in Missouri or going that way—a way that most of them will never return. we have men enough after them to annihilate them. Genl. Mower is in their tracks with 12000 good men. and Genl. Smith is East of them with a Still stronger force. and Thayer is west of them with 5 or 6.000. and Old Rosey is north of them with all the Militia and volunteers in his military district. . . . if they undertake to retreat, all of our force at this place, and Fort Smith, and Pine Bluff, and all the troops on the "line of the Arkansas" will oppose their retreating South again. so I think Pap Prices Army has got into a tight place. if he gets out, it will be a fault of our military leaders.

We are now building our Winterquarters. we will have them done in another week. it is quite a job to build So many houses. there has to be five for each Co. [Each one is] 15 feet square. they are made of Cyprus logs and covered with white Oak Shingles of our own manufacture. every man works all the time when not on duty. we will be very Comfortably fixed for the wet weather in a short time. Tents are a very poor thing to live in in rainy weather.[24]

The weather is still warm through the day. . . .

. . . Lincoln is gaining ground every day. "Little Mac" cant be spoken of in the same day with Lincoln.

I hope you can get William liberated. I think he could have been freed long ago if he had done his duty as a repentant rebbel Should. *Government will not keep a repentant Rebbl in Prison if he gives proof of his sincerity to return to his allegiance.* If William *promises* to do *right, do all you can to free him.* if not, *let him stay there untill the war ends.* I have as much Brotherly feeling as any man, but *I cannot forget my duty to my country.* When a Brother rises up in rebellion against his country, and he falls into the hands of the offended powers, let him suffer the consequences. or let him adjure his Traitorous principles

and become a man again. I will Say no more upon that Subject this time. it pains me. . . . your Affectionate Son, Charles

Little Rock, Ark   Oct 21st/64

Dear Sister: . . . The weather is Still pleasant and favorable to us.

Tell Frances and Henry if they wish to hear from me often, they must not neglect answering my letters, for I write two to their one. I do not neglect any of my relatives or friends if they do not first slight me. But I tell you, I wont buy friendship. There are only two or three persons that write regular to me. one of them is Father. . . . they write often and always get answers. if any one feels like getting offended at what I have wrote at any time, they have the undoubted right to do so, for I am not going to retract any thing I have said.

I am lonesom to day. . . . it is So dull here all the time. I would give $100 if I could get a transfer to some place where there is fighting every day. I dont care for the dangers. what is my poor, miserable life worth to me or anyone? life is only a dream—a few short years and we will all be gone and forgotten. and [there will be] nothing to show that we ever existed except the evil acts we do. for who does any good acts these times? alas, a very few, and the evil predominate.

I hope this shedding of Blood will soon cease So that we can Come home. but I dont want to come home untill the war ends. let that be ever so long, but I do not think it will be long untill the rebbels will lay down their Arms and return to their Allegiance. . . . your Brother, Charles O. Musser

---

When the votes were tabulated, the president emerged triumphant with a 500,000-vote popular majority. The electoral count was more impressive: 212 to 21. Lincoln owed no small part of his victory margin to the soldiers, nearly 80 percent of whom cast their ballots for the Union ticket. Uniformed voters might have tipped the balance in the president's favor in two close contests: New York and Connecticut. Nineteen states had adopted laws allowing their soldiers to cast absentee ballots in the field, and furloughs were granted to likely Republican supporters eligible to vote only in their home precincts.[25]

Little Rock, Ark.   Nov 1st, 1864

Dear Father: . . . It is raining to day, and I have nothing to do but to
write and read. . . . my stock of reading matter is very limited unless I
take up the "yellowback literature" that almost deluges every Camp.
but I dont much fancy Such "pass times." it is not profitable.

I got a *Nonpareil* to day but found nothing but *"old news"* in it. I
have been *takeing* the *Nonpareil* ever since I have been in the army,
with the ecception of a few months. I *take* it more to patronize the
town and the "Union party" in the Bluffs than because I think it is
a good Newspaper. it is much better than it used to be. it was at one
time a regular *Blackguarding Windy Paper.* I had almost concluded to
quit the Paper. but it reformed a little, and [I] thought [I] would let it
go onn.

The news from Virginia is very good. Sheridan seems to meet
with unusual success lately in his Campaign. but in his last Battle, the
rebs almost got the best of him in the fore part of the engagement. but
the tide of Battle soon turned and gave Sheridan a great victory, the
greatest he has yet . . . won.[26] I saw in a late paper that "Old Pap" had
got a check in Missouri from [Major] Genls. [Samuel R.] Curtis and
[Alfred] Pleasanton.

Such success to our Arms is very bad on the McClellan Party. . . .
their horse wont run in the next Tuesdays race. Our Party is gaining
ground fast here, and we will do our best when the time comes. there
are two regts that will give the "White Feather Party" a strong vote.
those two regts are the 40th Iowa and the 50th Indiana. but I think
they will not give "Little Mac" a majority. I would be sorry to hear of
one Iowa regt voteing the Copperhead ticket, but that regt has always
been called the Copp. regt.

The weather is still warm. there has been a few light frosts this
fall and a few cold rains, but otherwise the weather has been very
pleasant.

Our duty is still very hard, but we bear it and have no fears of
breaking down under it.

One thing there is that causes great complaint among the boys
[and] that is the scarcety of grub. . . . there is no cause why we should
be starved as we are now. it is all through the dishonesty of our Q.Ms.
[quartermasters]. they have to have their stealings out of our rations.
first, the Chief [of] Com[missary] of . . . this Army takes his toll, and

then the Divis. Com. must have his, and the Brigade Com. must also get his share. and finaly, the regtl Com. Sergt takes the last grab at our poor, unfortunate allowance of "Hardtack & Sowbelly," and we have to go Hungry or "Subsist on the country." a soldier will spend half his wages for nesessarys of life, the way we live. If the prayers of the wicked were heard, our "Army Thieves" are gone past all hope. . . . if them rascalls were caught two hundred paces from camp, they would get their past dues quicker than the *Officer favoring law in the army . . . [would] give it [to] them.* I could pull a trigger on such men as cooley as I could on a dog. None but a Villian can get into the "Commissary Department" at this place because the "Whole Business" is under the controll of a deep, designing Villian, a man whose heart is in the Treasury of the U.S. and not in the cause of his country.[27] . . .

. . . it has been only of late that I have been So very personal in my writeing, but you know there is a time when patience ceases to be a virtue. and *we, the Soldiers of this Department, have cause to complain of the unjust treatment that we receive at the hands of Villians wearing shoulderstraps: Officers that are appointed over us.*

We will be payed off in a few days, so it is rumored. we were mustered for pay yesterday. government owes us four months pay. most of the boys are deep in debt on the account of haveing to buy grub. I owe but little of my wages. . . . your Affectionate Son, Charles

Little Rock, Arkansas   November 9th, 1864

Dear Father: . . . yesterday, the *Election* came off. all went as quiet as a funeral (almost). we found but little opposition at the *Ballot Box.* our regt Polled 493 votes, and out of that number, Little Mac got 51. 33rd Iowa polled 431 votes, 42 for McClellan. 40th Iowa, 380 voters; Lincoln got 25 of a majority (much better than we expected). 3rd Iowa Battery polled 104 votes; out of that number, Mac got 14. 36th Iowa polled 140 votes; out of that, Little Mac got 6 votes (the rest of the regt are prisoners since last April, taken at Marks' Mills on the Saline). Iowa Soldiers in General Hospital polled 117 votes and gave 12 of them to McClellan. and last named but the best of all, comes the noble Iowa 1st Cavalry that polled 480 votes, and out of that number McClellan got *One* vote—and that *one* can neither *read nor write.* The 9th Wisconsin (German regt) gave a large maj[ority] for Lincoln. so did the 77th Ohio. the 23rd, 21st, and 20th Iowa regts at Devall's Bluff went almost unanimous for *Old Abe.* and the 9th Iowa Cavalry gave a very small number of votes to Mac. the 33rd, 35th, 27th, 28th Wisconsin Infantry, and 3rd Cavalry Wis. Vols. all gave Old Abe an overwhelming majority. Indiana & Ills. Soldiers are prohibited from voting in the field, or I could tell you of some more great Election victorys. I am Sorry to say that Co. "A" of the 29th Iowa gave almost half the Copperhead votes that was polled in the regt. I do not know as it would interrest you much to give the names of the men that are so lost to all pride of country and Patriotism as to vote for a man that was nominated by traitors. Still, for curiosity sake, I will give you the names, as follows: Sergt Hiram Lewis, Corporal [Dominic] Heagney, George Heagney, Saml Allen, Saml Underwood, Wall. McFadden, Jacob Case, Andrew McIntosh, Addison McIntosh, Chas Clare, Oliver H. Paine, Peter Deal, Harry Williams, Wm Reed, Edwin Ferris, Nephi Joseph, James Brookhousen, Stewart Caldwell, Christian Hack, George Brinkerhoff, Joseph Groff, Sergt Elwood Wilson = 22 out of 51 in the regiment. the rest of the Co., 29 in number, all voted the "Union War Ticket." I will now await with all the impatience in the world for the "returns" from Home. I do not doubt the Loyalty of one free State [to McClellan]. without [a doubt], it is New Jersey, and I have some hopes that it will turn the cold shoulder toward the "Chicago Platform." [28] . . .

we have been under "marching Orders" since the 1st of the month. we do no duty at all now. Our regt has been transfered from the 1st Div. to the 2nd, Hd Qts at Devall's Bluff, [Brigadier] Genl. [Christopher Columbus] Andrews Comdg [Commanding].

All the Cavalry left here for the purpose of cutting off the retreat of old "Pap Price." Genl. Thayers Comm[an]d at Fort Smith are on the lookout for the Old "Skedadler." he will cross the Ark River between Fort Smith and Gibson, and if he is not very cautious, he will encounter a force that will turn him in another direction. One of our best Genls was Ord[ered] to Shermans Army just as he was geting ready for the "Ark. Traveler." That Genl was Mower.

All is quiet around here except an occassional *Brush* with the *Bushwhackers*, which dont amount to much neither way—only the *Hanging of a rascal when caught.* you dont often see an account in the newpapers of the punishment of Bushwhackers. *but that is no sign that it is not done.*

Where we will go to when we march is more than I can conjecture at present. part of our Divis (2nd) is at Pine Bluff and part at Devall's Bluff, and it is uncertain where we will go—or whether we will go at all or not. for my part, I wish we would go out of the Department— any where but here—to serve my time out. Some seem to think that we will not have to serve more than this winter, as the rebs are almost *worn out*. I have heard so much of such talk that I dont listen to it any more. I will think myself very fortunate if I get home safe in 13 months from now. . . .

. . . I am very much obliged to you for them Postage stamp you sent me, for my stock was geting low, and [I have] no money to buy any with. but there is a prospect of geting some Pay soon, and I will lay in a new stock of writeing material. . . . your Affectionate Son, Charles

Little Rock, Ark   Nov 17th/64

Dear Father: . . . we are still under marching orders and cant tell when we will move. The "right-wing" of our regt has been out in the country Since the 11th and just returned this evening. we were Stationed at a government mill on the Benton Road five miles from town. we were relieved by the left wing today. we had Some little Skirmishing with Bush Whackers while there, but none of our boys got hurt.

The weather has been very pleasant untill last night. it commenced raining and is still raining—looks very much like winter (in the south), and [I] would not wonder if it rained for a week. the rain is not very cold.

Late news is that Price is crossing the Ark. River above "Fort Smith" with the remnant of his army, which is not very much reduced. he has men enough left yet to do us some harm when joined with Magruder at Arkadelphia. I dont believe half these tales about the rebs being so *badly beaten—all their Artillery taken and Trains destroyed*—though I hope he (Price) will not try Missouri again.

The best news I have heard lately is that Sherman had *burned Atlanta* and was on his way to Charleston. nothing has done me so much good in a long time as that news did. it was just what I have been wishing to hear: *Burn and lay waste; desolate the country and kill Traitors.* if that *Policy* was adopted in this Department, the Traitors would soon come to terms. I would like to see this *Town laid in ashes* and *every one* of any importance in Rebbeldom. [We should have] the torch in one hand and the sword in the other untill all Traitors yield and come back to their allegiance. we have been playing with *our enemys too long.* it is time to quit this mild policy of feeding with one hand and fighting with the other. If Grant takes Richmond and Petersburg, he ought to burn them down and Still march *on, on* untill all is served in like manner.

We have not yet heard the returns from the Election except from some of the States, and that is only rumor. I suppose by next mail we will know who is our next President. if the Home voters do as well as the Soldiers, Old Abe is all right in the "White House." he wont have to *move* next March. . . . your Affectionate Son, Charles

Little Rock, Ark. Nov 30th, 1864

Dear Father: I take up my pen this evening to Scribble you a few lines in answer to your letter. . . . I also got one from . . . Uncle Charley. . . . it was written before Petersburg. Uncle Charley Seems to like his situation better now than he did a couple of months after he enlisted.

The weather is very fine, almost like May. . . .

Our "Marching Orders" have been countermanded, and we have been assigned to "Post Duty" as Provost Guards, which is much easier than the duty we have been doing. we will not be exposed to the weather and will do no Fatigue duty. but you ought to see the Stile. we put on more airs than a french Dancing Master. we have to come out in our *best* at Guard Mount and Stand the closest inspection by an officer Specialy detailed for that purpose. when we march through town, our arms and accoutrements fairly dazzle the eye.

we are *putting down the rebellion very fast now. the rebs will soon be starved out, and they will submit.*

we have a very fine "Saxe Horn Band" to "Mount Guard" with every morning, and *Oh, what a Blow the Rebellion gets then.* it realy astonishes the natives.

Our rations are a little more plenty now than formerly. Some of the boys went to the Commissary Depot and *helped themselves* a short time ago. . . . hungry Soldiers will do most anything for something to sustain life. for a while, the Citizens Cattle Suffered Severely on the account of *our* short rations—enough on the *Grub* question.

I aint hungry now. am in a good humor. I am about as anctious to get where there is full rations and no *Hardtack* as any one and dont care how quick the war plays out—[just] So it is done honerably. I can eat Hardtack and Bacon several years yet rather than have a Dishonerable Peace. we have too many able Bodyed men in the north yet to give up to Jeff Davis and his "Band of Traitors."

I hope the war is as near its termination as most people anticipate. All we want to end the war speedily is to fill up our Armies and . . . *war in earnest*. give the rebs no time to settle down after they have been driven from one place but follow and wipe them out *entirely*.

I am glad to hear of the Draft. it did catch some of the Sore heads as well as good men. So we have no reason to complain of the partiality of the *"Wheel of fortune."* I seen the list of the names drawn some time ago. I supposed Mr King would have to delay building his *new House*. Mr Triplett [Charles's future father-in-law] will be hurt the worst of any man that I know of among the Union portion. Henry or Moses Nixon will neither pass the Board of examination if it is a competent one as it should be. we want none but able bodyed men in the army.

Old Pap Price is now away down in Arkansas on the Washita at Camden or Monticello, So it is rumored, rather worsted by his pleasure trip up to Missouri. . . . your Affectionate Son, Charles

Little Rock, Ark   Nov 30th/64

Dear Sister Hester: . . . Jane has entirely forgoten me. I have not had a letter from her for nearly five months. . . . I wrote & told her if She did not answer my letters, that she would get no more letters from me.

The weather is very warm and pleasant. yesterday, it was so warm that persons hunted for shade, the sun being so hot. today, it is cloudy but Still warm.

we have once more Settled down in Camp and have our regular duty. our regt is now doing "Provost Guard" duty in the City. we belong to no Brigade or Division. we are Detached and subject to the Orders of the "Commander of the Post," the Col. of the 40th Iowa. we do no "Picket Duty" or any "Fatigue Duty." we quarter in a good Brick House in town (not the regt but the daily detail). Our duty is now permanent untill the Spring Campaign opens, and then we will again "march on" as we have done many times before.

In looking over the list of Names drawn for the Army, I was pleased to see the names of some of our Copp[erhead] Citizens of the Bluffs. but [I] was sorry . . . to see the names of others that are not able to come into the Army. I dont suppose Mr King will like soldiering very well, but that is the case with a great many men now in the army. . . . like it or not, we have to go and make the best of our bargain. I do not dislike soldiering so much but what I would enlist again if it was nesessary. Henry will not be accepted if he is examined by a board of surgeons that have been in the Army for any length of time. but it is very likely that some *Jack Asses* (that clerked two months in some drug store and turned themselves out as Doctors) will be the Board of Examination to examine the subjects. . . . [letter incomplete]

Little Rock, Ark.   Dec 11th/64

Dear Father: . . . I will find it a great undertaking [to write] this cold morning. it froze quite hard last night, and there is a cold wind from the North blowing from off the snow at home, I suppose.

. . . about 35 of the Drafted men from the Bluffs arrived here a few days ago, and among them was Triplett, Babbitt, and several more that I know. they were all assigned to the 3rd Iowa Battery and seem well pleased with the Company. I am very glad they did not come to our regt.

Mr Triplett is in good spirits and wants you to let his family Know by me that he is well and hearty and satisfied with his lot. Charley Babbitt seems to feel the force of the Draft the most, but he will soon become initiated and all will run smoother. Poor Dave. Dunkle, Sutton, and the rest of the "Clique" had to go to [Major] Genl. [George H.] Thomas' Army where they will smell Powder right away. Henry went with the rest of the boys to Thomas' Army, the 9th Iowa Infty, so I learned by Triplett. I hope he will be more fortunate than when he was in the Army before.

Genl. Steele has been Superseeded by [Major] General [Joseph J.] Reynolds. I dont know much about the latter, but I hope the change is for the better. . . . your Aff. Son, Chas. O. Musser

By todays mail we learn that there is going to be an Armistice of Sixty days. I dont credit the rumore. I believe it is only a *Rumore*. . . .

Little Rock, Ark.   Dec. 13th/64

Dear Father: . . . We have some news from Tenn. and Georgia. Sherman seems to be going ahead nobly and meeting with no Serious opposition. Genl. Thomas had a very severe engagement with [General John Bell] Hood and defeated him with heavy loss. The Battle was not a very decisive one, but it learnt the Rebs caution. they will not again soon attack Thomas, even if he has an inferior force. There is yet to be some very hot work done in the Cumberland and Tennessee Valleys. but Thomas is the man for the emergency, or Sherman would not have entrusted the "Army of the Cumberland" to his care.[1] [Brigadier General Alvan C.] Gillems defeat by Breckinridge at Bull's Gap, Tenn, was quite a disaster. but we must expect a reverce occasionaly. we cant be victorious every where. . . .

The weather is quite warm again to day and has the appearance of rain.

You spoke of Wall McFaddens voteing the McClellan Ticket. he is like a great many other old, hard shell Democrats (dont want to give up Partyism), but he dont say much one way or the other. I read that letter that his wife wrote him. it hurt him pretty badly. . . . he tried to smoothe it over by jokeing about it, but I knew how he felt. Wall has some very good qualitys with his many faults. his faults injure him worse than they do any one else. he is a good soldier for all.

The *Conscripts* are all right yet. Mr Triplett is anctious to hear from home. I guess he feels uneasy about the family, though he does not "let on." I Should be very sorry to hear of his family Suffering, but I suppose the Neighbors will help them if they need it. Mr Triplett praised his Willie highly for his good management.

. . . The Drums are beating Tatoo, and I will have to go to Roll Call. . . .

Well, I will go at it again. . . . Gus Breese got a letter from Mr Holeman this evening. he is Still at Indianapolis. he belongs to the 5th regt, Vet. Reserve Corps, Co "E." he is well and hearty. he Says he Saw William in Prison a few days before he wrote. he was well and Hearty. I will write to Mr Holeman and see what I can find out about William, his circumstances, &c. I would like to know why he has been confined so long if he is repentant and wishes to take the Oath as I have often heard. . . . your Affectionate Son, Charles

Little Rock, Arkansas   December 20th,1864

Dear Father: . . . The weather is dull and gloomy to day and has been
for several days past. it has been raining for nearly a week.

Genl Steele left us on the 18th and is now on his way to Hd Qts of
the Dept of West Mississippi. his Successor has not yet arrived. we are
expecting him every day. Genl Steele isued a farewell address to the
troops of the 7th Corps. he reviewed our "Campaigns" and praised us
for the great "Success," for *our great military achievements*. . . . [He]
was sorry that he had to part with a command that he had been so
long with. he wears a Sword that his Corps bought for him (cost—
$1,500). I hope he will soon change *his Arkansas Willows for Laurels
of some other kind.*

It is reported that Fort Smith has been evacuated and the troops
on their way here. Pine Bluff is also reported evacuated.

I think that the 7th A.C. will soon be a little more compact than it
has been for several months. a part of the 19th A.C. at Devall's Bluff is
subject to Genl. Reynolds Command, but they now belong to the
Western Reserve Corps, Hd Qts. St Louis, Genl. G. M. Dodge Comm.

It is rumored among the troops here that an Expedition is fitting
out, ready for a forward movement at an early period. I have noticed
lately that a very large number of Wagons and Ambulances have been
shipped here, and all the repairing Shops are full of workmen. Harness, saddles, Gun carriages, and everything is being repaired, ready
for any emergency. and the evacuation of the two Posts above named
looks as if something was going to be done early. Our scouts report
quite a force of the rebs at Arkadelphia and a still larger force at Camden and Monticello. Magruder is in Command. his force is said to
number about 23000 strong and are inside of strong earth works. [Major General Simon Bolivar] Buckner is at Shreveport or Alexandria
with a large force. So we will find plenty of work to do as soon as we
reach the line of the Washita.

We have no news from Sherman lately and none from Grant. in
fact, we dont hear anything untill after all the rest of the world is
through with it.

I never was so sick of any place in my life as I am of this, and I
dont care how soon we leave for any other point. danger or no danger,
fighting is what we enlisted for. . . . your Affectionate Son, Charles

Little Rock, Ark   December 22nd/64

170   Dear Sister Hester: . . . I was very sorry to Hear of the death of Uncle John. I would not care half as much if he had fallen in Battle, but to be murdered in prison is very hard. (as I am writeing, the Big Guns on Fort Steele are booming away. they are fireing a Salute for our new General. The old 20 pounder Parrotts Thunder it off quite lively. it makes us think of Battle.)² sorry, too, that Frances is sick. . . .

you think I will be on my way home in a year, do you? well, I may be—at least I *hope so*—but who knows but what I may reenlist again right away if the war continues. it is not at all unlikely, for I want to *See* the Rebellion *played out* befor I go home. . . . your Affectionate Brother, Charles

Little Rock, Arkansas   December 24th, 1864

Dear Father: . . . The weather is quite pleasant yet hardly cold enough to freeze at night.

The boys are all well, as usual, and prepared to Spend tomorrow as any other day.

I was in town this morning a couple of hours, and it was full of citizens and soldiers, and yet it was dull. I cannot content myself anywhere now. I am lonesom wherever I go, in a crowd or any where. I wont associate with some of the *boys* that their only passtime is *drinking and gameing*. I can see no pleasure in such a waste of time and money. So I Keep clear of such "resorts." I occassionaly go to the reading rooms of the Sanitary Commision. I was down to the Episcopal Church yesterday, helping to decorate it for the Coming Christmas. I had a good time. there was quite a number of Ladys and Gentlemen helping. we used Pine, Cedar, Holly, Magnolia, and many other evergreenes that grow here, and Flowers from hot houses. The Pastor . . . gave me the invitation, and I spent the day quite pleasantly with the good members of the Fashionable Church of the City.

We have good news from Sherman and Thomas. the former has brought the rebs to a stand at Savannah. he captured Fort McAllister and has all communication cut off, and demanded an unconditional Surrender of the Garrison and works around the City, and gives a short time for them to consider.³ . . . Thomas, it is said, has given Old Hood another lesson in Yankee fighting and charged him only 39 pieces of artillery and 5 or 6.000 prisoners for the lessons.[4] Such news is cheering and bids fair to bring the war to the final struggle Soon.

Them intelligent Copp[erheads] you tell that joke on are almost as intelligent as the "Contrabands" down here. I have seen, in some of the Arkansas regts here, men that wear Shoulderstraps [and] are as ignorant as horses. . . . [They] dont know the names of our leading Generals, and dont know whether Hood and Lee are our Genls. or rebbels. I know a Major in an Ark. regt that [cannot] write his own name. . . . your Affectionate Son, Charles

Little Rock, Arkansas   Dec 30th, 1864

Dear Father: . . . The weather is warm and pleasant, but times are very dull—no stir or excitement whatever. . . .

There is quite a change of affairs going on here Since Genl Steele left and the arrival of General Reynolds.[5] The *loose ends* are being gathered up and the *Screws* tightened. Genl R. is a relegious man, and a strict temperance man, and is down *heavy* on all disloyal citizens. his first act was to take posession of the fine residence of a rich rebbel (and turn him out side of the lines) and establish his Hd.Qts. there. (the Genl. has his family, which consists of wife and two little boys along with him. . . .) the next act was the Stoping of the sale of Commisary stores to citizens unless [they are] in government employ, and [Reynolds] ordered *full* rations to be isued to the Soldiers. . . . another thing is being done that suits me and all the rank and file of the army and that is "Dishonourably Dismissing" all Officers that are found *Drunk*, whether on duty or off. a few nights ago, the Genl. was walking on the streets in citizens dress, and on passing a house of not *very good repute*, he observed some officers haveing a *good time* and very drunk. So he went to the Provost Marshall and ordered them arrested, which was done, and Mr Officers (three of them of the 3rd Regulars) were brought before the Genl. . . . their swords taken from them, and they [were] placed in arrest. . . . next day, they got their papers and found themselves citizens by a Dishonorable dismissal from the United States Service. Such doings meet the approbation of all good soldiers, and Genl Reynolds is gaining the good will of all loyal men at this place. I have wished long for such a change. all will turn out well yet.

As I am writeing, the Big Guns on Fort Steele are Booming away in honor of Genl. Shermans great victory, the capture of Savannah. One hundred guns are to be fired. they fairly make the earth tremble. the 20 pounder Parrotts make a big noise when fired at the rate of two a minit as they are now. Such news is very cheering. Our Armys seem to be victorious every where now. Genl Sherman and Thomas have been very sucessful this winter, and if Grant makes Lee strike colors soon, the Rebellion will "Play Out" in less than eight months. Lee's Army is the only one of any importance left, and that will not last long. Shermans capture of 15000 men, and over one hundred pieces of Artillery, and a large amount of rebbel Cotton is a very heavy blow to the rebbel Government. . . . Hoods several defeats are enough to dampen even a good cause, but the rebs are desperate and blind to their own interests.

Our Officers think that the war will be over by the first of April, but I dont expect it quite so soon. if I get home by the first of August, I will consider myself very fortunate. A great many of our Officers are resigning and going home. very few of our old officers are left—I mean the line officers. Major [Charles B.] Shoemaker will leave us soon. Capt [Edward T.] Sheldon of Co "I" left a short time ago. also, Lieuts [James] Munns [Jr.] of "D" Co, [John S.] Elliott of "H", [Frederick] Sommer of "H", [Isaac] Damewood of "F", and [John S.] Miller of "K" left a short time ago. the only excuse was [they were] tired of the service.[6] Capt. Gardner *will not* leave our Co. untill the time is out. Lieut Kirkpatrick will be here in a few days and report for duty. he has been away a long while on detached service. I guess he is tired of the service, too, and will not remain long with us. . . . Your Affectionate Son, Chas. Musser

Little Rock, Arkansas   January 2nd, 1865

Dear Sister: . . . I got a letter from Uncle Charlie to day. he was well and still before Petersburg.

The weather is very warm and pleasant and looks more like Summer than winter. I never Saw such warm weather at this Season of the year as we are experiencing now.

I am anxious to hear from Henry. I wrote a letter to him and directed [it] to the 9th Iowa at Nashville, but if the 9th is at Savannah, he will not get the letter. . . . Jane has at last written to me after six months delay. probibly she has not got much time to write, So I must overlook her appearant neglect this time.

I would like to be at some of your Spelling Schools this winter. I expect I have forgoten all that I Knew when I left home and will be almost ashamed of my ignorance when I get home. if I had . . . remained at home, I would have been a good Schollar by this time, but I am as ignorant as when I left. only in worldly affairs, . . . I am a little more experienced. . . .

I would have given considerable to have been at home for the past two weeks. I would have improved the time, I tell you. but *wait* untill next Christmas, and I will *call* around and see you. we are now *Slideing* down on our third year, and it will not seem long reaching the bottom. another year will end the war at farthest, and I want to *see* it end before I go home. The late Victorys won by our Armys are a heavy blow to the rebs, and they will not Stand many Such severe reverces.

. . . Sometimes I am almost ashamed to send my letters, but when I think the matter over, I say to myself it is only *me* that is writeing, and I make no pretentions to be a *fine writer*. . . . [I] think you will look over my many failings and consider that it is only an humble soldier that is writeing to you. . . . I wish you to write often and write long letters. . . . If we were Campaigning, I could write better, but we have been here so long that it is like an old Song *about played Out*.

. . . Give my love to all and best regards To all the Friends. reserve a liberal share for yourself. . . . your Affectionate Brother, Charles O. Musser

Little Rock, Arkansas   January 7th, 1865

Dear Father: . . . The weather is not quite so pleasant as it was when I last wrote, but still it is not cold. yesterday morning, it snowed very fast for a short time but melted as fast as it fell. so it turned out no worse than a small rain storm. . . .

The reformation of this Army is going on finaly. the Old Genl. is creating quite a panic among the "Shoulder straps." he is jirking them off quite lively. night before last, the Genl. went to the Theatre in citizens dress, and . . . he saw an officer *very drunk*. [the General] enquired his name, rank, and address and left the Theatre. . . . the next day, the drunk officer got an order which read thus: "Capt M. L. Wright of the 3rd Iowa Battery is hereby *Dishonerably* dismissed from the U.S. Army for being found so *drunk* in the little Rock Theatre that an *enlisted* man was required to *help him home*." this Cap. Wright is a very smart and intelligent young man (only 23 years old). he is the Son of the Secretary of State of Iowa. It is a pity that such a promiseing young Officer should throw himself away like *that*. his Father is a fine Old man and it will *hurt* him badly when he hears of the disgraceful conduct of his son.

Mr Triplett and the rest of the . . . [conscripts] are all right. . . . I am glad to hear from Henry and Know that he is all right yet.

I am glad to hear that Some of the Copp[erhead]s are coming to their senses. a great many will change their Political views before they get home. if they dont, it will only be contraryness that keeps them from it. *that* is all that is the matter with *Our* boys here. they dont want to acknolledge they are wrong, but *time* will tell wonders. . . .

you ask if I Know any thing about John Nixon and Jo Meginness. well, I know but little and that is, they are still at Camden in very good health and likely to be exchanged soon. All the Prisoners in this Department will be exchanged between this [Winter] and Spring. their folks need not worry themselves about the boys, for they will get home all right as soon as the rest of us does. One of our Co that was sent to Tyler, Texas, has been Parolled, and when we heard from him, he was at New Orleans, well and hearty. one of Co "F" was with him also. they were the only two out of 550 that belonged to our regt. the rest were mostly of Banks Army. and out of that 550 that left Tyler, only 340 got to Orleans. the rest all died on the way from the effects of bad treatment at the hands of the Traitors.

The news is good from all points. Sherman did not catch old [Lieutenant General William J.] Hardee as at first reported, but he gained a signal success. Thomas also gets along with his *Hood* finely, but Thomas dont suit the *Hood*.

I will be glad when the time comes for us to pack up for a march, which will be about the middle of March or there abouts. Our duty is not so very hard now, but this thing of being so long at one place dont suit me at all, and I dont care how quick the *forward* is sounded. I have plenty of exercise to Keep me in good health, but a little more wont hurt me in the way of marching.

Nathan Barton has concluded to settle down and go to Teaching, has he? well, he could not do any better unless he *enlisted again*, which

I *expect* he will do *very soon.* just like *I will when I get home.* Oh yes, we'll be *"regulars" no doubt....*

We have been expecting "Old Green Back" around for some time, but he has'nt come yet, and I am afraid he wont come before March. Government owes us six months pay now, and I would like to have a little of it, for I am *flat broke.* "haint got a cent" and dont want any credit, for I am opposed to this thing of runing into debt.

... excuse my scribbling, for I am nervous this morning. [I] was on duty last night and lost all sleep. . . . your Affectionate Son, C. O. Musser

Little Rock, Arkansas   January 19th, 1865

Dear Father: . . . I am about out of Postage Stamps and [have] no funds to renew my stock with. I am afraid the Paymaster will delay his comeing so long that [I] will have to quit writeing entirely.

... The only news I have to write is that a Garrison of our forces at Dardanelle (70 miles up the Ark River) was attacked by rebbels under [Brigadier General William] Steele and [Colonel Sidney D.] Jackman and repulsed with considerable loss. their loss is said to have been over two hundred killed and wounded while our loss was only 2 killed and about fifteen wounded. . . .

about ten days [ago], a Squadron of the 9th Kansas [posted at Dardanelle] was out on a Scouting Expedition, and these same rebbels surrounded them, but the 9th boys cut their way out with the loss of twenty five men. dont know how many the rebs lost that time but equal to ours no doubt, for them boys are not going to get out of such a trap without leaveing a mark. close quarters is what the Indians like.

I am very glad to hear that Mr Holeman has got safe home, for I guess his family needs his help.

The weather is very pleasant for this season of the year. . . .

I want to see that *Draft* come off soon and fill up the regts that have lost so many men during the fall and winter Campaigns. we dont want any of them here, for we have more men than is needed now. . . . your Affectionate Son, Chas O. Musser

Little Rock, Arkansas   January 19th/65

Dear Sister Mary: I was very much surprised and also much pleased to get a note from you. . . . I am glad you have come to the conclusion to learn to write letters. you should have commenced long ago, but you will yet make a good letter writer if you try.

The weather is warm and pleasant here, yet it looks more like May than midwinter. We are all well and enjoy the fine weather. . . .

Mary, I would like to send you my Photograph this time, but it is out of the question. I have none on hand at this time, and it has been a *good while* since I last saw the Paymaster. As soon as I can, I will send some home to all of you. . . . your Affectionate Brother, Charles

Little Rock, Arkansas   January 30th, 65

Dear Sister Hester: . . . Since I last wrote, most of the troops that were here have left on an Expedition to Some point farther South. where they are going the Genl. Knows, and that is sufficient for the present.

The weather is quite warm at present. . . . we have had during the past week quite a severe cold spell, but it has moderated down again.

Hester, I dont want you to throw up homesickness to me, for realy I am not and have not been since February 63 while we were in camp at Beach Grove near Helena. I am so tired of this peace. we have been tied here so long and doing nothing that I wish myself anywhere but here. I dont want to go home untill my time is out or untill the war is over. I want to be doing something for my country instead of laying here in indolence. So dont *twit* me with home sickness anymore, or I will be offended.

. . . You asked me if I did not wish I was at home so that I could gallant the young Ladys home when they come to visit you. well, I do not know as it would do any good for me to wish it or to have *that* pleasure either. I can have *that pleasure* here without going so far. there are plenty of young Ladys here—pretty ones too. . . . Your Brother, Charles

Little Rock, Arkansas   January 30th, 65

Dear Father: . . . A few days after I last wrote, we were Surprised by seeing all the troops around us pack up and march off to where none but the Genl's knew. none of the Citizens knew of any Movement untill the forces marched out of the City. the whole plan was kept a profound secret. Some of us suspected Some movement early but not in the middle of the winter. We have learned lately that the Pine Bluff forces under Genl. Clayton moved out the same time that our Division did and that they formed a junction at Bayou Bartholomew between

Pine Bluff and the Saline River. . . . [From there] they marched toward Camden. A force is said to have concentrated at Gaines' Landing on the Miss and are now on the march toward Camden, which is about the same distance from there as it is from here.

A large River Expedition was fitted out at New Orleans for another attempt to capture Shreveport. the Expedition is to be under the Command of Steele. it is even now rumored that he (Steele) has possession of Shreveport. this is only a *rumor*, but I hope the Genl. will be successful and prove old Banks out a greater blunderer than is known. but there could not be a poorer Genl. than old Ben. Butler as shown by his late great blunder: the attempted capture of Wilmington [North Carolina]. I do not see what the war department means by keeping such News Paper Generals in the Army.[7]

The news lately is good. the Capture of Fort Fisher by Admiral [David Dixon] Porter and [Major] Genl [Alfred H.] Terry is a great thing. it stops Blockade Running and releases a large number of war Vessels composeing the "Blockadeing Squadron." . . . Wilmington will fall soon if it has not allready fallen.[8] The news of to day says that Sherman had Captured a Fort 18 miles from Charleston [South Carolina]. twelve canon and quite a number of prisoners were taken with it.

Since the troops left here, our duty has been very hard. we are on duty *all* the time, day and night. yesterday, a brigade of troops (Colored) arrived from Fort Smith. our duty will be some lighter now unless the new arrivals are ordered still farther on, which is altogether likely.

The weather is tolerably pleasant now, but it has been quite cold since I last wrote you.

The two boys of our regt that was Paroled at "Camp Tyler," Texas, and sent to New Orleans by way of Galveston has got to the regt and are well and hearty.[9] they were separated from the rest of the boys— Nixon, Meginniss, and the rest—on the 22 of last June. . . . [They] were sent to Tyler, where they remained awhile, and then were sent to "Camp Grose" two hundred miles from Tyler. . . . after a long stay [there], they were sent to "Camp Ford" two hundred and fifty miles farther toward Galveston, where they remained untill they were Paroled, and got to Galveston on the 12th of Dec. they told me they marched over seven hundred [miles] during the time they were in the hands of the Rebbels, which was nearly eight months, and [they were] in the Hospital from Wounds two months and a half.

. . . it is geting late, and I must [go] to bed. I have to go on duty to morrow.

(Tuesday morning, Jan. 31st) . . . Four more regts left here last night on their way to joyn the forces that left before. . . . your Affectionate Son, C. O. Musser

Little Rock, Ark.   Feb 5th, 1865

Dear Father: . . . We have been busy geting ready to move for the last four days and are not quite ready yet. We expect to get Orders every moment. our guards have all been releived except one Post, and they will be relieved in the Morning. today, our Quarter Master "turned over" all the regimental effects to the Post Q.M., so we have nothing to encumber us when we move.

This time, I have some sad news to write you. Harvey Meginniss got a letter from his Brother Jo. yesterday. he is now at Camp Hood, Texas. Jo Said that John Nixon was dead, that he died at Camden on the 29th of Sept. he did not say how he died or what was the matter with him.[10] Jo is well and hearty. I feel sorry for Johns wife and his mother. the news of his death will hurt them very much. Poor John. he has been gradualy wearing away for the last eighteen months. he would not have been taken prisoner if he had been stout and hearty.

The weather is very disagreeable. it has been raining for several days, and it finaly turned into sleet and snow. but to night, it is freezeing a little.

(Feb 6th) . . . The rest of our Guards have been relieved, and now we have no men on duty at all—still no Orders to move. I would not be at all surprised if the Order would be countermanded before night, and we would yet stay here untill spring.

The weather cloudy this morning but not cold. I hope it will turn out fine if we have to march, for it would be very disagreeable on the river, such weather as this.

Two years ago this month is the time *that tried us*. Oh! how we Suffered then. I can never forget them times. we buryed from *two* to *seven* men a day at that time. Give me the dangers of the Battle field in prefrence to such dangers [and] Hardships as we underwent at the "Old Camp" near Helena. Near one hundred and fifty of the 29th

Sleeps beneath the sod on the Hills of Helena. I hope the last Funeral Ceremony has been performed for our regt as long as it is known as the 29th Iowa.

. . . I [just] got a letter but not from home. it was from Uncle Charlie. he is not well. he is about to get a Discharge from the Army for "Physical Disability." . . .

Some of the troops are just leaveing town—their destination the same as ours. we will probibly leave in the morning. . . . Yours as ever, C. O. Musser

Little Rock, Ark   Feb 8th, 65

Dear Father: . . . We are yet waiting for "Orders" and do not know when we will go. there are no Boats up yet, but they are expected every hour—so we heard by a Telegraph despach this morning.

The weather has cleared up, and the sun shines warm as ever.

I am sorry to hear that Julia is sick. I hope she will get well soon. . . .

I have Some Photographs of some friends and no way of Takeing care of them if we leave. so I thought I would send them home. you will find them enclosed in this, and among them is the Photograph of Genl. Grant. Please take care of them for me. . . . Your Aff. Son, C. O. Musser

---

The 29th Iowa split into two wings and boarded steamers for the journey southward. One wing, led by Colonel Benton, reached Algiers, Louisiana, opposite New Orleans, on February 14, 1865; the other, under Adjutant Lyman, arrived two days later. On February 20 the Iowans were transported from Algiers to Lakeport on Lake Pontchartrain, thence to Mobile Point, Alabama.

On Board the Steamer *St. Charles*
Port Hudson [Louisiana]   Feb 12th, 1865

Dear Father: . . . We left Island Station the Same evening I wrote last to you, and we run to Vicksburg by 8 Oclock next evening. I did not get to go ashore, for we did not stop long. I wanted very badly to see the City and vicinity by daylight.

yesterday, we made a good run and had but few stopages—only for wood. the country is generaly very low. once in a great while, we come to places where the bluffs come to the river. one place at a small town called Rodney, the Bluffs were very high [and] resembled the Vicksburg hills. the country looks desolate. most of the Plantations are deserted by all their former inhabitants, except some aged colored people and some children. the land is very rich and every . . . few miles on the sides of the river, we see large Plantations and long rows of slave quarters, which looks very like a country vilage. . . . . the desolateing hand of war has visited most every farm, for "Masters Mansion" is generaly in ruins and nothing but the tall chimney left standing.

We stoped at Natchez to day at 3 Oclock and stayed about two hours. I went ashore as soon as we landed and took a stroll over the City. Natchez is the nicest place I have Seen since I came south: fine houses, and the streets all clean and Paved nicely, and some of the most beautyful Gardens I ever saw, evergreens of every kind growing all round. . . .

We will get to New Orleans by the day after to morrow morning if nothing serious happens. . . . We will pass Morganza some time in the morning. . . . Only half of our regt is on the *St Charles.* there was not room for the rest on account of the Boat being so heavily loaded. the rest of the regt is close behind us and will get to our place of destination almost as soon as we will.

the weather has been very favorable since we left Little Rock.

[Brigadier] Genl [James C.] Veatch (the Commander of our Brigade) is on board on our Boat with his "staff."

The Boys are all well except Wm Reed. he is very sick—got the Lung Fever. it will go pretty [illegible] with him, but he has good care taken with him. . . . Your Affectionate Son, Charles

Algiers, La   Feb 15th, 1865

Dear Father: . . . We are quartered in the City of Algiers, La., opposite the Crescent City. We got here yesterday about Noon and are quartered in an Old Foundry about the centre of the City.

We had a pretty rough ride from Port Hudson down to here. The wind blew almost a gale, and it finaly began to rain, and when only ten miles from here, we had to tie up and wait untill the Storm abated.

We touched at Baton Rouge. I did not get to go ashore but had a very good view of the City. I do not like it as well as Vicksburg or Natchez. it looks more deserted and dirty. Still, it is a fine City. the State House is a very large Building. it is near the Levee and overlooks all the City.

From Baton Rouge to New Orleans, the River on both sides is lined with Plantations. . . . the Mansions, the slave quarters, the shugar Mills, the Ware Houses, makes every Plantation look like a flourishing Vilage. This is the nicest country I ever saw. the only objection I have to it is the lowness of it. but it is well protected by Levees, and only in extreme high water it overflows.

I have always heard that this was a rich country. now I know it. we can get every thing cheaper down here than at any point north that I have been at.

We Stoped at Lafayette awhile and put off some stock and then run down to the city. The wharf is lined with Vessels and Steamers. there are "sloops of War," Barques, skooners, and some Ships of the line. there is a French Barque laying at anchor (off the city) with the tri color at masthead. and a little way down is an English Vessel anchored. There is over two hundred vessels laying here, most of them Govt Vessels.

I will give you a table of the distances between places that we have passed since we left Little Rock: From Little Rock to Devall's Bluff, 55 miles; From Devall's to mouth of White River, 175 miles; from White River to Vicksburg, 240 miles; from Vicksburg to Natchez, 120 miles; from Natchez to Morganza, 90 miles; from Morganza to Port Hudson, 30 miles; from Port Hudson to Baton Rouge, 20 miles; from Baton Rouge to New Orleans, 130 miles; From Little Rock to New Orleans, 860 miles.

We had a pretty long ride since we left the rock, and considering all things, we made a pretty quick trip. And if we get on the Gulf, we will think it is a rough time when we get sea sick, as we certainly will if we get on salt water. . . .

I would like to tell you where We are going, but that is out of the question, for I have not the remotest Idea where we are going. Some say we are going to Mobile, and some to Galveston, and others say we are going some where in the coast of Florida. . . . I suppose we will know where we are going when we get there and no sooner. . . . Your son, Chas O. Musser

Algiers, Louisiana   Sunday, Feb 18th, 1865

182   Dear Father: . . . We are still quartered in the "Bellville Iron Works" and awaiting Orders.

yesterday, we Boxed up our extra clothing and put them into the hands of Parkers Express Co to be sent home. I had a few articles that I did not want and could not take with me, so I Boxed them up . . . and [had] them sent to Jo. Boulden where you can get them. . . . I will name the articles: One Woolen Blanket, One Oil Blanket, One Dress Coat, One Pair of Pants, one Knit shirt, One pr of Drawers. The clothing is not worth much, but I had a chance to send it, and the Expressage would not be much. We are . . . allowed to take with us but one change of under clothing—no Over Coat, no extra pants, only just such articles as we actualy need on a campaign.

We can yet form no Idea where we are going. troops are still arriveing from the north. there are ten Regts of Infantry in Camp close around us. and how many are in the rear of New Orleans I can not tell, but a large number must be there if they have not [all] left since the 17th. there is a Brigade of Colored troops near us and another one expected soon, so there will be one whole Divis of Regulars with us.

The weather looks gloomy this morning and has the appearance of rain.

The health of the Regt is not so good as it was when we left Little Rock. there are several cases of the Small Pox in the Regt and a few of Pnewmonia. but I think we are geting along fine, considering the sudden change of climate. if we never fare worse as regards health, we will do well.

two months will find the 29th considerable smaller than it is at present. Our "Feather Bed soldiering" has been too good for us, but it is played out now, and I am not sorry at all. Genl. Steele is in the City and is to take Command of the forces concentrateing. So we will be under our Old Commander. Well, I dont care who [commands us, just] so we are in the field and doing something for our country.

the rest of our Brigade, the 33rd Iowa and 50th Ind, has not yet arrived but are expected every hour. the 23rd Iowa is some where about here, but I have not had the chance to hunt them out. there are several boys in it that I would like to see. . . .

I was over to the city yesterday and strolled around for three or four hours, viewing the sights that were to be seen. New Orleans is a fine City. it is low, but there is no mud to be found. the sts are all Paved with stone and kept very clean. but one fault I found [and] that was the streets are a little too narrow. the sun does not shine long enough in the Streets. I visited most of the most attractive places and found that I could spend several days in viewing the city and then not be satisfied. St Charles Hotell [is] one of the finest houses in the city, large and commodious. it is built of grey lime stone. it has been neglected since the out break of the Rebellion. Still, it is a fine Building. French Cathedral is another nice building. it is too grand for me to describe, so I will say it is the finest Work of the kind I ever saw. Academy of Music is a great affair. it is on St Joseph Street. I heard some fine music there but did not have time to stop long. so I walk on to St Charles Theatre, the greatest Theatre in the City. the "stars" shine there in all their brilliancy. I will go on to the Convent of St Catharine. I can say nothing of the inside of that ancient "Stone Pole," but it looks like a Prison to me. I got a glimps of a few of the Nunns. they were mostly French, I should judge from the looks. next to the Convent is the Hospital of St Louis. I could not see much of the inside. it looked nice and clean and roomy. it is the Principal one of the City. The Alms House I did not look around much, but what I saw I did not like much. . . . New Orleans Medical College is also a fine work. I was hurryed too much to look much at it. Mercantile College, now the U.S. Genl. Hospital, is a very large Building near the Wharf. it is the largest House in the City. we can see it from our quarters. it towers far above all other houses around. But the nicest scenery in the City is Jackson Square, the Old Battle Ground. in the center is a statue of the old Genl. on his War Horse, and at each corner of the Square is a statue of the Goddess of Liberty. [There are] Evergreens of every kind, Flowers, and every kind of shrub that grows in this climate, neat walks paved with shells of the shell fish, and nice Bowers, and seats to accomodate visitors. you could get any thing you wished to buy there. . . . Pedlars (of every kind of Fruits and refreshment) brought it to you. well, I will have to move on to St Marys Market, the best one in the City. Cincinnati, St Louis, Memphis, or any markets I ever saw before cannot be called markets by the side of St Marys, N.O. it is large and too grand for me to describe. . . . The Monument of Henry Clay in Canal Street is a fine sight. I could spend weeks in viewing the City and surroundings.

. . . Some how or other, I cannot write as well as I used to. I cannot get my mind settled down to it. But I know you like to hear from me often. . . . I like to get letters from home often and thereby another reason for writeing often. . . .

We have not been Payed off yet. almost eight months Pay [is] due us. if we are going to move right away, I dont care much if we are not Payed off now. but if we stay here a week or two, I want some money. we cant Borrow any more. all are Broke. if I was at the Rock now, I could get money at any time, but several hundred miles lies between me and that City. About the only pleasure a soldier has is his letters from home and what he can buy with his little Sum of Green Backs. . . . keep[ing] us out of the use of our money almost eight months is too bad. I dont believe Government intends to treat her soldiers in that way. I think it is the rascals and sharks in her employ. A soldier is bad enough when he has plenty of money and not *forced to appropriate.* but when deprived of his dear earnings, he is not over concientious about *appropriateing* what he needs for his especial use. If we get our pay soon, I will send you some money, for I will have *some* more than I will want to use between Pay Days. . . . Your Affct Son, Charles . . .

Pontchartrain Par. [Parish], La   Feb 21st, 1865

Dear Sister: . . . We left Algiers about noon yesterday, . . . came across the river and got on the cars at the Lake Pontchartrain R.R., and run out here (six miles). . . . are now awaiting our Regimental train that came around by the wagon road. We are encamped on the shore of Lake Pontchartrain at a little town of the same name.

There are several Steamers at the Pier, waiting for their load of soldiers who are also here waiting Orders to get on Board. We are going to Dauphin Island, Miss Sound, 40 miles from the City of Mobile, Ala. it is 175 miles from here by the way of the Lake and Sound. we will go on Steam ship from here to our destination. as the wind is now blowing, we will have a stormy time crossing the Lake. the waves run high now, and the gale is increasing.

We are now on salt water for the first time in our life, and it is quite a novel sight for us. Barques and other sail Vessels rideing gracefuly over the waves is a sight worth seeing at any time. The Pier or Landing is built on pileing and extends about four hundred paces out into the Lake. the R.R. runs out to the extent of the trussel work, and the largest sea going Crafts can tie up to the Pier without any danger of geting into shoal water. Lake Pontchartrain is a larger lake than I had any Idea of. it is, at the widest place, about 56 miles wide, and the length of it is about 165 miles. the country between the Lake and the City of New Orleans is nothing but one great Cyprus swamp, and nine tenths of the land is under water, and the water looks almost as black as Ink—the very quintessence of disease. I cannot see how the people live there. they must certainly be sick most of the time. they get their fire wood by runing out in the swamp with canoes and cutting the Cyprus, which is the only kind of wood here. the people live in water, work in water, and are a kind of water animal.

The weather is warm and pleasant, when we can get out of the wind. the sea Breeze is not cold but troublesome on the account of it carying away our caps.

. . . I have got a goodly number of letters to answer, but most of them will have to lay by untill I get more . . . Paper, Envelopes, and Postage stamps. and what is worse still, my Purse has been long empty, and *consequently*, I will have to *dry up* for a while. . . .

I am very glad to hear that Julia has got well again, for when there is sickness at home, I am continualy uneasy. I dont care for myself at all, but I hate to hear of any of the Dear ones at home being ill.

. . . I do not expect to get mail very frequently while we are on a campaign, but I will write all the same . . . if I can get the material, which is not a very easy job now when most all of the Boys are in the same unfortunate condition as myself.

Hester, I hope you learn fast this winter, for I want to see you get a good education and not be like your Brother: Ignorant and sorry that he did not improve the time while he had a chance. You will make a good Teacher if you study hard and do your utmost. . . . Your Affectionate Brother, Charles . . .

7 ← **PEACE AGAIN**   February–July 1865

Aside from its value as a rail center, Mobile ranked second only to New Or-
leans among Confederate ports. Grant saw this and more: the city's potential
as a base for a thrust deep into Alabama. In January 1865 the general-in-
chief ordered Canby to seize Mobile. For Canby, the chief obstacles would
be Spanish Fort, commanding the mouth, and Blakely, commanding the
head of the Appalachee River. Opposing forces consisted of no more than
10,000 Rebels under Major General Dabney H. Maury. One Federal col-
umn, 32,000 strong, assembled at Canby's direction on Dauphin Island and
prepared to march on Spanish Fort. A second column, 13,000 men under the
command of General Steele, concentrated at Pensacola, Florida, with
Blakely as its objective.

    On February 23, as the campaign began to take shape, the 29th Iowa
was bivouacked at Navy Cove near Fort Morgan. Reorganization brigaded
the Iowans with the 91st Illinois, 50th Indiana (five companies), and 7th
Vermont, all led by Colonel Henry M. Day.[1]

Camp Navy Cove   Mobile Point, Ala   Feb 24th/65

Dear Father: With my Portfolio on my lap and seated near the Beach,
where the Breakers roll almost to my feet, I attempt to again pen you
a few lines. . . .

    About noon the 20th, the assembly was sounded, and we "fell in"
and marched to the [Algiers] Wharf. got on Board the *Jennie Rodgers*,
crossed the River to New Orleans, and layed some time at the R.R.
Depot. it was almost night when we got to Lakeport, only 6 miles from

the City, and when we got there, our teams that started before we did . . . by the way of the wagon road had not yet arived, and we must await their comeing. night passed away and no teams yet and a large detail was sent to help them through the mud. finaly, about 1 P.M., they got to the Pier, and we comenced to load them [the wagons] onto the Steamer by takeing them all to pieces so that we could stow them in [the] Hold. about 4 oclock, the steamer was ready to receive the Regt on Board, so we were all piled in—or rather on—for we all crouded on the upper deck, there being about 75 mules and Horses between decks besides a large ammount of freight. Our steamer (the *Clyde*) was a 2nd Class Gulf steamer—low pressur Engine. Crouded was no name for the way we were stowed into that old tub: 600 men all on one deck. we had about 6 inches square to the man. and the worst of all was about the time we got settled down, it began to rain. the wind had been blowing almost a gale for several days. finaly, we weighed anchor and started across the Briney Waters. about 9 P.M., we came to a shoal, and the Captain of the steamer said we must anchor untill morning. I was glad, for the Wind and rain did not seem to beat so bad when we stoped, but there was no sleep for us. I cast anchor on my Knapsack, covered my head with my Poncho, and told the storm it might rage for all I cared. but Oh! what a squeezeing I got: men before me, men on each side and behind me. I thought my ribs would be caved in before morning, but thank providence, I weathered it through. but the storm still raged with . . . increased fury. the Boat rolled and tumbled on the waves.

[On the] 22nd, we Weigh anchor at 6 1/2 A.M. and run steady. we were almost out of sight of land several times. the rain and wind beat us heavy. about 10 A.M., we get to Fort Pike at the mouth of Rigolets Strait, the connecting stream between Pontchartrain and Lake Borgne. Fort Pike commands the Inlet. it is a very strong work, an Old government work. it was surrendered to our forces at the Capitulation of New Orleans. there is a Light House at Pike. about 1 P.M., we get into Lake Borgne. the Waves still run higher. some of the Boys geting sea sick. about 2 1/2 P.M., we run out of the Lake into Mississippi Sound, Pass Cat Island at 3 1/2 P.M., at 4 1/2 [P.M.], Pass Ship Island— Still storming. The Boat rocks worse than ever. Oh! What a sight. every man nearly is geting sick. many of them is leaning over the lea railing and casting up accounts. it is laughable and still pretty hard. I began to get drunk myself. my stomache feels very queer. I lay down but get worse—Oh, how sick. I felt as if I would just as soon die as live. but we soon got into smoothe sea again, and the Boat did not rock so much. I feel better [and] will soon be strait again. we get into shoal water at 7 P.M. and Cast Anchor, the storm abateing. once in a while, a gust of wind and rain comes.

[On the] 23rd, Weigh Anchor at 4 1/2 in the morning—raining and blowing hard as ever. another sleepless night I have passed. I begin to feel very unwell. The Vessel rolls and rocks as bad as ever—more of the Boys sick. I am afraid I will get sick if the Boat continues the rock. . . . geting into shoal water, [we] are in sight of Fort Powell and Grant's Pass when just at the mouth [of Mobile Bay], the Old *Clyde* gets aground and labors hard to get loose but no go. a Gun Boat comes in sight. we Signal for help. she comes to our aide but does no good. two or three more Vessels come in sight, one astern and two out of Mobile Bay. we again signal for help, and a steam tug from the Fort comes just as the steamer comes that was astern of us. she provs to be the *Genl. Banks* with Genl Veatch, our Brigade Commander, on board. one of the steamers over our Bow comes up, and Genl Veatch has her stop and lighten the *Clyde*. we are all Ordered to sling Knapsack and get on Board the *Warrior*. we are soon on the steamer, but our Commissary stores, cooking utensils, and a guard is left [behind] to take care of the Mules and Horses. the *Clyde* gets loose and starts through but again runs aground. we pass on and leave here. the last we saw of her, the Tug was hitching to her for the purpose of towing her through the mud, 1/2 mile from Fort Powell. (There are no guns on the Fort. a squad of men stays there to keep the Light House, which is a short distance from the Fort. Powell was evacuated when [Admiral David G.] Farragut took Gaines and Morgan.) The *Warrior* gets through the Pass all right. We are now in Mobile Bay. Dauphin Island, the Key to the Bay, is in sight. Mobile Point is also in sight. Fort Gaines is on a Point of Dauphin Island, about four miles from Mobile Point where Fort Morgan is situated. we stoped about an hour at Gaines and then moved off for this Place, which [is] four miles from Morgan. here the Point is scarcely a half mile wide. on the Bay side is Navy Cove, a small town where all our troops land for the Point. on the other side is the open Gulf where the Breakers roll high and keep a continual roar. They say we are now 25 miles from the City of Mobile and 20 from the nearest Rebbel force, which is at a Point not far from the main defences of the City. their is about 7 or 8 thousand troops at this Point and about twice that number at Fort Gaines. three regts landed since we did, and many more are on their way here. their will, in one week, be over 50000 men near Mobile, besides the Naval force. three Monitors are lying off the Cove, and some half dozen men of War, besides about 8 or ten Musquito Boats. their is about fourty sail Vessels at anchor here, and I do not know how many steamers.

The *Clyde* has not yet arrived, and we have nothing to eat but Oysters, which we can get by the quantity by going about a half a mile around the Cove. . . . we can pick them up by the Bushel. . . . fish of all kinds are very Cheap. if we had money, we could live well here, but no Green Backs yet, and it will be a long while before we can get any. . . .

It has begun to rain again, [and] a strong breeze is blowing off the Gulf.

. . . this [letter] takes my last Stamp, last sheet, and last Envelope. so if I do not make a raise soon, my letter writeing has stoped. . . . your Affectionate Son, Charles

(Feb 25th) . . . The weather is still cloudy and damp. . . .

The steamer *Clyde* came in this morning—or rather her cargo—for the Boat is still aground in Grant's Pass. Troops are still arriveing. . . . I do not think we will remain long here for the Campaign. Genl Steele is here and is in command of the forces. Genl Canbys Hd Qts is at Pensacola, only a short distance from here. there is some talk of us moveing across the Bay to Cedar Point and move from there upon the City of Mobile.

Some seem to think the Rebbels will not stand but will evacuate as soon as we advance. I do not believe such talk. they have not been spending millions of money and years of work upon the defences to run at the approach of our Army and Fleet. I think we will have a chance to dig and Bombard a while before we catch the Johneys.

I will now quit for this time. My Pen is [illegible] like writeing with a stick. this is the third Pen I have spoiled by carying them in my Knapsack. . . . Your Son, Charles . . .

Camp Navy Cove   Mobile Point, Ala   March 7th, 1865

Dear Father and Sister Mary: . . . I would answer your letters separately, but I have not the *material*. it was through the generosity of a friend that I am able to answer your letter at all—no money and no credit here on this wilderness of sand. there is some talk of Paying us

off soon, but that *soon* is forever coming, and we will move before any
Paymaster can accomodate us this time. . . .

the weather is quite pleasant.

Some of the forces move in the morning. others will soon follow,
and the whole army will move in a very Short time. . . . Yours as Ever,
C. O. Musser

P.S. Our Boys that hav been prisoner since last spring are now
at New Orleans, Paroled for exchange. Jo Meginniss is well and
hearty. . . .

March 16th/65   Navy Cove   Mobile Point, Alabama

Dear Father and Sister Hester: . . . we have orders to move forward at
Daybreak. . . . we have to "fall in" at four in the morning.

. . . nothing of any importance has transpired—only a few slight
demonstrations, such as the shelling of a Battery as the Johneys try to
build some around the City. last saturday, the monitors and Gunboats
moved up the Bay toward the City and near the mouth of Dog River
Channel. they encountered a Battery, shelled them out, and fell back
to their moorings, with only one of the Torpedo Rakes of a monitor
slightly damaged.

we are now ready to try *them* both by land and sea. the whole force
on Mobile Point moves "forward" immediately. old Col Thomas H.
Benton is now a Brigadier Genl., Brevetted very lately. "Old Tommy"
is the man for the 29th yet. the Boys like him better every day. A
Brigadier Genl., [William P.] Benton, Commands our Division, the 3rd
of the 13th A.C. Major Genl. Gordon Granger Commands the 13th
Corps. Genl. Canby [is] Commander in Chief [Military Division of
West Mississippi].

The weather has been varied since we came here: rain, wind, and
sunshine following each other in rapid succession.

The news from all points seem favorable. but we scarcely ever get
any news, and when it does come, it is stale.

. . . I have found quite a number of old acquaintances. the first I
came across was Charles Sanborn, a young man from the Bluffs, a
school Teacher. . . . Mr Sanborn belongs to the 77th Ills Infty. I also
found some of *our* old Ohio Neighbors (from Millwood and vicinity)
in the 96th Ohio Infty. . . . the 33rd Iowa is here. the 96th is a Veteran
[Volunteer] Regt., and the boys have been at home lately. . . .

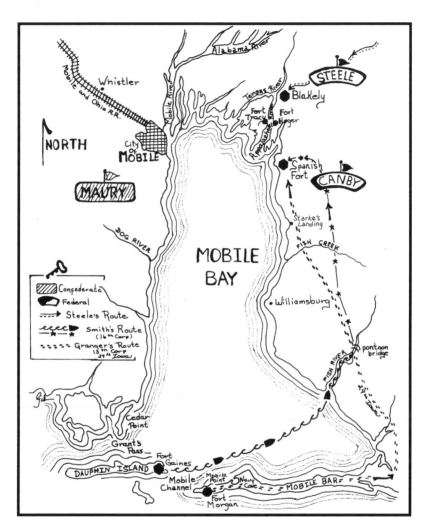

Siege of Mobile, March–April 1865. Map by Gaile Beatty.

. . . Many thanks for those Postage Stamps you sent. were it not for them, you would not get this letter. they cannot be had for either love nor money here, and I was in a remarkable streak of luck when I got this sheet of Foolscap from a man in another regt. . . . your Affectionate Son, C. O. Musser

The campaign for Mobile opened March 17. Major General Andrew Jackson Smith's Sixteenth Corps boarded transports at Fort Gaines while the Thirteenth Corps of Major General Gordon Granger marched overland from Fort Morgan. Smith's and Granger's commands were to rendezvous at the Fish River before closing on Spanish Fort. Brigadier General William P. Benton's Third Division, which included the 29th Iowa, led the march of the Thirteenth Corps. It was slow going for the infantrymen, as the roads were sodden after an eighteen-hour rain.

By March 26 the two Federal corps were poised before Spanish Fort. They completed the investment of the fortifications next day, driving the Rebel skirmishers back to their rifle pits. Within easy range of the Confederate batteries, Day's brigade maintained its position throughout the day under heavy fire. Immediately after nightfall, the 91st Illinois and 29th Iowa began to construct breastworks. By daybreak they had sufficient cover from the annoying fire of Rebel sharpshooters.

The blue ring around Spanish Fort inexorably tightened—Day's skirmishers were within 100 yards of their objective by March 30. General Benton reported that "the operations of my command from this time . . . shows . . . incessant toil in the trenches night and day, a gradual and sure approach to the enemy's works by means of the pick and spade . . . , the construction of batteries . . . , bringing up and mounting of siege guns."[2]

On the other side of the lines, Brigadier General Randall L. Gibson commanded a garrison of 1,800 men, 6 siege guns, 14 field guns, and 12 cohorn mortars (a small brass mortar invented by Baron Menno van Coehoorn). The initial response of General Maury, Gibson's superior, was to order reinforcements to Spanish Fort, including sharpshooters with Whitworth rifles. After losing more than 300 men March 30, Gibson received additional reinforcements, but he realized that the garrison was being bled to death. Determining that preemptive measures were called for, Gibson ordered an artillery bombardment of the closest enemy force. Shortly after sunset on March 31, seventeen Southerners sortied from their rifle pits in Colonel Day's sector, capturing twenty-two members of the 7th Vermont without the loss of a man. But this small break in the Union siege lines was quickly repaired.

Relentless artillery and sharpshooter fire continued to wear down the defenders both physically and psychologically. As the Yankees closed the range, they brought massive fifteen-inch seacoast mortars into operation, lobbing shells capable of plowing through six feet of earthworks before ex-

ploding. The Southerners were demoralized by the sight of these shells, but, of course, they were powerless to do anything about them. Equally dispiriting was an acute ammunition shortage that handicapped the Southerners' ability to shoot back. The supply was so low that Gibson urged his men to gather stray shot, shells, and bullets for recycling by the Ordnance Department. Before long, only sharpshooters in forward rifle pits were allowed to fire their weapons. So many cannon and mortars were concentrated around Spanish Fort that Rebel artillerymen were pinned down most of the time. Gibson ordered the garrison's black cooks to help his exhausted men strengthen the works. This cover was desperately needed April 4 when the Yankees let loose a two-hour artillery barrage. The people of Mobile could plainly hear the noise of siege guns and feel the earth shake.

Finally, under cover of a massive bombardment on the evening of April 8, Federal infantry overran a 300-yard section of Gibson's trenches. Lacking the necessary force to seal the breach, he concluded that further resistance would risk the capture of the entire garrison. The Southerners spiked some fifty artillery pieces, and, under cover of darkness, most of the defenders were able to make their way to safety. At 11:45 P.M., skirmishers from Benton's division entered the Confederate works.

Meanwhile, on March 20, Steele set out from Pensacola with the other Federal column, arriving at Blakely April 1 and laying siege to the place. A general assault on April 9 took the fort with 3,700 prisoners and 40-odd guns. (Benton's division had marched eight miles to Blakely and was preparing to support Steele when this attack was made.) The fall of Spanish Fort and Blakely caused Maury to draw up plans for the evacuation of Mobile, as he had lost half his effective force in the sieges, expended a great deal of ammunition, and saw no prospect of relief. The evacuation of the city commenced April 10. Forts Tracy and Huger, the last defenses standing between the Yankees and Mobile, were abandoned and blown up the evening of April 11. That same evening, Day's brigade marched to Starke's Landing and boarded transports, crossing Mobile Bay with the rest of the Thirteenth Corps. The Federals entered the city on April 12 just as the defeated Maury departed, retreating to Meridian. The 29th Iowa camped on the outskirts of Mobile with Day's other regiments. The Iowans could look back on the campaign with some relief, having lost few of their number: one killed, fourteen wounded, and four captured or missing in action.[3]

Camp of 13th A.C. on Fish River, Ala   March 24th/65

Dear Father: . . . I will begin with our March from Mobile Point, which was comenced on the morning of the 17th. It was almost noon before our forces got on the route. . . . we did not march over 12 miles this day. the roads [were] very bad: Sand Banks and Swamps continualy. Camp No 1 [was] on the Bayside and within hearing of the Gulf Breakers. The Country is covered with Scrubby Pine and Live Oak.

We struc Tents early next morning. Our regt [was] Vanguard of the Divis. roads geting worse and worse fast. we have been Traveling almost an easterly cource since we started, sometimes a little south of east. we halted at noon for dinner at an old rebbel Camp . . . 9 miles from Camp No 1. Forward is Sounded soon, and again we move on. 5 miles farther and we pitch Tents on Camp no 2. The country presents almost the same appearance as the first days march: the timber a little heavy and all Pine.

I have as yet told you nothing about the Orders of march or Field Orders. First, we are allowed to cary only one change of under clothing; namely, one shirt, one pair drawers, one pr socks, and one Woolen Blanket, one Rubber Blanket, an extra pr shoes, and one half of a shelter Tent. . . . we *have* to cary 4 days rations in our haversacks, and 50 rounds of Cartridges, and for every 12 men, one ax and one Shovel or spade. just think of *that* load. and the soldier has to march from 5 to 20 miles a day, . . . wade swamps, haul Artillery and subsistence wagons by hand, sometimes fifty yards through mud and water waist deep, and when we stop for the night, fortify our camp with a line of rifle pits or a Breast Work of fallen Timber—and by three Oclock next morning, be up and ready to perform the same labor again. . . . sometimes our Blankets and Tents get wet, and wet or dry, we must cary them. . . .

. . . next morning came but us still in camp. to day, we are Rearguard and have to await the slow progress of the subsistence Train. [The] Pioneer Corps, and in fact, the whole forces had to . . . make the roads Corduroy. this day, we build over one mile of that kind of road through a swamp. most of the Train crosses. we move about 1/2 mile and form Camp No 3. Vanguard of 1st Divis comes up to our rear just at night.

[March] 20th, Train moves on, and we march 7 miles and enter Camp No 4. Genl Granger joins the command.

to day, we changed our direction and marched in a northerly course. . . . Camp No 5 [is] 4 miles from last nights camp. to day was one day that we will never forget. the rain poured down in torrents. the whole country almost flooded. about 1 P.M., it stoped raining, and we came to a halt to help the Artillery and Wagons through the now almost impassible swamps. we unhitched the Horses and hitched the Prolong or Manropes and about 100 men to each . . . [cannon] in water and mud Waist deep. we hauled them over 200 yards, got them on ground that would hold them up, and then hitched the Horses to them. one may judge how the roads is when 8 large Horses cant move a 12 Pounder Napoleon gun. Well, finaly, our troubles were over for the day and us wet and mudy as could be and no dry clothing to put on, so we built large fires of Pine Knots and stood in the smoke untill we were more like contrabands than white men.

[March] 22nd, Ordered to move on to Hd Qrs 2 miles farther. get there by the middle of the afternoon, stack guns, and go to road working again. I believe we have built, so far, ten miles of Corduroy road. this is the worst country I ever saw for an Army to march through. the ground in most places seems firm, but as soon as half dozen teams goes over it, down they go to axels, and then it's "halt," "front," "Stack Arms, Boys and help those teams out of the mud." as hard as the work is, we hear no grumbling. I never saw as lively and light hearted an army since [we] came south. they all seem in the best of spirits and care not what comes. they are prepared to meet anything. . . . Today, we heard some heavy fireing up . . . [Mobile] Bay. I learned that it was our gunboats shelling the Woods where a rebbel force was seen. and our Transports were landing the 16th A.C. at the mouth of Fish River, some ten miles from here up the Bay.

[March] 23rd, We move out of Camp No 6 at daylight and arrive at Fish River at Noon, halt for dinner, and then cross the Pontoon Bridge and go into Camp on the North side of the River. we found the 16th A.C. here and some Gunboats at anchor in the River. We had a very fatigueing but not a long march to get here. we are between 40 and 50 miles from Fort Morgan by land and hardly half that distance by water. . . . I am certain that we are not far from the Johney Rebs, for they feel of us occasionaly. rumor says there is some very strong rebbel Works 8 miles from here near a little town called Williamsburg. but we will not mind them. when we get ready to move, Our Army is able to sweep all before it in this state. Our Subsistence Trains are being loaded, and troops are still arriveing both by land and water. at a rough guess, I would now estimate our force at 45.000, and several Divisions of the 13th and 16th A.C.s has yet to come, and Genl Steeles Column from Pensacola is on the way across from West Florida toward the Alabama River. . . . [letter incomplete]

Before "Spanish Fort," Mobile Bay   April 1st, 1865

Dear Father: . . . This is the 6th day of the Siege of the "Spanish Forts" or the main defences of the City of Mobile.

. . . about noon on the 25th [of March], we Struck Tents and moved off, the 16th A.C. in the Van. our Divis (3rd of the 13th A.C.) was in the rear. we marched very late and went very Slow—only got 7 miles. As large an Army as this cant move fast. the roads was very good, but we were nearing a stronghold of the enemy. consequently, we had to feel a little ahead. early next morning, we moved off, 16th Corps on the right in Column, one Brigade of . . . one Corps was . . . marching in a parallel line with the other two columns. toward evening, there was Slight Skirmishing in front. the Army come to a halt at sundown, . . . made a line of breastworks, and remained under arms all night. we were then three miles from the Rebbel Works, 16th Corps on the right, 13th on the left.

. . . The old Spanish Forts are on the Bay, opposite and in plain view of Mobile. this is called the "Key of Mobile." The main work is in front of our Corps. it is a very strong work, . . . mounts many heavy guns, and has a strong line of outer Works. it commands all the country around. the work next on its right is a Square Work called the Watter Fort, as it is low down and built more to operate against the Navy than Army. it mounts some 100 pounders of the best kind. next work is a long work and is very formidable. it is farther from our line than the left Works and gives them a cross fire upon our lines. and Still farther to our right is another work of the same kind and mounts Some very heavy guns. still farther to the [right] is similar works. but on the extreme right is a very Strong Fort and gives our lines more trouble than all the rest of the Works on the 16th Corps line. these Works are all built on high hills overlooking the Bay and country in the rear. they are about three miles long.

We have completely invested the Works. our right rests on the Bay. Our Fleet lays about one and three forths miles from the Rebbel Works and near our left. We have Batteries in position at short intervals all along our line. Operations have barely begun yet. still, we have had some Warm work, I assure you.

. . . early on the morning of the 27th [of March], the whole Army was put in order of Battle. 2nd Divis, 16th Corps, was the advance line of that A.C., and the 3rd Divis of our C. was in advance. our regt was [in] front of our Brigade and close in rear of the advance line. we moved up slowly but surely, by the way. our Company was put in front on the Skirmish line. it was not long before we pressed the Johneys close, and the work got prety warm. bullets began to fly. . . . we kept moving up, the rebs falling back toward the works. finaly, we were too close to suit the rebs, and they opened upon us with Grape, Shot, and Shell, and soon our guns were in position, and we returned the compliment. our line of Battle was halted and ordered to ly down while we, the skirmishers, followed them to their works and advanced to within Speaking distance. we covered ourselves behind logs and kept up such a fire upon the rebbel gunners that they could not use their guns. whenever they would Show their heads in an embrasure, a dozen rifles would belch forth their deadly contents among them. night came on, and the fire slackened on both sides. (our line of Battle was strengthened by falling timber and building heavy breast works. by morning, our whole line was strongly fortifyed with field defences.) as soon as it was dark, our company was relieved from the Skirmish line and fresh men sent out. our works are about 900 or 1000 yards from the rebbel Works. first day, the loss in killed and wounded of our Divis was only 50, and our regt lost the heavyest of any other regt in the Divis. our loss was 9.

[March] 28th, the fighting comenced at day light and continued all day with but light loss on our side. we [were] still erecting works— work all night and all day, sometimes with Ax, sometimes with Shovel, and sometimes with gun. we have our impliments of warfare all with us: tools to build works with and arms to defend them with. today, Capt [Lewis K.] Myers of our regt was wounded by rebbel riflemen.[4] our monitors are moveing up slowly today, . . . feeling for Torpedoes and occasionaly throwing a shell at the forts. our skirmishers advance nearer the rebbel works and throw up some breastworks. we relieve the skirmishers regular at dark every night so that the rebs cant see the movements. last night, a squad of our boys missed our line, and the first thing they knew, they were right upon the Johneys. both partys were badly scared, but a sharp little Skrimmage ensued. the rebs run, and our boys run. one reb was Killed and a few wounded. one of our boys was Killed, and the "Officer of the Day" that was with our boys was wounded in the hip, a flesh wound.

[March] 29th, no material change in the appearance of things along [the] lines, only . . . heavy works being made. some Siege Trains are coming up. in a few days, they will be in position. Not as much fireing today. . . .

[March] 30th, heavy fireing comences at the dawn of day. last night, the rebs came out of their works and tried to dislodge our Skirmishers but failed with the loss of a good many men. last night, a squad of rebbel Skirmishers made a mistake and got in to the rifle pits of the 33rd Iowa and was Bagged and sent to the rear. several such incidents has occured since the investment of these works. if our boys make such a mistake, they have a little fight over it, but the Johneys generaly give up when they find they are . . . [surrounded]. a regt of the 16th C. charged the rebbel skirmish line last night and captured about 20 rebs and lost only one Killed and three wounded. Our Artillery is now all quiet [and] dont reply to rebbel fire. works being built for Mortar Batteries and Siege Guns. 26 pieces of Siege Ordnance came to the front last night.

[March] 31st, Our regt [was] relieved from the advance lines and sent to the rear lines today. fresh regts sent to the front. the total loss in our regt so far is not great. . . . it is between 20 and 30, three in our Co—none that you know. Boys all well and full of fight, just as soon fight as not. this is the 6th day of the investment of Spanish Forts. as soon as our Heavy Batteries get fixed, there will be a big fuss between the two works. The Monitors are at anchor close to their works, ready to open as soon as the signal is given. The rebel forces inside the works is variously estimated from 6 to 15000 men. . . . they have received reenforcements since we came here. I saw three regts land from Transports. there are several rebbel Gunboats and Transports in sight of our fleet, but when these works are taken, then look out for news of a big naval fight in Mobile Bay—or a big destruction of crafts by the rebs.

. . . [Steele is] near Blakely, a town on the Alabama River, about 25 or 30 miles from here. one Divis of our Corps was sent to reenforce him. he is going to operate against the Mobile and Ohio R.R. and the Communication between Mobile and Selma and Montgomery. Steeles Column numbers about 15000 strong, and moreover, it is said that he is going to cooperate with Genl Thomas as well as Canby. . . .

. . . [Major General John M.] Schofield, Sheridan, Sherman, Grant, and all are doing well. it seems to me that the rebellion is playing out fast. still, it will take time to crush such a gigantic Rebellion. I want to see the end of this war before my time is out. . . .

While I am writeing, the Peace commissioners are flying over us. they are [the] rebbels [shells]. ours are going the other way. . . .

I am glad to hear that William is geting along all right. hope he will go home. I should like very much to see him.

I hear that Capt [James L.] Trenor caries a high head since he got home. if he receives such a kind reception at home, how ought *true old soldiers* to be used when they return from the war? I will tell you how he got his 2nd Lieutenantcy. in the first place, he had not men enough to muster him in as captain, and there was a 1st Lieut in the Co allready, so he had to take the 2nd Lieut or go back to his old regt as sergt. so he chose the Shoulder Straps. he got dissatisfied and began to neglect his duty. . . . once or twice he was put in arest for it, and finaly, his Col prefered Charges against him for neglect of duty, disobedience of orders, and drunkenness. he was tried by a Genl. Court Martial and Dishonerably dismissed from the service. now you have the sum and substance of the story. I know the circumstances as well as any one, for he told me all himself, and I saw a copy of the Charges and sentence.[5]

I got a letter from Uncle Charley yesterday. he was well and still before Richmond or Petersburg. he was in the Battle of Hatchers Run. . . . your Affectionate Son, Chas O Musser

Before Blakely, Ala   April 10th, 65

Dear Father: Since I last wrote you, we have had quite a lively time with the Johneys. . . . there was fighting every day untill the night of the 8th. we charged a part of the enemys right works, carried them, and captured 200 rebs. at midnight, our whole line was to open on the Forts, but the rebs began to evacuate, and over and in to the works we went and got there in time to bag about 450 more rebs. the main force had all left. the guns were all temporarily spiked. they numbered about 45, nearly all heavy [caliber]. a good many dead rebs were strewn all through the works. one Brigade of our Corps ocupied the works.

marching Orders came to our Divis right away. part of our regt was sent off to Ship Island with the Prisoners, and the rest went along with the Brigade. after a quick march of 6 hours, we joined Steeles forces before this place. this is 12 miles from [the] Spanish Forts. We had hardly got here when part of our Corps and [Brigadier General John P.] Hawkins Divis (Colored) of Steeles Corps Charged and captured the entire line of rebbel works and Garrison—guns, stores, and all. 3,500 Prisoners were taken and many heavy guns. I have not yet learned the number. two rebbel Gun Boats fell into our hands, both disabled from our 100 pounder Parrott shot. the loss on our Side in the charge was, as near as I can learn, 250 killed and wounded. a great many were blown up with Torpedoes that were planted around and in the approaches to the works.[6]

our losses so far in the Campaign has been comparatively light while the rebbel loss has been great. we have destroyed quite an Army. 1800 will cover our whole loss thus far in Killed, wounded, and missing. over one half of the wounded are but Slightly hurt. the rebbel loss at the Spanish Forts is about 1700 total. the loss at Blakely [is] 5.000 since the beginning of the siege to the capitulation. 14 days the siege lasted. . . .

The news from Virginia is cheering. Sherman and Grant is going to drive the Johneys to their last ditch. while we were marching yesterday, one of Genl Canbys Staff Officers rode by us on a run, and as he passed us, he Said, *"Boys, Richmond has fallen."* . . . such cheering I never heard before. he passed the word to every Regt as he passed, and when he would come to . . . Brigade Hd. Qarts., he would stop and give them the news. . . . Brig. Genls., staff and all, would off with their hats and give three Cheers for Grant and Sherman. It is generaly believed that Richmond has fallen. still, we have no official paper to that effect.[7]

When we move again, we will be in the rear of Mobile, and maybe the next letter from me will be written in the city. it is only 12 miles from here to the city, and a few hours quick march will bring us there, but there are *obstructions* in the way that might imped our progress. 10 or 15000 rebbels in strong works are no mean enemy to contend with, but we have an Army that could suround a work of most any size. Blakely is on the Tensas Bayou (or River). we cross it on a Pontoon Bridge. the River is about 1/4 of a mile wide.

another rebbel gun Boat came up to our lines and surrendered to day. among the Trophys of our victory is the far famed Ram *Nashville*. it was on the stocks at Mobile at the time of Farraguts Victory and capture of the Ram *Tennessee*. the *Nashville* is larger and said to be stronger than the *Tennessee*.[8] . . . your Affectionate Son, Charles

P. S. . . . to day, 200 guns were fired over the glorious news of the surrender of Lees Army to Genl. Grant.[9] this evening, a rumor is circulated in Camp that Genl. Johnston had surrendered his Army to Sherman—too much good news at once. . . .

On April 13 Day's brigade marched through Mobile to the Mobile & Ohio Railroad. The 91st Illinois and 29th Iowa followed the tracks to Whistler, north of the city, where they encountered Confederate cavalry. The 29th was formed for battle on the 91st's left while the 50th Indiana and 7th Vermont were brought up in support. The infantry advanced, driving the Rebels back more than a mile. The enemy scattered after losing four men killed and two wounded, while Colonel Day lost one man killed and two wounded.[10] This was the last action of the war for the Iowans.

The 29th subsequently marched with the Third Division to the Mount Vernon Arsenal, north of Whistler. On April 22 the Iowans were detached from the division to guard the arsenal, performing this duty until May 12, when they returned to Mobile.[11] Good news arrived May 4. Lieutenant General Dick Taylor, after hearing the news of Johnston's capitulation in North Carolina, surrendered all remaining Confederate forces east of the Mississippi.

Fort Stoddard, Alabama   May 1st, 1865

Dear Father: . . . We left "Whistler Station" on the 19th of last month, marched up here (50 miles from Mobile) on the Mobile River near the Junction of the Rivers Alabama and Tombigbee. our regt is stationed at the U.S. Arsenal, Mt Vernon, 3 miles from Fort Stoddard, which is the old Govt Landing. our Co is quartered here in the Warehouse.

we have a good time—the best we have had since we have been in the Army. there are no rebbels within a weeks march of us. they did not stop until they got over 100 miles from us after they left Mobile—

with the exception of a few hundred scouts—and they wont fight any more. *there is no more fighting for us during this war*, and how thankful I am for it.

Our Army is now all over the state of Alabama, from Mobile to Florence. [Brigadier] Genl. [James Harrison] Wilson cleaned out Central and East Ala, and we cleaned out southern Ala. Wilson is now in Georgia, beyond Columbus, and is still marching on unopposed.[12] the people are very tired of the war here and all are willing to submit to the U.S. authorities. men and officers of the Rebbel army are surrendering themselves up to our forces every day by tens and almost hundreds. they take the oath of allegience willingly. the Prisoners that Genl Wilson took at Selma and Montgomery and Paroled are going home, and they swear that they will not again take up arms against their country—what ever their officers say to the contrary.

They all feel sorry that President Lincoln was murdered.[13] they say that he was more of a friend to them than the Villain [Jefferson] Davis was. ah, the whole south will curse the day that that diabolical murder was committed. that will cause more bloodshed than a hard fought Battle. the whole Army is enraged. the bitter feelings toward the Rebbels are greater than ever. . . . revenge will be had, and it will be bloody vengeance. it is wrong to retaliate upon the rebbels in the ranks, but the leaders Should hang. every one of them should suffer the Penalty due a Traitor. we have but little confidence in President [Andrew] Johnson.

our Divis . . . is at McIntosh Bluffs, 25 miles above here on the Tombigbee. the rest of our Corps is up the river still farther, except Andrews Division/2nd, which is at mobile. Genl. Steele and Smith is between here and Montgomery Somewhere. It is rumored that Genl. Dick Taylor Surrendered his forces to Granger at Mobile. his Head Quarters was at Meridian, Miss, after the evacuation of Mobile.

everything is turning around again, and the Mashine will be runing after the old fashion again in a month or two. the whole country around Mobile is crowded with deserters and Paroled Prisoners from the Rebbel Army. and Niggers by the thousands are flocking there. they have allready organized 7 new regts, and they are filling up rapidly.

this is a rich country, and we live well—almost as well as at home. . . . this is my last Scrap [of paper], last stamp and Envelope. I have begged untill I am ashamed to beg any more, and there is no more to beg in our regt. there is some talk of us being payed off Soon. I think it is time, too. yesterday, we mustered the 5th time since last payed. so ten months wages is due us. If I had writeing material, I would not care if I got no pay untill I am mustered out of the service, which I think will be done before the 1st of Aug.

Lee's surrender dishartened the whole South. Johnston will [surrender] in a short time if he has not already. . . . Yours as ever, Charles

Fort Stoddard, Ala   May 7th/65

Dear Father: . . . we live on the fat of the land and have nothing to do but "pleasure ride" in our little Sail Boats, "go fishing," and visit our *neighbors*. they are geting quite reconciled to the presence of the *Yanks*. Paroled Rebs are all round us. . . . [They] are quite sociable and willing to let bygones be bygones and once more be *Americans* . . . not Confederate and Federal as heretofore.

Genl. Taylor Surrendered his army to Genl. Canby last Thursday. the meeting was held at Citronelle, a town on the Mobile and Ohio R.R. 16 miles from here. immediately after the terms were agreed upon (they were the same as those between Grant and Lee, Johnston and Sherman), Taylor started for Meridian (his Hd Qrts) to carry out the terms. . . . his surrender includes East La, East Miss, Ala, and Florida—in fact, all the country between the Department of Johnston and E. Kirby Smith on the Trans Mississippi. So the war is over in this Dept. [of the Gulf], and Kirby will soon come under the same Leenient terms. the rebbel Fleet under Com[modore Ebenezer K.] Farrand Surrendered to Admiral [H. K.] Thatcher at Citronelle, also. the fleet consisted of 17 Transports, 3 Gun Boats, and three Ocean steamers (Blockade Runners).

our Fleet is all comeing down the Rivers, and the Army will fall back to Mobile in a few days. our Division, now at McIntosh Bluffs, received marching Orders yesterday, and as soon as the Captured Transports comes down—they are 200 miles above on the Tombigbee—they will move down to Mobile. our regt will remain here, in all probability, untill we are ordered to the North to be mustered out, which I dont think will be long hence.

Our Divis at the Bluff was building a Fort to cut off the retreat of the reb Boats. . . . when Genl Benton (Divis Commander) heard of the Surrender of the reb army and fleet, he mounted his horse, rode out to where the boys were at work on the Fort, rode up among them and said, "Boys, the war is over, throw down your spades and let the Fort go to H——ll. we dont want it." and then you ought to have heard the Noise. all the wild savages in the far west cant make Such a noise. the Piney woods rang again, and the old monitor *"Octorara"* at anchor there opened with her 200 pounders, and the very earth shook with the concussion. . . . we could hear the heavy guns at Mobile, nearly 50 miles [distant], about the Same time.

This evening, we hoist the old Garrison Flag over the Arsenal at Mt Vernon. a salute of 34 guns will be fired in honor of the event. the Rebbel *rag* has hung over it for the last four years, and now the Glorious old Stars and Stripes will wave proudly over the reclaimed property of Uncle Sam.

In a late paper it is rumored that the Traitor Davis has been captured in North Carolina. I hope it is so. he ought to suffer the extreme penalty of the law. he ought to be tried, convicted, and executed by a Nigger executioner. I have a little charity for a brave soldier if he is a rebbel. but Davis—no punishment is too great for him. . . .

Tell Hester it will not be long long before I will get to tell her (by the word of mouth) the news, and then [I] will make up for the neglect (unavoidable) of our correspondence. . . . your Affct Son, C. O. Musser

Camp Near Mobile, Ala   May 14th, 1865

Dear Father: . . . We are back again to Mobile. came here on the 11th. we were relieved by a Co of Veterans from the 1st Divis and are here now prepareing for an Expedition into Texas. a reorganization of the forces is going on and a reclotheing, also, for a two months Campaign. (The weather is geting *very hot* here now.) I dread the coming Campaign, but old Kirby [Smith] must submit, and we will be, before this reaches you, on our way to Texas. Some Seems to think that the rebbels will surrender as soon as an army mennaces them. I hope so, for I am tired of marching and fighting and want to get where I will no longer hear the Drum and fife or Bugle or the Booming of canons or the rattle of Musketry. a few short months and the olive branch will flourish, and the old Banner of freedom will wave over a once more united people. and *we* will let foreign nations know that *our* flag cannot be insulted with impunity by any one. *we* will let them know that man is capable of Self-Government. and *we will* be respected by those Powers that remained *so neutral* as John Bull did. . . .

The 13th A.C. is all here, and the 16th is arriving as fast as it can come. in a day or two, Canbys whole Army will be here. It is rumored that the Veterans and Recruits of the whole army is going to be organized into one Corps and be sent to Texas to cooperate with forces that are now [there]. . . . the report may be true, but I put no confidence in it, for we are *all* drawing clothing and other materials for a new Campaign. If our Regt is mustered out three years from the day it was enlisted, I will consider ourselves very luckey. . . .

. . . we will not stay [at New Orleans] longer than four days at farthest, so I was told by an officer that Knows pretty well how the machine runs. Glad that Box of goods got home safe for the Sake of Mrs. Nixon. She wants some relic of Johns, and his Uniform Coat is a good thing to Keep. the things I sent was hardly worth the charges, but I didnt care for that. If we get Pay before we start on the Campaign, I will send some money home by Express when [I] get to Orleans. we will get all that is due us this time. we will be payed up to the 1st of march.

There is great talk here among the boys about *emigrateing to Mexico* as soon as [we are] free from this Army. the Emperor [Ferdinand] Max[imilian] will find a very difficult Job in siting upon his usurped throne in the course of six months. [Benito] Juarez will have many old Veterans from the Armys of the Union as soon as this war closes—not alone from the north but thousands of the men that were once Rebbels will go and fight Side by side with men that were once their foes.

. . . it is quite dull here now, so it Seems to us, but to the Citizens it is very lively. the Cars are runing now quite lively on the M. and O.R.R. [Mobile & Ohio Railroad]. the road is open to Jackson and Corinth, Miss. trains come in every day loaded with Paroled Rebbel Prisoners. the city is full of them all the time. still, they are leaveing as fast as they can get transportation to their homes. Our boys have no difficulty at all with them. you will see "Graybacks" and "Blue Coats" in crowds on the streets most any time in the day, talking about the war and jokeing as if they had not been trying to kill each other only a short time before. a Soldier is a Soldier, and if they are enemys, they will naturely hold up for each other only because they are *Soldiers*.

We have received no Pay yet and no telling when we will get it. our Pay Rolls are all at New Orleans. I will have to try Borrowing off some of the regt that have been payed off. . . . your Affectionate Son, Chas. O. Musser . . .

(May 15th) . . . Two large Trains just came in, loaded with Paroled Prisoners of Taylors and Forrests Armys. Several thousand have come in within the last three days, all bound for home . . . , All glad that they are out from under the Rebbel yoke. . . .

Mobile, Ala   May 22nd/65

Dear Father: . . . I have been quite sick for about a week but feel a little better today. I have had the Fever. To tell the truth, I have not seen a well day since the middle of last February, but I have managed to wear my way through So far without going to the Hospital. When we were at the Siege of Spanish Fort, most all of us had a touch of the Scurvey from liveing on nothing but Bacon, Hardbread, and Coffee— No vegetables at all. after we went up to Mt. Vernon Arsenal, we got Some Fresh meat and vegetables, and most of us were geting well when we were ordered away, and now we have come to the same old "Quintescence of Scurvey." but it will not certainly be long before we get to where a person can get food that is fit for a dog to eat. I have Stood the life of a soldier very well untill the begining of this Campaign. When we left Little Rock, I weighed 146 Pounds. now I weigh 118.

our army is still all here—that is, in the Dept. Some are at Montgomery, Some at Selma, and the rest at this city. there is not much talk of any going home yet for a while. An Order came around yesterday to the different Comm'drs to make out an estimate of the troops that their time expires before the 1st of Sept. I do not know what it is for unless it is to reorganize and consolidate the recruits and Veterans to retain them in the field. most all of the troops of [the] '62 Call [for volunteers] will go out of the service in Aug, but Our regt [muster in] dates 1st Dec. So we will, in all probibility, remain in the field untill the finale disbandenment of all the Volunteers, which will be some time next fall, about Oct or Nov. Some thinks we are going home soon, and others say we are going to help fight Old Kirby Smith. I would like to get home in time to celebrate the aniversary of American Independence there, but I am afraid *that* celebration will be in 1866. but who knows. . . . we may be among the luckey ones to get home first from this Army.

we are at the tail end of all creation away down here in the Swamps of Alabama. Government hardly knows that she has an Army down here, or els it has forgoten us, or it would not certainly keeps us nearly a year without pay. Probibly we do not deserve pay. all the attention of Government has been directed to the Armies of Sherman and Grant, and our insignificant Army of 50.000 men is not worthy of the attentions of the Great men of our Nation. Well, all will be right after awhile no doubt.

I am glad that all Paroled men of our Army and all the men absent from their regts will be Discharged. Jo Meginniss will never be exchanged 'Cause . . . [there is] nobody to exchange with.

The Rebbel Government (old Jeff.) was captured by some of Genl. Wilsons Cavalry in Georgia. the Papers say he was dressed in his wifes clothes. he was runing across a field at regular, masculine Strides. Some of the Boys saw the lady runing and saw that the Lady wore *high top Boots*. they smelled a [illegible] and captured the Lady, and Lo, it was the Southern Confederacy runing for dear life. I hope they will hang him on the same Gallows that John Brown hung on.[14]

Since we have been here, the weather has been very hot. I never felt the heat so much in my life. probibly it is because I have been unwell. . . .

. . . people say that it begins . . . [to] remind them of the times of before the War. Business is becoming quite brisk in the City. . . . your Affectionate Son, Charles

Mobile, Alabama   May 25th/65

Dear Sister: . . . I get so lonesome. times are so dull. Since the campaign is over, time drags along so slow—to me at least. While we were *active*, I never thought of geting lonesome or anything of the kind. We are laying here now in suspense, expecting either to go home or to *"Texas"* soon. If I have got to soldier, I want it to be *active soldiering*, not loungeing around in camp and in town as we are now doing. (I ought not to say we, for I have been confined to my Tent for quite a while, but I think I am geting well now. I hardly make a shadow now, I am so thin. . . . I would make a good Ghost for Hamlet.)

. . . it is so hot now that we cant write in the middle of the day.

We are in camp 2 1/2 miles from the City, just outside of the outer line of Fortifycations and on the East side of the Rail Road in a Grove of Pine. we go to a station about 1/4 of a mile up the track, get on the cars and go to the City for 15 cts, and [go] back when ever we choose, for trains are runing continnaly up and down the R.R., repairing the Track.

the 13th A.C. is all here around the City and also Hawkins Division of U.S. Colored Infty—plainly speaking, niggers. they are very good soldiers when they have good White soldiers *to lead and back them.* they are too wild and reckless. 10 of them will get killed in Battle where 1 white soldier will fall. they do not try to protect themselves from the enemys fire while they are engaged. they forget in their excitement that they are in danger. consequently, more get killed while we lookout for our own Scalp and that of the enemy, too.[15]

. . . We have been payed off lately and can [buy] plenty of writing material now. . . .

Hester, I want you to give me Cousin Joseph Mussers Post Office Address so that I can write him a letter. I will risk his corrupting my political principles if he is a Copperhead. I will cure him of that disease in a letter . . . if he will not break off writeing as some Cop. Correspondents have since [I have] been in the Army.

I am glad to hear that Mrs Triplett is geting along so well and Mr Triplett also. he can go home and Say that he had an easy time soldiering, but there are many that cant say that. Well, I dont envy them their easy times. when I soldier, I want to soldier. . . . your Affectionate Brother, Charles

Mobile, Alabama   May 26th, 1865

Dear Father: . . . no prospect for a move, as I can See. to day, the regt moved camp about 1/4 of a mile farther up the R.R. than we were before.

I am geting well slowly. this hot weather is hard on me. I am still confined to my tent.

We were payed off a few days ago. we only got 8 months pay. I started (yesterday) $100 by Express to you. . . . it had been so long since we were last payed that out of the little we drew, we owed considerable. . . . I dont think it will be long before we Sign our "Muster Out Rolls," but it may then be a month before we start homewards.

I am glad to hear that Henry is standing the Service so well. I was afraid that he would not stand it, but it is hard to tell who will stand such a life the best.

I am afraid you will be disappointed in your expectations of us geting home in June. we will have to leave here very soon if we [are to] get home by the 1st of July. . . . your Affectionate Son, Chas. O. Musser

---

Less than a month after the guns fell silent, troops were being sent to Texas to reassert Federal authority there. The Stars and Stripes replaced the Stars and Bars in Texas towns. Officers paroled Confederate soldiers, inventoried captured military stores, helped to establish reconstructed governments, and liberated slaves. Enlisted men became restive, eager to go home now that the job, as they saw it, was done.

Camp of the 3rd Divis, 13th A.C.
Island Brazos De Santiago, Texas   June 9th, 1865

Dear Father: You will no doubt be somewhat surprised to get a letter from this part of the world. when last I wrote you, 700 miles of salt sea tossed her dark billows between me and this barren Island, the extremity of the Territory of the United States.

. . . On the evening of the 31st of May, we broke Camp at Mobile, marched to the wharf, and that night, we went in to "Bivouac" on the Pier, awaiting Transportation. next evening, we Embarked on the U.S. Steam ship *Margerette* of Mobile (a Vessel that was built there for Blockade runing and was not quite finished when we ocupyed the City). there was not Transportation for the whole of our regt, so the left wing was Ordered back to Camp. Cos "A", "F", "D", and "I" embarked on the *Margerette*, and Co "E" got on the *"Bellvedier"* with another regt. early [the] night of [June] the 2nd, we Weighed anchor, run up Mobile Channel to Spanish Pass, thence into Spanish Channel and down into the Bay, and on to Mobile Bar at Forts Gaines and Morgan. we Cast anchor for the night. our fleet consisted of four Vessels, all Ocean steamers: The *Clinton* (Flag Ship, Genl Steeles Hd. Qts.), the *Continental, Bellvedier*, and the *Margerette*, all crowded with troops. the *Clinton* run out side the bar into open sea that night and on for this place while we waited untill morning, then run out to sea. then comenced our fun. the Vessels rolled and pitched awfuly, disturbing our stomachs considerably, though Soldiers are toughened to all kinds of hardships. on the 4th about noon, we arrived off the [illegible] and was in hopes that the Vessels would Signal for Pilots and run us up the old Father of Waters. but alas, vain hopes, for we left the mouths of the Miss 20 miles to the right, and on we went. we soon run into blue water, and land was soon out of sight. many an anxious eye was turned toward the north while the Good ship *Margerette* was wafting us still farther away from there that we love.

we could not see the use in sending us away off here to this desolate sand bank when there was no longer an enemy to fight. the news papers say that peace is restored, and Uncle sam now has whole control of her Territory from the St Lawrence to the Rio Grande. then why send such an Army here? We are not at war with the French or with the Usurper Maximilian.

I long for the time when I can say that I am a free man and not bound down by military law. Well, Well. all will come round right by and by. It's kind in Government to allow us to see so much country at her expense, aint it?

Well, it took us 5 days to run from Mobile Bar to Brazos Bar. we got here yesterday but did not land untill this morning. of all the places I ever saw, this is the most detestable and lonely looking. ther is scarcely an herb to be seen on the Island and not a drop of water to drink, only that which is *purified* and made fresh by Machinery on the Island. . . . it is Isued out to us as a ration, and such water it is: filthy, warm, and not fit to wash with. but it is the best we can do, for ther is no water nearer than 10 miles that is fit to drink.

We will not remain here many days but will move up to Brownsville, which is 30 miles from here by land and 50 by water. but we are almost in sight of the town of Brownsville on our side and Matamoros on the Mexican side of the Rio Grande. the mouth of the river is only 6 miles from here. We can also see the town of Bagdad south of the rivers mouth and a French Fleet of 32 sail laying off that town. the fleet is too far off to see what kind of Vessels, whether armed or not. . . . there are some large vessels, but most of them are Skooners, Barques, and Morphodite Briggs. a small craft from the fleet sailed up to our Fleet to day with the French Try Color at masthead. it stoped about an hour and sailed away again for the Fleet.

. . . I cant write anymore long letters like I used to. I do not feel

like the same person that I was a year ago. . . . I am not yet well, but
I worry the time through as best I can. I feel tolerable well to day. . . .
your Affectionate Son, Charles

Camp on the Rio Grande River

Near Clarkesville, Texas   July 6th, 1865

Dear Father: . . . We are not geting home as quick as most people anticipate. we will see the end of our term of service before we start for
home. The 33rd Iowa left here for home about ten days ago. there time
was not out as soon as ours by nearly two months, but they happened
to be the luckey ones. ours is the only Iowa regt now in this Department. there are one Indiana, one Vermont, and three Wisconsin regts
here, and they are all the White troops that are here. there are about
25.000 colored troops: Inft, Artillery, and Cavalry, all of the 25th A.C.

The 4th passed off as most any other day, with the exception of a
National salute being fired, and an Oration being delivered by a Chaplain of the Army.

The Weather is and has been intensly hot. We do not run about
any more than is actualy nesessary.

the duty is light, but the fact is, *we make it light ourselves.* very
little duty is done by white soldiers now a days.[16]

Col Benton left to day for New Orleans on business connected with
the Commisary of Musters. Capt Gardner has left on a furlough, or he
has resigned. I dont know which but guess at the latter. Co. A and the
Capt cant agree, and they have separated. and if he has not divorced
himself allready, he will Soon. Lieut Kirkpatrick is in Comm[and].
he is *very good* since he returned to the Co. Well, it is to his interest to
be so.

The Whole regt has lost all confidence in Col. Benton. they all
blame him for our comeing to Texas, and they curse him for his imbe-
cility and slowness. The Greatest dissatisfaction prevails among the
boys here. it sometimes almost breaks out in open mutiny. Officers
have no controll of the men, and every day it is geting worse and
worse. I am sorry to see it, but now the only way to avoid some of these
difficulties is to muster the troops out as quick as possible.

We are all in the best possible state of health for people liveing as
we do.

Every thing is quieting down over in Mexico. the *Emperors* foot hold is giveing way, and he is geting scared. the Imperial Troops are becomeing discouraged. Genl. Negreette of the Liberal party has quite a force of Americans under him and just walks through all opposition lately. We wish him success.

. . . it is needless for you to write any more. . . . we will not certainly remain here long, but it is *very* certain that we will not *Soldier* long. Our time is fully out about the Middle of August. Genl. Steele examined our original muster rolls, and he decided that we were mustered in on the 7th day of Nov. to serve three years from the day of enlistment and not three years from the day of muster, as Col. Benton represented it to Genl. Canby. . . . consequently, we were sent to this state, *where instead*, we would have been at home at this time.

. . . I think the 1st of next month will find us on the Miss River on our way home. when we start from here, it will take us over 30 days to go home and [get] all squared up in the mean time. . . . Your Affct. Son, Chas. O. Musser

Camp on the Rio Grande River
Near Clarkesville, Texas   July 8th, 1865

Dear Sister: . . . when we were at Mobile, I thought we would be at home by the 4th of July, but now I think we will be lucky if we get home by the 4th of September. There is talk of us going to New Orleans soon, but there are so many rumors about that, we can put no confidence in them at all.

The weather is awful hot here. I never knew what long *days* were untill we came to Texas. At Sunrise, the sun looks like a ball of fire comeing out of the Gulf, and it feels like one at noon. . . . it seems as if it never would go down when it gets low in the horizon as we look over the low, sandy Plain toward the west. *This is the last place that was made when the world was created and the material run out.*

Our Idolized Captain left this morning for Council Bluffs. he says he is going direct for that City. So you may expect him in that part of the Country in about fifteen days. I hope you will give him a *warm reception* if he comes to our house. He left the Company under *peculiar circumstances*. . . . I will State a few plain facts to you concerning C. V. Gardner. Firstly, *we run him off.* we refused to do duty under him and, the Col releived him from the Comm[and] of the Co.; Secondly, he was an abuseive and tyrannical officer and abused his men without cause;

Thirdly, he done all in his power (with others) to get our regt sent to Texas when we might have been at home now, the same as other regts in our Brigade that came out the same time as ours; Forthly, he has appropriated money that belonged to the Co for his own use. [It was] a mess fund or Co funds.[17] I will prefer no more charges. of what I have Said, the whole Co (to a man) will vouch for. If we stay in the army ten years, he can never Command Co "A" again. *That we will not bear.* we have born insults and wrongs from him long enough. we have come to the conclusion that patience is no longer a virtue. last evening, he came to us when we were atending roll call and asked us if we wished to send any letters to our folks by him. we told him that when there was no possibility of geting any stamps to send our letters by mail, we would think of it. he should be the last one to ask us to trust him that far. I suppose he will go around palavering, trying to smoothe over his meanness to our folks at home. John Boulden, Rube Barton, and myself were the last ones to condemn him, for we thought he was a Gentleman, but we found that we could bear no more. and now, when I am on equal grounds with him, I never wish him to trouble me or try to reclaim his lost confidence with me. He is not free from the service, only on leave of Absence for 30 days.

The officers of our regt are playing out fast. The Col is on sick leave, the Lieut Col is on detached service, the Major has resigned. the Adjutant is also on detached service. the Senior Capt is on detached service. the next in rank is Capt Gardner. . . . the 6th Capt is now in command of the regt. his name is Andrew Johnston, Capt of Co "G", of Ringgold County, Iowa, a tolerable good officer.

. . . You can look for us home any time after the 15th of August—but not Sooner—and three to one if it is not that late in Sept before we see Iowa. . . . your Affectionate Brother, Chas Musser

Camp near Clarkesville, Texas   July 15th, 1865

Dear Father: . . . there is a fair prospect of us spending the fall in the Army. A few days ago, a detachment from the 19th and 20th Iowa regts (nearly 200 [men]) arrived here from Mobile to be put into our regt. they were recruits. the recruits of the 23rd Iowa is also assigned to our regt and are on their way here. So our regt is to be filled up and remain in the Service while nearly all the regts that came out in 1862 are being mustered out. It is an outrage and a wrong that if we *are men*, we will resent it. we are not brutes to be bought and sold by a set of Ambitious villians—undermineing, Scheming officers. we offered our services to our country to help put down the rebellion. that object has been accomplished, and our time is out, and we are no longer needed.

. . . there is not a single sick man in Co A, and we now number over sixty from the recent Transfers. our regt numbers now 850 strong all told, but a great many are absent that will never return to duty.

This is a healthy country [even] if it is a barren sand waste. the heat through the day is almost unbareable, but the nights are very beautyful, So cool and pleasant, always a refreshing breeze off of the Gulf. and as soon as the sun is down, the Camps are almost deserted for the Gulf Shore. up and down the beach as far as we can see, the Shore is lined with the Clothing of the boys, and they out in the breakers batheing. it is the nicest place to bathe I ever saw—no danger of geting the ague or Chills and Fevre by being in the water a little too long as is generaly the case where we bathe in fresh water. Sometimes a Shark Shows itself along shore, and then you ought to see the scatterment among the boys. he invariably gets cropped by a Minnie ball or two before he gets out of reach of our rifles. . . .

Some of the "Foreign Legions" of Maximilian embarked at Bagdad yesterday and night before last. they were going to Tampico . . . [to] take Shipping for Europe. they were from Matamoros [and] Composed of French, Austrian, and Belgians. They wore the picturesque Uniforms of the French Chauceurs: red pants, blue coats, and red caps, Turkish Boots with yellow tops. they also wore a Scarlet sash. they looked fine, but "the Cocked hat does not make the Warrior" nor the gay Uniforms good soldiers. it is rumored here that the "Foreign Legion" in Mexico is going to be withdrawn and that the would be Emperor is going back to his Dukedom in Austria and give up the idea of forming an Empire upon the ruins of a Republican Government. . . . your Affectionate Son, Chas. Musser

Camp near Clarkesville, Texas July 18th, 1865

Dear Sister: . . . We are Still in Texas and [have] poor prospects of geting out Soon. but we will have to make the best of a bad job. we are all in a good state of health. still we want to get out of the Service. I have

been geting Stouter ever since we left Alabama. I feel about as Stout now as ever.

. . . we get no papers, and when our mail comes, it is about five weeks old. times are awful dull here now.

I would have been happy to be at your 4th of July Celebration, but it's all over with now, and you can get a Christmas Dinner ready for us. . . . we will be at home by that time if ever we get there. . . .

the 29th Iowa will not be mustered out [as a unit]. the old soldiers in the regt will be mustered out by detachment as their time expires. our regt is now about 800 strong, and half of them are recruits, and they will be held after we are discharged. . . .

I am glad to hear that you are going to school all the time. I believe I will go next winter if [I] get home in time. I dont think I am too old yet to learn a little. do you think so? [I am] only 23/past and look and feel as boyish as ever. I dont believe that I look one year older than when I left home. I hope Nathan Barton and all the young chaps at home will get married before I get [there], for then I will have no opposition and stand a better chance of geting a wife. . . . Your Affectionate Brother, Chas. Musser

---

Charles and his comrades were finally mustered out August 10, then transported by steamer to Davenport, Iowa. On August 25, the regiment was formally disbanded and the men returned to their homes. Answering the final roll call were 765 officers and enlisted; 415, including Charles, had served with the regiment since its organization.[18]

New Orleans, La   July 25, 1865

Dear Father: The 29th got here yesterday after a four days run from Brazos Santiago. We are quartered in a large, empty Building in the City and will be mustered out in a few days and on our way to Davenport. on the 22nd, we got Orders to report to New Orleans immediately, so on the 23rd, we marched to Brazos, and on the 24th, we Embarked on the Steam Ship *Wilmington*. on the evening of the 25th, we touched at Galveston, lay at anchor all night and untill noon of the 26th when we again moved off. . . . about midnight of the 27th, we got to mouth of the Mississippi. a little after daylight, we got to Quarrantine, stoped a short time, and again moved up the river. arrived here about 1.Oclock P.M. yesterday, all well and hearty and in good spirits.

I got *Sea sick* coming across. Oh, how sick I was. I thought I never was so sick in my life as I was then. but we was on our way home and did not think so much about it as we would had we been going the other way.

We will lay here about ten days. it will take nine days to go to Davenport. [We] will lay there about six days, and then it will take us six days from there home. so you can look for us home about the last week in August.

. . . I dont suppose we will get any new mail while in the service. . . . your Affectionate Son, Chas. Musser

THREE UNDATED LETTER FRAGMENTS

The weather is very warm and Sultry to day. Mercury has several times rose to 110 in the Shade and is Steady heat all the time.

The boys are all well and enjoy themselves as well as they can [in] this hot weather.

The grain that was raised in this Section of the Country has been harvested nearly three weeks ago. Some Apples are about ripe. there will [be] but little fruit this season here on account of late frosts. Vegetables are very Scarce and high.

We dont get any vegetables at all and live harder than we ever did since [we have] been in the army except while [we were] out to Camden. Still, I am giting Stouter every day. this rough liveing seems to agree with me better than I agree with it. . . . Your Aff Son, C. O. Musser

→ ←

The weather is Still very warm, only this morning there is a cool breeze. . . .

I am glad you are geting along so well with your hay. I was afraid you would have a hard time geting it this fall.

I am sorry Benton Marshall has been so unfortunate as to fall into the hands of the Rebbels. I heard of the failure of [illegible] Barton in geting his proper Discharge. it is prety rough to have to soldier when he is a Citizen.

I am glad to hear that you are so Successful with your garden. it is better than farming on a large scale. . . . I hope you will hav good luck with your Molasses making this Season. The money I sent you will be a great help to you in arrangeing matters for winter. I expect to hear from [you about] it soon. it is about one month since I started it for home.

The news boys are around with late Northern papers. I will Get one and read the news. . . . your Affectionate Son, C. O. Musser

→ ←

. . . you Spoke of the *Advocate* and asked if i still received it and if i wanted it still sent to me. Well, i tell you, i do not for this reason. for the time you had it sent [to] me, i only got four copies, and they were a month old when i got them. So you see, it does not pay to lay out money for papers to send to the army. I also Subscribed for the *Nonpareil* last february and have never received one fourth of the papers due me. i payed for one year. Burke may keep the rest of his papers and the money, too, if he needs them wors than i do. I had rather you would buy postage stamps and paper and send me more letters than lay out your money for me, and i never get any good from it.

The weather is Still very Showery. we had a very hard shower last night, but to day, it is warm enough to roast an egg in the Sun.

I want to know what doings you are going to have the fourth of July—dont suppose there will be much done, though.

Has Capt Gardner ever wrote you a letter yet? dont think he has. Shoulder straps takes his attention too much. got the swelled head a little. the boys lost all the confidence they used to have in him. not the man we supposed him to be. very passionate and Tyranical. Stutters wors than ever. all the rest of the Officers in the regiments laugh at him for his blunders. he was one of the best Orderlies in the regt but is out of his element now. I have nothing against him myself—has allways been a good friend of mine. you must not think hard of what i write—only want to show you what changes there is in some men in high life [compared] to what there is in low life. Office and position makes a great chang in some men. . . . your Affectionate Son, Charles O. Musser

NOTES

Introduction

1. Briggs, "The Enlistment of Iowa Troops," 354–55.

2. Ibid., 355, 358.

3. Iowa ranked tenth among states that contributed white troops to the Union army but only seventeenth among those that provided black troops. Only 1,069 African Americans resided in Iowa in 1860, however, compared to 674,913 whites. Using these figures as a baseline, 41 percent of the state's black population served in the military, compared to 11 percent of the white population. Free blacks across the North were mindful that military service would support their claim to equal rights. Fox, *Regimental Losses*, 532, 536; Rosenberg, *Iowa on the Eve of the Civil War*, 10 n.16.

4. Statistics for Company A drawn from Iowa Adjutant General's office, *Roster & Record*, vol. 3, hereafter cited as *Roster & Record*; Wiley, *The Life of Billy Yank*, 303. Benjamin A. Gould, an actuary for the U.S. Sanitary Commission, found that 10,233 Yankees were under eighteen years of age and 5,213 over forty-five years old when they enlisted (Wiley, *The Life of Billy Yank*, 298–99, 302).

5. "Historical Sketch," in *Roster & Record*, 1351.

6. The principal source for the biographical sketches of Charles and William Musser is the Military Service/Pension Records in the National Archives.

7. Wiley, *The Life of Billy Yank*, 38; Company Muster-In Roll, Military Service/Pension Records of Charles Oliver Musser, National Archives.

8. Untitled, undated newspaper clipping, Musser Papers.

9. Untitled newspaper clipping, March 11, 1938, Musser Papers.

10. Faust, ed., *Historical Times Illustrated Encyclopedia*, 110–11.

11. William Musser to Father, April 4, 1867, Musser Papers.

12. William Musser to Charles, December 20, 1921, Musser Papers. Recent attempts to document William's stay here were unsuccessful.

13. In researching his classic study of the North's fighting men, Bell I. Wiley read 20,000 of their letters. Wiley concluded that the overall reaction to soldiering was "good-natured conformity," leavened by "chronic growling." Wiley, *The Life of Billy Yank*, 28.

14. Most Billy Yanks, if they thought about it at all, were in the war to save the government, not to free the slaves. Perhaps one in ten was genuinely supportive of the abolition of slavery while the rest, early in the war, either had no opinion of slavery or a favorable one. Revelation of the value of slaves as a manpower resource—manual laborers, teamsters, cooks, scouts—persuaded many of the latter to go along with emancipation. Ibid., 39–40, 42, 44; Berlin et al., *Free at Last*, 12.

Charles swam with a strong current of white supremacy in the army—not surprising, considering where he was raised. During the antebellum period, Iowa legislated black codes depriving African-American residents of civil rights enjoyed by whites and an exclusion law prohibiting the further immigration of free blacks—a law that remained on the books until after the war. Wiley, *The Life of Billy Yank*, 109; Dykstra, *Bright Radical Star*, viii, 23–24, 112–13.

1. To War: December 1862–April 1863

1. "Historical Sketch," in *Roster & Record*, 1343.

2. Yankees frequently attempted to supplement their rations by appropriating food from enemy civilians. Foraging was to be done only by authorized details under an officer's command, but a great deal was done by individuals without the necessary orders.

3. According to the "mess system," an individual soldier would cook for four to eight men on a rotating basis. Once the unit left camp on a march, however, individuals usually cooked for themselves.

4. The Battle of Belmont, Missouri, fought on November 7, 1861, was the baptism of fire for a freshly minted brigadier general, Ulysses S. Grant. Forces under Grant's command briefly overran a Confederate camp across the Mississippi from Columbus, Kentucky.

5. These observations on contrabands/contraband camps are based on a reading of Berlin et al., *Free at Last.*

6. Sperry, *History*, 58.

7. This incident took place December 27, 1862. A military tribunal investigated and found Davies innocent of any wrongdoing. War Department, *The War of the Rebellion: A Compilation of the Official Records of the Union and Confederate Armies*, hereafter cited as *OR*, ser. 1, vol. 22, pt. 1, 176–77.

8. Most Yankees did not like the country (too backward) or the climate (too hot) of the South. But some areas did draw favorable comment in their letters. Wiley, *The Life of Billy Yank*, 96–100, 105–6.

9. Sources for this account of the White River expedition include Rea, ed., "Diary," 306–7; *OR*, ser. 1, vol. 22, pt. 1, 216–19; "Historical Sketch," in *Roster & Record*, 1344.

10. Gorman to Curtis, January 20, 1863, in *OR*, ser. 1, vol. 22, pt. 1, 218.

11. Brigadier General Clinton B. Fisk, commander of the Thirteenth Division, initially endorsed the outcome of the abortive expedition: "The satisfaction of *knowing* what was going on in the interior of this State, and making the demonstration we did, was worth the *cost.*" But Fisk's ardor evidently cooled as the casualty returns mounted. He complained a month later about "men of my command who were murdered outright by crowding them into dirty, rotten transports, as closely as slaves in the 'middle passage.'" Fisk to Curtis, February 10, 1863, in *OR*, ser. 1, vol. 24, pt. 3, 43; Fisk to Ross, March 25, 1863, in ibid., 144.

12. On January 11 Fort Hindman succumbed to a severe pounding by Lieutenant David Dixon Porter's Union fleet.

13. Principal sources for this analysis of the soldiers' health include Wiley, *The Life of Billy Yank*, 124–30, 133, 136–37; McPherson, *Battle Cry of Freedom*, 471–72, 487–88; Dykstra, *Bright Radical Star*, 196; Roberts and Moneyhon, *Portraits of Conflict*, 81, 143, 147. Iowa mortality statistics were drawn from Fox, *Regimental Losses*, 516, 528–29. The 33rd Iowa, which like the 29th Iowa saw most of its active service in the Trans-Mississippi, lost three men killed by disease and other noncombat causes for every man killed in action. Ibid., 516.

14. Sperry, *History*, 8; Roberts and Moneyhon, *Portraits of Conflict*, 85.

15. Fisk to Curtis, February 10, 1863, in *OR*, ser. 1, vol. 24, pt. 3, 43; *OR*, ser. 1, vol. 41, pt. 2, 714.

16. Leonard, *Yankee Women*, chap. 2.

17. Shadden, a native Missourian and resident of Council Bluffs, enlisted August 13, 1862, and died February 1, 1863. *Roster & Record*, 1441. Henry P. McElroy, a native Ohioan and Council Bluffs resident, enlisted August 11, 1862, and died January 31, 1863. Ibid., 1413. Boyle, Ohio-born and a resident of Council Bluffs, enlisted August 6, 1862, and died February 5, 1863. Ibid., 1358.

18. Yankees were voracious readers. Newspapers invariably topped their reading lists: hometown weeklies, metropolitan dailies, and illustrated newspapers such as *Frank Leslie's*. These were followed in popularity by *Harper's* and other weekly literary periodicals, religious tracts, and books, especially dime novels. Publishers supplied books to soldiers at half price, and regiments established lending libraries while in winter quarters. Wiley, *The Life of Billy Yank*, 153–57.

19. The army allowed each regiment one sutler, a civilian authorized to sell soldiers consumer goods, including food, tobacco, newspapers and books, razors, plates and cups, and illicit alcoholic beverages. All too often the vendor took advantage of his monopoly by price gouging and extending credit to soldiers between paydays. It was not unknown for angry customers to descend on the sutler's tent or hut and commandeer his inventory.

20. Sources for this account of the Yazoo Pass expedition include *OR*, ser. 1, vol. 24, pt. 1, 372, 389, 393–99, 415–17, 419–21; Carter, *The Final Fortress*, 135–38; Rea, ed., "Diary," 307–9.

21. The turtle gunboats, or "Pook Turtles," made up a class of seven armored vessels designed by Samuel M. Pook. Their sloping, ironclad casemates and rounded bow suggested the appearance of a turtle.

22. In volunteer regiments enlisted men elected lieutenants and captains while company officers elected majors and colonels.

23. The gunboat *Marmora*, accompanied by the 29th Iowa, had been detached to escort the expedition's slow-moving coal barges. At this time, the main fleet was still on the Tallahatchie. *OR*, ser. 1, vol. 24, pt. 1, 393.

24. After Ross's failure before Fort Pemberton, Brigadier General Isaac F. Quinby returned to the scene with the intention of launching another assault, but Grant recalled his forces.

25. This incident occurred on March 20 near Moon Lake. The *Luella* sank rapidly as water rushed in through an opening in the hull, and the first deck was awash when half the crew jumped overboard. The

steamer *Jenny Lind* came to the rescue. Rea, ed., "Diary," 308–9; *OR*, ser. 1, vol. 24, pt. 3, 144.

26. At the age of thirty-six, Clark was old for a private. A native New Yorker and resident of Council Bluffs, he enlisted August 6, 1862. *Roster & Record*, 1368.

27. As the Union divided along sectional lines, so did the Democratic party. Most members of the Northern faction—"War Democrats"—supported the policies of the Lincoln administration. When the administration embraced emancipation as a war aim, however, a vocal minority of Northern Democrats—"Peace Democrats"—rose in opposition, resisting the draft and clamoring for a negotiated settlement with the South. To Republicans they were "Copperheads," that is, poisonous snakes threatening the life of the Union. It was argued, with some justification, that Copperhead opposition to the war effort only encouraged the South to fight on. Lincoln reacted with arrests, suspension of *habeas corpus*, and press censorship. The Copperheads were especially strong in the Midwest, a region that feared a tidal wave of black immigrants should slavery be abolished.

Copperhead activity had its effect on soldier morale. It inspired some men, like Charles, to fight harder but broke down the morale of others. Wiley, *The Life of Billy Yank*, 286–88.

2. Soldier Boy: April–July 1863

1. On March 3, 1863, Congress passed the Enrollment Act, which provided for the first national draft in the history of the Union. (The Confederacy had already adopted a conscription law of its own.) Names were to be drawn from a pool of men eighteen to thirty-five years of age. Only 6 percent of those who were drafted ever served, however. Faust, ed., *Historical Times Illustrated Encyclopedia*, 160–61; Briggs, "The Enlistment of Iowa Troops," 391.

2. Williams resigned February 18, 1863. *Roster & Record*, 1456.

3. Privates were paid thirteen dollars per month, raised to sixteen dollars in 1864. More often than not, the paymaster was late in coming.

4. Charles was apparently referring to the Western Sanitary Commission, a nonprofit civilian organization established to aid Union soldiers. Among other benevolent activities, the Sanitary Commission dis-

tributed food, clothing, blankets, medicine, personal care, and other items to troops in the field.

5. During the war, Federal wounded died at a rate of 14 percent, compared to 2 percent for the Korean War and a mere .25 percent for the Vietnam War. Large-caliber bullets combined with the low muzzle velocity of rifled muskets produced ghastly wounds, and contemporary medical science was unequal to the task of treating them. Army surgeons, for instance, were unaware that a dirty instrument could cause a fatal infection in a patient. McPherson, *Battle Cry of Freedom*, 485–87.

6. The Holemans resided at Council Bluffs and enlisted August 12, 1862. George died of disease May 24, 1863. Joseph, his father, was transferred to the Invalid Corps September 28, 1863. *Roster & Record*, 1392.

7. The "plates" were probably tintypes. In this process, the photographer registered an image on a small piece of sensitized sheet iron. Images could also be made on glass plates, called ambrotypes. Soldiers generally preferred tintypes, though, because they were cheaper and, being virtually unbreakable, could be sent safely through the mail. Kelbaugh, *Introduction*, 15, 27.

8. Sergeant Burroughs, a native New Yorker and resident of Council Bluffs, enlisted August 11, 1862. He died May 6, 1863. *Roster & Record*, 1359.

9. Each volunteer regiment had a surgeon and an assistant surgeon commissioned by the state's governor. As a result, many of these appointments were made on political, not professional, grounds. While the majority were competent, enough were so unfit for this duty as to arouse a widespread mistrust of army doctors among the men. In fact, they would often avoid seeking medical attention in the early stages of an illness, when it might be easily—and successfully—treated. Wiley, *The Life of Billy Yank*, 129–32.

10. This skirmish took place May 1, a mile from La Grange. A detachment of 160 men from the 3rd Iowa Cavalry clashed with an estimated 600 Confederates, killing and wounding about 40 of them. The captain commanding the detachment reported 41 casualties. *OR*, ser. 1, vol. 22, pt. 1, 316–18.

11. Conrad resigned June 2, 1863. *Roster & Record*, 1353. Each volunteer regiment was authorized one chaplain, elected by the field officers and company commanders. Soldiers complained about chaplains more often than not, particularly their alleged neglect of spiritual duties. As the war went on, however, the situation improved as the worst of the lot was

weeded out and the qualifying standards were raised. Wiley, *The Life of Billy Yank*, 263–64, 266.

12. Vicksburg would fall July 4; Port Hudson, July 9.

13. This regiment was the 2nd Arkansas Infantry (African Descent). Though not mustered in until September 4, 1863, the regiment would be present as a unit at the Helena fight, reporting no casualties. Dyer, *A Compendium*, 1000; Bearss, "The Battle of Helena," 295.

Blacks did not always enter the Union army of their own volition. Escaped slaves were sometimes rounded up and impressed into service. Berlin et al., *Free at Last*, 398, 436.

14. Haynes resigned May 25, 1863. *Roster & Record*, 1392. The Virginia-born Surgeon Grimes resigned June 8, 1863. Ibid., 1352.

15. This report was ten days premature. On July 9, 5,500 Confederates surrendered at Port Hudson. Boatner, *The Civil War Dictionary*, 663.

16. By the spring of 1863, most Northerners had concluded that blacks should shoulder muskets. As Iowa's Governor Kirkwood expressed it, "When this war is over & we have summed up the entire loss of life it has imposed on the country I shall not have any regrets if it is found that a part of the dead are *niggers* and that *all* are not white men." The Lincoln administration, too, had moved gradually toward the policy of arming African Americans. Finally, on January 1, 1863, the president gave his formal endorsement in the Emancipation Proclamation, which authorized their recruitment for combat duty. Slaves who enlisted were given their freedom, but free blacks as well as contrabands responded to the call, and within six months more than thirty regiments were organized. Approximately 180,000 African Americans served during the war, representing almost 10 percent of the Union's military manpower. Kirkwood to Halleck, August 5, 1862, in Berlin et al., *Free at Last*, 67–68, 101; Cornish, *The Sable Arm*, 95, 158–65, 288. For a discussion of Confederate treatment of African-American POWs, see chap. 4.

17. Charles never had a furlough during his term of service.

18. Sources for this account of the engagement at Helena include *OR*, ser. 1, vol. 22, pt. 1, 385–91, 395–97, 408–12, 436–37; Bearss, "The Battle of Helena," 256–97; Castel, "Fiasco at Helena," 12–17.

19. *OR*, ser. 1, vol. 22, pt. 1, 409.

20. Ibid., 388.

21. Ibid., 411.

22. Ibid.

23. Ibid., 386.

24. Two of the wounded Iowans later died. All told, 57 Federals were killed, 146 were wounded, and 36 were captured or missing. Casualty figures from *OR*, ser. 1, vol. 22, pt. 1, 391.

25. Johnson survived and served with the regiment until mustered out, August 10, 1865. *Roster & Record*, 1401. Nixon survived and was discharged for wounds at Memphis, Tennessee, August 25, 1863. Ibid., 1425.

26. These Rebels were Brigadier General L. Marsh Walker's cavalry covering the retreat.

27. Charles was referring either to the kepi, a cloth cap with a leather visor, popularized by the French army, or its variant, the forage cap. Many Federal soldiers, especially in the western theater, preferred slouch hats made of soft felt. Davis, *Memorabilia*, 7−8.

28. Target practice was a rarity in the Union army. One imaginative officer had his men shoot at representations of Jefferson Davis. Wiley, *The Life of Billy Yank*, 26−27.

29. Wilson, the regimental quartermaster, resigned August 22, 1864. *Roster & Record*, 1352.

30. In his official report, Colonel Benton himself acknowledged Patterson's leadership during the battle as well as "the thorough instruction previously given by him to both officers and men." *OR*, ser. 1, vol. 22, pt. 1, 397.

3. Army of Occupation: July−December 1863

1. The New York−born Steele graduated from West Point in 1843 near the bottom of his class, but he served with distinction in the Mexican War and held the rank of major in 1861. Steele's star rose quickly: he was promoted to brigadier general in January 1862 and major general fourteen months later. On January 30, 1864, he assumed command of the District of Arkansas. Warner, *Generals in Blue*, 474; Boatner, *The Civil War Dictionary*, 794.

2. Sources for this account of the Little Rock campaign include *OR*, ser. 1, vol. 22, pt. 1, 470−71, 474−77, 520−22; "Historical Sketch," in *Roster & Record*, 1346−47; Rea, ed., "Diary," 311; Huff, "The Union Expedition," 223−37; Roberts and Moneyhon, *Portraits of Conflict*, 120−21, 127.

3. Clayton commanded the cavalry brigade, comprised of the 5th Kansas and 1st Indiana.

4. Reed does not appear as a deserter on the regimental roster.

5. By June 1863 the War Department realized that a manpower crisis was in the offing. Half of all units then in the field would see their terms of enlistment expire by the end of 1864. If allowed to go unchecked, the mustering out process would deprive the Union of thousands of badly needed veteran soldiers. In consequence, a Veteran Volunteer program was initiated. Volunteers could extend their enlistments three years or the duration of the war in exchange for a $400 bounty and a thirty-day furlough. The program resulted in the reenlistment of 200,000 men who would make a significant contribution to victory. Wiley, *The Life of Billy Yank*, 342–43.

6. "Historical Sketch," in *Roster & Record*, 1347.

7. Marmaduke had supposedly accused Walker of cowardice at the Battle of Helena. Lucius Marshall Walker, a nephew of President James K. Polk, was mortally wounded by pistol fire. Warner, *Generals in Gray*, 321–22.

8. Gambling was a favorite pastime of Union soldiers, especially on payday. The principal game of chance was poker ("bluff") followed by chuck-a-luck ("sweat"). Wiley, *The Life of Billy Yank*, 249–50.

9. Benton's brigade included the 29th Iowa, 33rd Iowa, and 28th Wisconsin.

10. William's regiment fought at Helena, but he was already a prisoner at Indianapolis.

11. The Third Division crossed the Arkansas River September 15.

12. In June 1863 Emperor Louis Napoleon of France launched a campaign to extend his empire to the Americas. On Louis Napoleon's order, a 35,000-man expeditionary force took Mexico City and ousted Benito Jaurez's republican government. The emperor of France planned to replace Jaurez with Hapsburg Archduke Ferdinand Maximilian as emperor of Mexico. The Confederacy extended an offer of diplomatic recognition to Maximilian if he would help persuade Louis Napoleon to recognize the South. But the Lincoln administration resorted to diplomatic pressure and a show of military force to nudge Louis Napoleon toward abandoning his grandiose scheme.

13. Charleston did not fall into Union hands until 1865. Chattanooga was occupied by Union forces September 9, 1863.

14. Loynd, a resident of Council Bluffs, was a native Englishman. He enlisted August 4, 1862. *Roster & Record*, 1408.

15. Peck, a resident of Council Bluffs, enlisted August 15, 1862. *Roster & Record*, 1429.

16. Smith, a resident of Council Bluffs, was a native Tennessean. He enlisted August 7, 1862, and died August 14, 1863. *Roster & Record*, 1441.

17. Cox, a resident of Council Bluffs, enlisted August 11, 1862, and died September 7, 1863. *Roster & Record*, 1368.

18. The Enfield rifle musket, of British manufacture, was widely used by North and South alike. Weighing nine pounds, three ounces—bayonet included—this weapon had a bore diameter of .577 inch. It was capable of firing a smooth-sided, conical bullet up to 1,100 yards with some accuracy. Boatner, *The Civil War Dictionary*, 266.

19. Rosecrans was actually holed up in Chattanooga, and Burnside was preparing to defend Knoxville, Tennessee.

20. Yankees generally had unkind things to say about Southern women, comparing them unfavorably to Northern females. Still, hundreds of the boys in blue, some already married in the North, wed Confederate girls and settled in the South after the war. Wiley, *The Life of Billy Yank*, 100–102, 107.

21. William M. Stone won the election.

22. Major General Silas Casey's 1861 work was the Union army's official training manual.

23. Ohio-born Clement Laird Vallandigham was an attorney, an editor, a U.S. congressman, and the North's leading Copperhead. In 1863, Vallandigham was banished to the Confederacy for making a speech hostile to Lincoln and the war effort. He was allowed to return to the North the following year after waging an unsuccessful campaign *in absentia* for the governorship of Ohio.

24. This skirmish was fought about nine miles from Benton on December 1. Fewer than 100 Confederates were probably involved, a detachment under Captain H. S. Randall of the 3rd Missouri Cavalry. Lieutenant A. D. Mills, commanding the Union patrol, reported a loss of three killed and two wounded. Randall put the Federal losses at two killed, four wounded, and one captured. His own casualties went unreported. *OR*, ser. 1, vol. 22, pt. 1, 767.

4. Battle: January–May 1864

1. Rea, ed., "Diary," 313.

2. Having successfully applied the stick to the Confederacy at Gettysburg, Vicksburg, and elsewhere, Lincoln determined it was time to extend the carrot. On December 8, 1863, the president issued a Proclama-

tion of Amnesty and Reconstruction offering full pardons to Rebels—with certain exceptions—who swore an oath "to resume their allegience" to the United States and its laws. At the same time, Lincoln announced a generous Reconstruction policy intended to bring rebellious states back into the Union as soon as possible. Once 10 percent of the citizens of a state who had voted in 1860 took the loyalty oath, that state could apply to the president for recognition.

Loyal state governments in Louisiana and Arkansas were subsequently organized under this plan. In January 1864 Unionists met in occupied Little Rock and rewrote the state constitution, revoking secession and abolishing slavery. A provisional governor was appointed and statewide elections were scheduled for the following March. More than 12,000 citizens voted—20 percent of the 1860 total. The new constitution was approved and Isaac Murphy elected governor. Though sanctioned by Lincoln, this new, loyal state government did not receive Congress's blessing. It nevertheless functioned through the balance of the war. Election figures from Roberts and Moneyhon, *Portraits of Conflict*, 121.

3. Besides four cavalry (mounted infantry) regiments, Arkansas eventually contributed nine regiments and one battalion of infantry and two batteries to the Federal army. One battery and six of the infantry regiments were of African descent. Dyer, *A Compendium*, 997–1000.

4. In March Grant was promoted to lieutenant general and given overall command of the Union armies.

5. Charles was referring to bounties, a system of monetary rewards offered to attract volunteers. A bounty could run as high as $1,500 for a three-year enlistment. Bounty jumpers took advantage of the system by enlisting, collecting a bounty, then deserting to enlist under a different name in another regiment and collect another bounty—much to the chagrin of legitimate volunteers and their families.

Despite complaining about "greenback patriotism," Charles did accept a $100 bounty for volunteering. Company Muster-In Roll, Military Service/Pension Records of Charles Oliver Musser, National Archives.

6. Most recruits joined newly organized regiments because the states preferred it. New regiments meant officer commissions, which could be dispensed as political patronage, and states took pride in the number of regiments each contributed to the Union army. In 1862 only about 12 percent of three-year volunteers entering the army went as replacements to established units. McPherson, *Battle Cry of Freedom*, 326.

7. Sergeant Trenor, a native of Ireland, was discharged for promo-

tion to lieutenant in the 113th USCT on January 20, 1864. *Roster & Record*, 1450.

8. Army life apparently disagreed with Eggleston. He deserted August 16, 1864. *Roster & Record*, 1382.

9. Sources for this account of the Camden expedition and Jenkins' Ferry include Bearss, *Steele's Retreat*; *OR*, ser. 1, vol. 34, pt. 1, 657–58, 661–62, 669, 684–86, 692–95, 700–701, 726; "Historical Sketch," in *Roster & Record*, 1348–50; Rea, ed., "Diary," 313–17; Kerby, *Kirby Smith's Confederacy*, 288–89, 299–300, 311–12; Atkinson, "The Action," 38, 41–50, 45 n; Richards, "The Battle," 3–15; Stuart, *Iowa Colonels and Regiments*, 448–50; Nicholson, "The Engagement," 506–12.

10. Steele complained bitterly that his department was "the last to be served" supplies. Roberts and Moneyhon, *Portraits of Conflict*, 159.

11. *OR*, ser. 1, vol. 34, pt. 1, 700.

12. Casualty figures from ibid., 701.

13. Ibid., 686.

14. Stuart, *Iowa Colonels and Regiments*, 448.

15. The 29th Iowa suffered the loss of two men wounded in the various actions at Prairie De Ann. *OR*, ser. 1, vol. 34, pt. 1, 692.

16. Ibid., 661.

17. Matériel shortages often resulted in Confederates using captured Union uniforms and equipment.

18. Private Shoemaker survived his wound and was mustered out with the regiment August 10, 1865. *Roster & Record*, 1441.

19. The fatigue details corduroyed muddy roads to make them passable for heavy wagons and artillery pieces. Tree branches or trunks were laid across the right-of-way.

20. *OR*, ser. 1, vol. 34, pt. 1, 726.

21. Nicholson, "The Engagement," 510–11.

22. Casualty figures from Bearss, *Steele's Retreat*, 160, 178; "Historical Sketch," in *Roster & Record*, 1350. Surgeon Nicholson commanded a detail of men left behind to care for the nonambulatory wounded. They were subsequently taken prisoner. Ibid., 1349.

23. Rea, ed., "Diary," 317.

24. This was the fight at Poison Spring. Some 300 of the 1,200-man Union escort were shot or captured; Confederate losses totaled only 114. Bearss, *Steele's Retreat*, 6–7, 37.

25. This was a Confederate feint to cover a crossing of the Washita by mounted forces.

26. This was the engagement at Marks' Mills. All but about 200 of the 1,500-man Federal escort were lost, most of them taken prisoner. Ibid., 55, 76.

27. As previously noted, when the battle opened, Salomon's defensive line included only two regiments of infantry: the 29th Iowa and 9th Wisconsin. Later that morning, elements of Engelmann's brigade and Thayer's division were brought forward to reinforce it.

28. Soldier descriptions of battle typically mention noise: the "rattle" of musketry and the "roar" of artillery. Minié balls "hum" like bees or "zip" while artillery shells "scream." Wiley, *The Life of Billy Yank*, 78.

29. Unfortunately, the bullet carried pieces of Rice's spur into his right ankle and shattered the bone. The general was taken home to Oskaloosa, Iowa, where he died July 6. Warner, *Generals in Blue*, 401–2.

30. Bearss, *Steele's Retreat*, 35, 37, 144; Nicholson, "The Engagement," 511–12; Faust, ed., *Historical Times Illustrated Encyclopedia*, 277–78.

31. On April 20 Confederate forces under Brigadier General Robert F. Hoke captured a Union garrison at Plymouth. This success was the result of a combined operation involving Hoke's land forces and a newly constructed ram, *Albermarle*.

32. As a young man, the Ohio-born Quantrill journeyed west to become a schoolteacher but soon graduated to murder and robbery. With the outbreak of war, he declared allegiance to the Confederacy. In 1862 Quantrill embarked on a new career, guerrilla fighter, demonstrating a penchant for shooting prisoners. After winning promotion to the rank of colonel, he led his band in the sack of Lawrence, Kansas, which resulted in the deaths of more than 150 men, women, and children. While on a raid in Kentucky, Quantrill was mortally wounded by Federal troops and died June 6, 1865. Faust, ed., *Historical Times Illustrated Encyclopedia*, 606.

33. Major General George G. Meade's Army of the Potomac, accompanied by General-in-Chief Grant, opened its spring campaign May 4. Subsequent battles with Lee's Army of Northern Virginia at the Wilderness (May 5–6) and Spotsylvania Courthouse (May 7–19) ended in tactical draws. Both sides sustained high casualties—the difference being that Meade could make good his losses while Lee could not.

34. John Nixon and Jo Meginniss were captured at Jenkins' Ferry.

35. Charles H. Hunter of Company K, a native Virginian, had been in the army only a few months. Hunter was promoted to seventh corporal shortly before mustering out with the regiment August 10, 1865. *Roster & Record*, 1400.

36. Trans-Mississippi Confederates were mounting their infantry whenever possible, hoping that enhanced mobility would compensate for lack of numbers.

37. This turned out to be a false report.

5. Home Front: June–November 1864

1. Roberts and Moneyhon, *Portraits of Conflict*, 166–67, 169.

2. Sickles led the Third Corps, Army of the Potomac, at Gettysburg. On the second day of the battle, July 2, 1863, he lost his right leg to Confederate artillery fire. After recuperating, Sickles was sent by Lincoln on an inspection tour of occupied Southern territory. He never returned to field command. Warner, *Generals in Blue*, 446–47.

3. Three Prussian-born Salomon brothers served the Union. Charles E., whatever his drinking habits, rose to the rank of brevet brigadier general. Edward S. was governor of Wisconsin from 1861 to 1863. Frederick S., fighting with distinction at Helena and Jenkins' Ferry, won a brevet as major general. Boatner, *The Civil War Dictionary*, 718–19.

4. Sherman's objective was Atlanta.

5. A commutation clause in the draft law allowed a conscript to buy his way out of the army for $300. Half of all Civil War draftees ruled eligible for military service paid this commutation fee—a fact that did not sit well with the men in uniform. On July 4, 1864, the clause was repealed for everyone except conscientious objectors. Faust, ed., *Historical Times Illustrated Encyclopedia*, 155–56; Wiley, *The Life of Billy Yank*, 286.

6. On June 5, at Piedmont, Hunter's column routed Southern forces under Brigadier General W. E. "Grumble" Jones. Jones was killed, and the Federals occupied Staunton the following day.

Sturgis was under orders to hunt down and destroy "that devil Forrest" and his pesky Confederate raiders. But on June 10, at Brice's Crossroads, Mississippi, Forrest turned on his pursuers and won a smashing victory. Sturgis lost more than one-fourth of his men, all but two guns, and his entire wagon train.

7. Roberts and Moneyhon, *Portraits of Conflict*, 157–58, 175, 178, 185–87; Kerby, *Kirby Smith's Confederacy*, 331–63.

8. Carr's forces caught up with Shelby June 26 at Clarendon. Carr reported the capture of two guns in the ensuing fight at the cost of one killed and sixteen wounded. Shelby's raiders broke off the engagement and headed north. Carr pursued for the next two days, but a shortage of mounted troops—he had only 750—and other factors forced him to give up the chase. Shelby, whose operations were just briefly interrupted, reported losing thirty men. *OR*, ser. 1, vol. 34, pt. 1, 1047, 1052.

9. Cooper, a white man, had been U.S. agent to the Choctaw and Chickasaw tribes before the war. He subsequently organized Indian troops for the Confederacy, leading them at Pea Ridge (1862) and Honey Springs (1863). In 1864 Cooper's Indians cooperated with Price during the Missouri incursion. They had a reputation for being undisciplined and functioned best as scouts, skirmishers, and raiders. Faust, ed., *Historical Times Illustrated Encyclopedia*, 164; Boatner, *The Civil War Dictionary*, 174.

10. On July 25 the 29th Iowa, 10th Illinois Cavalry, and Battery K of the 1st Missouri Light Artillery were ordered to march to Lewisburg for outpost duty. The 29th and Battery K returned to Little Rock on August 28. *OR*, ser. 1, vol. 41, pt. 2, 384, 910–11.

11. McCoid, a resident of Council Bluffs, enlisted as a corporal August 11, 1862. He was mustered out with the regiment. *Roster & Record*, 1413.

12. The Battle of Tupelo was actually fought in Mississippi, July 14–15. Smith beat off a succession of uncoordinated attacks by Confederate forces under Lieutenant General Stephen D. Lee. Forrest's cavalry, which bore the brunt of the fighting for Lee, incurred heavy losses. Forrest himself was wounded.

13. In June Lieutenant General Jubal A. Early set out with 14,000 men with the intention of reprising the 1862 Confederate invasion of Maryland. Early's primary objective was to draw Federal troops from the siege lines at Petersburg, Virginia, thus relieving pressure on Lee's army there. In this Early succeeded, although he was forced out of Maryland July 12 after encountering heavy opposition on the outskirts of Washington, D.C. A badly organized Union pursuit allowed the raiders to escape across the Potomac with all their booty.

14. Lax discipline was a problem in the Federal army, a military or-

ganization, for the most part, of citizen volunteers supervised by amateur officers. An insubordinate soldier might use intemperate language, disobey an order, refuse assigned duty, or, in extreme cases, assault an officer. Garrison troops in isolated outposts were especially prone to lapses in discipline. Wiley, *The Life of Billy Yank*, 198–200, 220–21.

15. Shoemaker was apparently on sick leave, having been wounded at Prairie De Ann on April 12, 1864. He enlisted August 22, 1862, and was mustered out with the regiment. *Roster & Record*, 1441. Sherratt, a native Englishman, enlisted August 14, 1862, and also served with the regiment until it was mustered out. Ibid., 1441.

16. Eggleston deserted August 16, 1864, after serving seven months in the army. *Roster & Record*, 1382. Fletcher deserted the same day, having served eight months. Ibid., 1385.

17. General William S. Harney—"Mad Bear" to his adversaries— was a ferocious Indian fighter of the antebellum era.

18. The 29th Iowa played only a peripheral role during this excitement. Detachments guarded two steamboats that had run aground on the Arkansas, thirty-five miles upriver from Little Rock. *OR*, ser. 1, vol. 41, pt. 3, 138.

19. Profanity was endemic to soldiering in the Union army. Though officers were to be fined a dollar for each offense, they were as guilty as the enlisted personnel. Commanding officers and chaplains who tried to stop it enjoyed no success. Likewise, efforts to curb drinking came to naught, and military discipline suffered as a result. Paydays and holidays were invariably marked by mass consumption of "the ardent" or "Nockum stiff." Wiley, *The Life of Billy Yank*, 248–49, 252–54.

20. Fort De Russy, Louisiana, was a Rebel garrison captured March 14, 1864, at the start of Banks's Red River campaign. On April 9 elements of Banks's army, now in retreat, fought a successful rearguard action at Pleasant Hill.

21. Lincoln issued four calls for troops under the conscription law, setting a quota for recruits from each congressional district. If a district failed to meet its quota, a lottery draft was imposed.

22. Third Winchester, fought September 19.

23. On September 29 elements of Grant's army seized portions of Richmond's outer defensive works: Fort Harrison and New Market Heights. The latter action is especially noteworthy, as thirteen black soldiers won the Medal of Honor.

24. In summer, the men were usually housed in tents, the most com-

mon variety being the shelter or dog tent. Two men carried half a tent and fastened them together when bivouacking. Soldiers built log huts in the winter when poor weather usually brought an end to campaigning.

25. McPherson, *Battle Cry of Freedom*, 804–5.

26. Cedar Creek, fought October 19.

27. Food shortages were not unknown in the Union army, occurring in every theater of operations. As Charles indicated, one major cause was the breakdown of the distribution system. The Commissary Department, responsible for issuing rations, was organized in army, corps, division, brigade, and regimental units. Staff officers at army headquarters would siphon food for themselves and their families, with corps, division, and brigade headquarters following suit. The regimental commissary, which distributed rations to the men in the ranks, was at the end of the food chain, so to speak, with the result that there might be little or nothing left to hand out. Soldiers often made up this shortfall with purchases from the sutler—at inflated prices—or by foraging from Confederate civilians.

As to the food itself, hardtack, a biscuit made of flour and water, and salt pork, called sow belly, were staples of the Yankee diet. Hardtack possessed the consistency of sheet iron and was frequently infested with worms. Soldiers on the march, unable to light campfires, ate their salt pork raw. Wiley, *The Life of Billy Yank*, chap. 9.

28. McClellan carried New Jersey.

6. Garrison: November 1864–February 1865

1. On November 30, 1864, at Franklin, Tennessee, Hood tried unsuccessfully to destroy two Federal corps on their way to join Thomas at Nashville. A half-dozen Confederate generals were killed.

2. The twenty-pounder Parrott was one in a series of rifled, muzzle-loading artillery pieces invented by R. P. Parrott. Capable of firing a conical projectile two miles and more, Parrott rifles were widely used by both sides.

3. On the night of December 20 the Confederate garrison at Savannah, Georgia, managed to slip across the Savannah River to South Carolina. Sherman's army occupied the city the next day, ending its famous March to the Sea.

4. In a well-planned battle at Nashville, December 15–16, Thomas wrecked Hood's army. He reported 4,462 Rebels captured, including 3 general officers. Boatner, *The Civil War Dictionary*, 579–82.

5. On December 22, 1864, Major General Joseph J. Reynolds assumed command of both the Seventh Corps and the District of Arkansas, succeeding Steele. The native Kentuckian served on the Texas frontier and in the Indian Territory after graduating from West Point in 1843. (Ulysses S. Grant was a classmate.) Reynolds saw action at Cheat Mountain, Hoover's Gap, Chickamauga, and Missionary Ridge, where he functioned as chief of staff of the Army of the Cumberland. Reynolds would continue in the Regular Army after the war, only to resign in disgrace in 1877, having inexplicably broken off a successful attack against Chief Crazy Horse's village. Boatner, *The Civil War Dictionary*, 694–95; Warner, *Generals in Blue*, 397–98.

6. Shoemaker resigned January 7, 1865. *Roster & Record*, 1352. Sheldon resigned December 20, 1864. Ibid., 1448. Munns resigned October 22, 1864. Ibid., 1420. Elliott resigned November 9, 1864. Ibid., 1384. Sommer was mustered out with the regiment August 10, 1865. Ibid., 1448. Damewood, a native Tennessean, resigned August 16, 1864. Ibid., 1379. Miller, wounded at Terre Noir Creek, was mustered out with the regiment August 10, 1865. Ibid., 1424.

7. "Beast" Butler made up in political influence what he lacked in military acumen. He was relieved of command, however, after the 1864 presidential election was safely out of the way.

8. Wilmington would fall February 23, 1865.

9. A paroled prisoner was one released with the understanding that he would not return to duty until exchanged for an enemy captive.

10. John Nixon, a resident of Council Bluffs, enlisted August 15, 1862, and was promoted to third corporal August 8, 1863. Nixon was buried in the National Cemetery at Baton Rouge, Louisiana. *Roster & Record*, 1425.

7. Peace Again: February–July 1865

1. Sources for this account of the Siege of Mobile include Johnson and Buel, eds., *Battles and Leaders*, vol. 3, 411; Bergeron, *Confederate Mobile*, 151, 173–92; *OR*, ser. 1, vol. 49, pt. 1, 216–19, 221–22; "Historical Sketch," in *Roster & Record*, 1350.

2. *OR*, ser. 1, vol. 49, pt. 1, 217.

3. Ibid., 112. Federal losses at Spanish Fort totaled 52 killed, 575 wounded, and 30 missing. Gibson reported his losses as 93 killed, 395

wounded, and 250 missing, but upwards of 325 Rebels might have been
taken prisoner April 8. Bergeron, *Confederate Mobile*, 182; *OR*, ser. 1,
vol. 49, pt. 1, 318.

4. Captain Myers commanded Company H. He survived his wound
and was mustered out July 6, 1865. *Roster & Record*, 1422.

5. On January 20, 1864, Trenor was discharged for promotion to lieutenant in the 113th USCT. *Roster & Record*, 1450.

6. Torpedoes and land mines were considered to be in violation of
the laws of civilized warfare, but both sides used them. They first appeared in May 1862, when Confederate forces retreating from Yorktown
buried artillery shells designed to explode when stepped on or moved.

7. Richmond fell April 3.

8. On August 5, 1864, a Union fleet forced its way into Mobile Bay as
Rear Admiral David Glasgow Farragut issued his legendary order,
"Damn the torpedoes. Full speed ahead!"

9. Lee surrendered April 9.

10. Casualty figures from *OR*, ser. 1, vol. 49, pt. 1, 223−24.

11. "Historical Sketch," in *Roster & Record*, 1350−51.

12. Wilson led three cavalry divisions in a raid on Selma, Alabama,
capturing the town April 2. His horsemen went on to take Montgomery
and Columbus, Georgia. At Macon on April 20, Wilson learned of the end
of hostilities. His raid eliminated the need for Canby to move beyond Mobile after occupying that city.

13. President Lincoln was shot April 14 and died the next morning.

14. Davis was captured near Irwinville, Georgia, May 10. He was
imprisoned at Fort Monroe, Virginia, for two years but never brought
to trial.

15. United States Colored Troops, as they were designated, served
under white commissioned officers. At least one modern authority agrees
that they fought with abandon, offering this explanation: "Time after
time black units as a whole acted bravely, because they were so afraid of
accusations of cowardice. They fought aggressively, even recklessly, and
no one could challenge their valor or commitment to the war. Black
soldiers knew full well what was at stake, and they were willing to
take greater risks in hopes of postwar rewards." Glatthaar, *Forged in
Battle*, 153.

16. From the day they were first enrolled in the Union army, blacks
were assigned a disproportionate share of fatigue duty. In June 1864 the

adjutant general, moved by the protests of black enlisted men and their white officers, decreed a "fair share" of such duty for African Americans. Berlin et al., *Free at Last*, 459–60.

17. The Union army allowed company commanders to return unused rations to the commissary in exchange for money. These proceeds were to be deposited in the company fund and spent on supplementing the men's diet. Unfortunately, captains sometimes absconded with these funds. Wiley, *The Life of Billy Yank*, 225.

18. The 29th Iowa had a total wartime enrollment of 1,485 officers and men. Of these, 41 were killed outright or mortally wounded in action; 107 were wounded; 249 died of disease; 157 were discharged for wounds, disease, and other causes; 65 were captured; and 38 were transferred. "Historical Sketch," in *Roster & Record*, 1351.

BIBLIOGRAPHY

Atkinson, J. H. "The Action at Prairie De Ann." *Arkansas Historical Quarterly* 19 (1960): 38−50.

Bearss, Edwin C. "The Battle of Helena, July 4, 1863." *Arkansas Historical Quarterly* 20 (1961): 256−97.

————. *Steele's Retreat from Camden & the Battle of Jenkins' Ferry*. Little Rock: Eagle Press, 1990.

Bergeron, Jr., Arthur W. *Confederate Mobile*. Jackson: University of Mississippi Press, 1991.

Berlin, Ira, Barbara J. Fields, Steven F. Miller, Joseph P. Reidy, and Leslie S. Rowland, eds. *Free at Last: A Documentary History of Slavery, Freedom, and the Civil War*. New York: New Press, 1992.

Boatner, Mark M. *The Civil War Dictionary*. New York: David McKay Company, 1959.

Briggs, John E. "The Enlistment of Iowa Troops during the Civil War." *Iowa Journal of History and Politics* 15, no. 3 (July 1917): 323−92.

Carter III, Samuel. *The Final Fortress: The Campaign for Vicksburg 1862−1863*. New York: St. Martin's Press, 1980.

Castel, Albert G. "Fiasco at Helena." *Civil War Times Illustrated* 7, no. 5 (August 1968): 12−17.

Cornish, Dudley Taylor. *The Sable Arm: Black Troops in the Union Army, 1861−1865*. Lawrence: University of Kansas Press, 1987.

Davis, William C. *Memorabilia of the Civil War*. New York: Mallard Press, 1991.

Dyer, Frederick H. *A Compendium of the War of the Rebellion*. Dayton: Morningside Press, 1978.

Dykstra, Robert R. *Bright Radical Star: Black Freedom and White Su-*

premacy on the Hawkeye Frontier. Cambridge, Mass.: Harvard University Press, 1993.

Faust, Patricia, ed. *Historical Times Illustrated Encyclopedia of the Civil War.* New York: Harper and Row, 1986.

Fox, William F. *Regimental Losses in the American Civil War 1861–1865.* Dayton: Morningside Press, 1985.

Glatthaar, Joseph T. *Forged in Battle: The Civil War Alliance of Black Soldiers and White Officers.* New York: Meridian, 1992.

Huff, Leo E. "The Union Expedition against Little Rock, August–September, 1863." *Arkansas Historical Quarterly* 22 (1963): 223–37.

Iowa Adjutant General's Office. *Roster & Record of Iowa Soldiers in the War of the Rebellion,* vol. 3. Des Moines: Emory H. English, 1910.

Johnson, R. U., and C. C. Buel, eds. *Battles and Leaders of the Civil War.* 4 vols. Seacaucus: Castle, 1983.

Kelbaugh, Ross J. *Introduction to Civil War Photography.* Gettysburg: Thomas Publications, 1991.

Kerby, Robert L. *Kirby Smith's Confederacy: The Trans-Mississippi South, 1863–1865.* Tuscaloosa: University of Alabama Press, 1991.

Kilburn, Lucian M., ed. *History of Adair County Iowa and Its People.* Chicago: Pioneer Publishing Company, 1915.

Leonard, Elizabeth D. *Yankee Women: Gender Battles in the Civil War.* New York: W. W. Norton, 1994.

McPherson, James M. *Battle Cry of Freedom: The Civil War Era.* New York: Oxford University Press, 1988.

Musser, Charles Oliver. Papers. In the possession of the family.

National Archives. Military Service/Pension Records of Charles Oliver Musser. RG 94.

National Archives. Military Service Records of William A. Musser. RG 109.

Nicholson, Dr. William L. "The Engagement at Jenkins' Ferry." *Annals of Iowa* 2 (October 1914): 505–19.

Rea, Ralph R., ed. "Diary of Private John P. Wright, U.S.A., 1864–1865." *Arkansas Historical Quarterly* 16 (1957): 304–18.

Richards, Ira Don. "The Battle of Jenkins' Ferry." *Arkansas Historical Quarterly* 20 (1961): 3–16.

Roberts, Bobby, and Carl Moneyhon. *Portraits of Conflict: A Photographic History of Arkansas in the Civil War.* Fayetteville: University of Arkansas Press, 1987.

Rosenberg, Morton M. *Iowa on the Eve of the Civil War: A Decade of Frontier Politics*. Norman: University of Oklahoma Press, 1972.

Sperry, Andrew F. *History of the 33rd Iowa Infantry Volunteer Regiment*. Des Moines: Mills and Company, 1866.

Stuart, A. A. *Iowa Colonels and Regiments: Being a History of Iowa Regiments in the War of the Rebellion*. Des Moines: Mills and Company, 1865.

War Department. *The War of the Rebellion: A Compilation of the Official Records of the Union and Confederate Armies*. Washington, D.C.: GPO, 1880–1901.

Warner, Ezra J. *Generals in Blue: Lives of the Union Commanders*. Baton Rouge: LSU Press, 1964.

———. *Generals in Gray: Lives of the Confederate Commanders*. Baton Rouge: LSU Press, 1959.

Wiley, Bell Irvin. *The Life of Billy Yank: The Common Soldier of the Union*. Baton Rouge: LSU Press, 1971.

INDEX

Blood and anger, bragging and pain, are all part of this young Iowa soldier's vigorous words about war and soldiering. A twenty-year-old farmer from Council Bluffs, Charles O. Musser was one of 76,000 Iowans who enlisted to wear the blue uniform. He was a prolific writer, penning at least 130 letters home during his term of service with the 29th Iowa Volunteer Infantry.

Soldier Boy makes a significant contribution to the literature of the common soldier of the Civil War. Moreover, it takes a rare look at the Trans-Mississippi theater, which has traditionally been undervalued by historians. Early in the war, the cream of the Confederacy's manpower in the region left to join the fray east of the Mississippi. The Union troops in the Trans-Mississippi theater were chronically hampered by supply shortages, reflecting the low priority that Washington assigned them. Large-scale, pitched battles were rare, small unit actions and hit-and-run raids being the order of the day. Still, hard fighting and real dying took place.

Musser was present in the midst of the action on Independence Day, 1863, and lived to graphically describe one of the bloodiest Civil War battles west of the Mississippi, when a federal garrison repeatedly turned back Confederate attempts to capture Helena, Arkansas. He survived his baptism by fire at Helena and served ably for the balance of the war, holding the rank of sergeant when mustered out.